THE
SHAHNAMEH

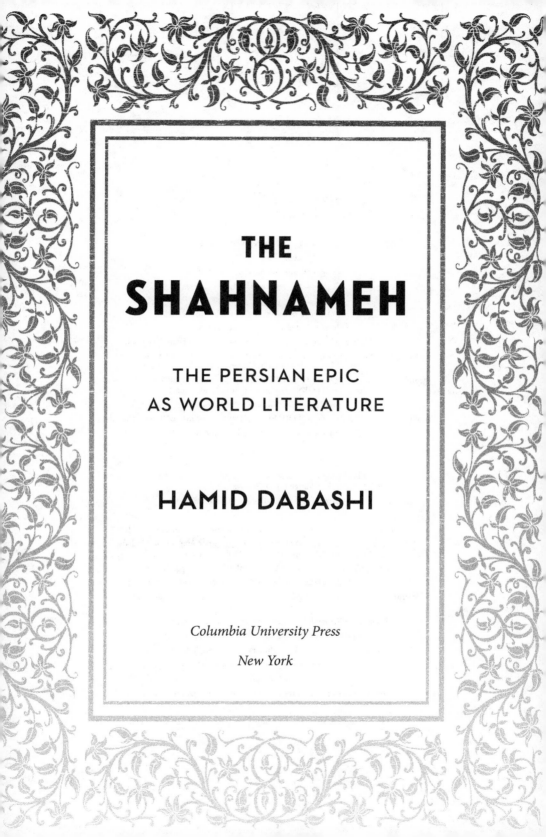

THE
SHAHNAMEH

THE PERSIAN EPIC
AS WORLD LITERATURE

HAMID DABASHI

Columbia University Press

New York

Columbia University Press
Publishers Since 1893
New York   Chichester, West Sussex
cup.columbia.edu

Library of Congress Cataloging-in-Publication Data
Names: Dabashi, Hamid, 1951– author.
Title: The Shahnameh : the Persian epic in world literature / Hamid Dabashi.
Description: New York : Columbia University Press, 2019. | Includes bibliographical
references and index.
Identifiers: LCCN 2018019466 (print) | LCCN 2018020311 (ebook) | ISBN 9780231544948
(electronic) | ISBN 9780231183444 (cloth : alk. paper)
Subjects: LCSH: Firdawsī. Shāhnāmah.
Classification: LCC PK6459 (ebook) | LCC PK6459 .D33 2018 (print) | DDC 891.55/11—dc23
LC record available at https://lccn.loc.gov/2018019466

Chapter opening art: Folios from an illuminated manuscript. Made in Iran, Tabriz.
The Shahnameh (Book of Kings) of Shah Tahmasp. Author Abu'l Qasim Firdausi
(935–1020). Paintings attributed to Qadimi (ca. 1525–65).
Metropolitan Museum of Art, Gift of Arthur A. Houghton Jr., 1970.
Preface: The Shah's Wise Men Approve of Zal's Marriage, Folio 86v, ca 1525–30
Introduction: The Angel Surush Rescues Khusrau Parviz from a Cul-de-sac,
Folio 708v, ca 1530–35
Chapter 1: Zal Expounds the Mysteries of the Magi, Folio 87v, ca 1525
Chapter 2: Tahmuras Defeats the Divs, Folio 23v, ca 1525
Chapter 3: Siyavush Recounts His Nightmare to Farangis, Folio 195r, ca 1525–30
Chapter 4: Bahram Recovers the Crown of Rivniz, Folio 245r
Chapter 5: Nushirvan Greets the Khaqan's Daughter, Folio 633v, cz 1530–35
Conclusion: Afrasiyab on the Iranian Throne, Folio 105r, ca 1525–30

Cover image: Rustam and Isfandiyar Begin Their Combat, Folio 461v, ca 1525

For Sultan Mahmoud Omidsalar

The generous patron of this book on the *Shahnameh*

CONTENTS

PREFACE

The *Shahnameh* is a long beautiful poem in my mother tongue. It was composed in Persian with poise, patience, perseverance, as if performing an act of poetic piety, of moral obligation, of the ritual ablution of a people. It has been loved and admired since its completion in the year 1010 in the Khorasan region of Iran, the singular lifework of one poet who in more than fifty thousand couplets summoned the full historical imagination of a people. It is the longest epic poem in the world composed by one poet.

The *Shahnameh* is the surviving relic of many beautiful and exquisite tales informing bygone and forgotten empires. It is forever loved, beautifully written, ceremoniously read, happily recited, and then, generation after generation, memorized, performed, painted, praised, critically edited, and even revered by Iranian and other Persian-speaking people around the globe. People name their children after its heroes. They call their loved ones names immortalized in these tales. Living histories are made of stories told in this book.

The *Shahnameh* is an epic of many empires. Its stories date back to time immemorial. It tells stories of legends and heroes and histories long since otherwise forgotten—the Sassanids, the Arsacids, Alexander the Great, the Parthians, the Kiyanids . . . stories of who knows what other forgotten gathering of unending pride and enduring prejudices.

Hakim Abolqasem Ferdowsi Tusi is the name of the poet who wrote the *Shahnameh*. He finished it around the year 1010 in the Christian calendar, though he lived on a different calendar, an Islamic, an Iranian calendar. The original text of the epic is carefully researched, judiciously documented, impeccably preserved—every single word of it lovingly cherished, meticulously honored, thoroughly documented.

Beyond and above its imperial pedigree, the *Shahnameh* has been the companion of multiple nations across the colonial and postcolonial worlds, deeply rooted as these nations are in a common moral imagination. The Persian epic is the shared memory of that active and enduring imagination.

The poetic gift at the heart of the *Shahnameh* extends the *totality* of its mythic, heroic, and historical narratives deep into an open-ended *infinity* they collectively invest in those who read it. When the narrative roots of this text began, we do not know; when it will end, we have no clue. The Persian epic remembers and perpetuates itself—in and of itself. It has sustained itself through the thick and thin of a history that has always had but limited, passing, fragile political claim on its unfolding poetic horizons. The *Shahnameh* is a renegade epic.

The paramount question today is, how are we to read the *Shahnameh* beyond its past and lost glories—today meaning almost two decades into the twenty-first century in the Christian calendar, which is not the calendar in which the Persian epic was written, or in which it is now read in countries where people can read and recite it in its original?

The *Shahnameh* has been widely translated into various languages and admired by readers around the globe. To read it in a language other than its original Persian, people have had to read it mostly in English, some in French, and less so in Arabic, Turkish, German, Russian, Chinese, Japanese, or Spanish. That fact is not accidental to the way the *Shahnameh* is read today. The primacy of English in reading it in its translation reflects the colonial context of its reception over the past two hundred years plus. Ferdowsi wrote the *Shahnameh* in Persian, once an imperial language of its own. Today people around the world, the world in which this Persian text is to be or not to be considered as part of what is called "World Literature," mostly read it in English. In that factual paradox dwells the ironic power of an epic living beyond its destiny.

In reimagining the *Shahnameh* as a piece of *world literature* first and foremost that Eurocentric *world* needs to be reassessed and reimagined. The "World" in "World Literature," as we use the term today, is a fictional ("Western") world—an imperial, colonial fiction, a fiction that has factually impaired the larger world in which we have lived. It is a decidedly European world, positing a Euro-universalist imagination upon the moral and normative universe in which humanity lives within multiple worlds. It is a colonial confiscation of the real world. It is the imperial appropriation of a world that has been denied its own inhabitants and their varied and multiple worldliness. Any text from any part of that real world that wants to enter this warped world of "World Literature" must first and foremost ask permission from a fictive white European literary critic and thus distort itself to the aesthetic, poetic, and above all mimetic particularities of that European world he represents before it is admitted, and once it is thus admitted it has ipso facto disfigured itself. In making the case for *world literature*, we must first and foremost dismantle and overcome the European fiction of that "World Literature" as theorized from Goethe forward. What Goethe and his followers have theorized is not "world" literature. It is the imperial wet dream of European literature. It is theirs. It is their world. It is not worldly, it is not real, it is fictive, imperial, cherry-picking aspects of other people's literature and twisting and turning it to its liking. It is therefore innately abusive of the world it wishes thus to appropriate and narratively (as politically) to rule. The world, the real world, the world at large, is entirely outside the parameters of that European manufactured, colonially fictional "World."

Where exactly is this "World," we can now ask in earnest, when they say "World Literature"? Can we question the location and the logistics of this world? Might this world perhaps be a specific world, a Eurocentric world, a world mapped to look dominant under the sign of "Europe," a world in the shadow of Europe, a world imagined by European cartographers, philosophers, world conquerors, and enlightened thinkers, and all their North American descendants? If so, might we perhaps think of another world, a world ravaged by European colonialism and now rising from the enduring conditions of its postcoloniality to claim a dignity of place for itself, including a claim on *world literature* beyond the limited imagination of "World Literature" perhaps? If so, can the *Shahnameh* be read as a piece of *world literature* in *that* world—the real world, the postcolonial world—as part and parcel of a global claim on the pride of place not mapped in "World Literature"? Can we reverse the order of these worlds and begin theorizing from "the wretched of the earth" upward, rather than the other way around, the way "World Literature" has been theorized?

To enter this real, larger world, to become part and parcel of *world literature* (without any imposing Euro-universalist capital letters), my argument in this book is very simple: the *Shahnameh* must be read and remembered for the imperial worlds it once occupied and the postcolonial world it now inhabits—the world in which it was created, the world it envisions, and the world in which it has been read. My consistent argument throughout this book is that to place the Persian (or any other non-European) epic in the context of real (not the colonially fictional Eurocentric) *world literature*, we must detect the ways in which its epic nature consistently overcomes its imperial uses and abuses and theorize the manner in which its poetics triumphs over its passing politics. To do so we need to see how its stories tower more prominently over its histories and show how its form trumps its formalities. Above all, you will see me consistently demonstrate how its Oedipal (or what I call *Sohrabaneh*) trauma dismantles its patriarchal order, and how its subdued eroticism undermines its flaunted warmongering, or how its festive *bazms* undermine its fighting *razms*. Ultimately this line of argument leads to my basic proposal that the sense of tragic in the *Shahnameh* embraces its sense of triumph, and how its *subversive* narrative foreshadows its triumphalist prosody. The result of this decidedly worldly reading of the *Shahnameh* places it against the very grain of the triumphalist reading of European epics from the *Iliad* to Virgil, a sentiment now evident in the very imperial diction of the idea of "World Literature."

By placing the *Shahnameh* far beyond the foreclosed totality of Eurocentric "World Literature," we open up its expansive vistas onto the infinity of a planetary conception of *world literature* that will liberate the very ideas of "modern epic" and "world text" into far more emancipatory literary and moral horizons. Ferdowsi's *Shahnameh* is neither triumphalist nor defeatist, if we were to place it on a common Eurocentric classification of epic. It is a decidedly defiant epic, drawing attention to its own form by the power of its expansive poetics. It is to that poetic force that I first and foremost draw your attention in this book. The *Shahnameh* is rich. It is diversified. Historians can draw historical evidence, biographers biographical data, emperors seek legitimacy, tyrants fish for justification, as could linguists rely on its syntax and morphology for their own purposes. But it is first and foremost as a poetic act of ingenious originality and power that I emphasize the enduring significance of the Persian epic in order to place it in the context of a radically reconfigured conception of *world literature*.

The *Shahnameh* began from the scattered sources in both Persian and Pahlavi. It was gathered and composed into a singularly beautiful and compelling narrative by a gifted, driven, and visionary poet. It was then loved, celebrated, admired, produced in beautiful illustrated manuscripts and, as such, served successive empires as the talismanic touchstone of their always fragile legitimacy. All those empires eventually collapsed, and European colonial modernity dawned on the Persian-speaking world—from India to the Mediterranean shores. Postcolonial nations emerged and laid varied claims on the Persian epic, as did states seeking legitimacy from the bygone ages the Persian epic represented. It was a mismatch, but it worked. The varied worlds the *Shahnameh* has historically inhabited are no longer there. The world in which it now lives is no longer a Persianate empire. It is an American empire—fragile, clumsy, dysfunctional, self-destructive, abusive, vulgar, producing its own unconvincing epics, therefore in no need of any "Persian epic."

The poetic power of the *Shahnameh*, however, was never contingent on any imperial anchorage or abuse. It gave those passing empires the symbolic legitimacy they needed and lacked but kept the substance of its own poetic sublimity to itself. It is now precisely that poetic sublimity that must be matched and mixed with the fragile world the *Shahnameh* today inhabits. The fragmented world in which the *Shahnameh* now lives, and in which it can lay a claim to being *world literature*, renders its stories allegorical, as indeed the closed-circuited totality of this world opens up the infinity of its poetic possibilities, its intuition of transcendence, now as forever definitive to the *Shahnameh*. My book is about this matching, this approximation: bringing the Persian epic to a close encounter with a fragmented empire it now inhabits, it can never legitimize, and it will ipso facto, discredit.

The *Shahnameh* is a long beautiful poem now mostly read in English, the language of an empire upon whose flag "the sun never set." It is reported that Herodotus once used that phrase for the Persian empire. From the Achaemenids to the British and now the American, empires rise and fall, all reflected in the shining pages and magnificent stories of a Persian epic that has endured and survived them all—to teach them a lesson or two in humility, and give the rest of us the good tidings of resistance, resilience, and triumph, so we can all learn that if empires lasted the whole world would be reading the *Shahnameh* in its original.

ACKNOWLEDGMENTS

The idea of this book on Ferdowsi's *Shahnameh* was first suggested to me years ago by my good friend and longtime editor Sharmila Sen. It took much longer than I had hoped or anticipated to write this book. But I still remember Sharmila's enthusiasm about the idea and am happy to have delivered what I promised her I would do.

Mahmoud Omidsalar is a world authority on the *Shahnameh* and a dear and close friend of mine. Without making sure he had read every word I wrote here in this book I would not have dared writing on the Persian epic. He is not on the same page with me on many of my thoughts in this book about a seminal text we both love and admire. But he was exceedingly generous and patient reading me out and being tolerant of my speculations. Dedicating this book to him is the only way I know how to publicly acknowledge my gratitude.

Another good friend and colleague, Ahmad Sadri, is an equally authoritative scholar and translator of the *Shahnameh*. He, too, has read portions of this book and given me valuable comments. It is not easy to write on the Persian epic with so many towering scholars in the field. But their grace and friendship have seen me through the task—at once daredevil and joyous, exacting and exhilarating.

Two anonymous readers generously took time to review my manuscript and offer me extraordinary comments helping me revise my book in purposeful and sometimes even unanticipated ways. I don't know who these distinguished scholars are but am indebted to them beyond words. One of these two reviewers was particularly helpful in passages of my book where I take on the issue of "World Literature." I am thankful to this colleague. I cherish the time-honored practice of such selfless service. I have done it for others and am privileged to have received it from these colleagues, too.

My Columbia University Press editor, Philip Leventhal, has been a constant source of support and unwavering professional integrity to see my book through publication. I am grateful for his constant patience and extraordinary editorial care. Lisa Hamm, senior designer at Columbia University Press, has been exemplary in her aesthetic taste, patience, and grace to give my book the look of a quiet elegance in which it has now reached you. I am ever so grateful to her. I thank Sheila Canby, Patti

Cadby Birch Curator in Charge of Islamic Art at the Metropolitan Museum of Art in New York, for her gracious help with illustrations on the cover and chapter headings of my book.

My research assistant, Sumaya Akkas, had an uncanny ability to procure obscure sources for me at a moment's notice. This book will always be indebted to her.

The two successive chairmen of my department as I was writing this book, Timothy Mitchell and Mamadou Diouf, have been exceptionally supportive of my work during their tenure. I am blessed by their friendship and collegiality.

As in my all other work, I have written this book on the *Shahnameh* while away from Iran, not in exile—an expression for which I have no use—but in an enduring distance from a homeland I can claim only in my scholarship, in a perpetual sense of loss I can remedy only when I read and write (about) "Iran."

New York
Spring 2018

THE
SHAHNAMEH

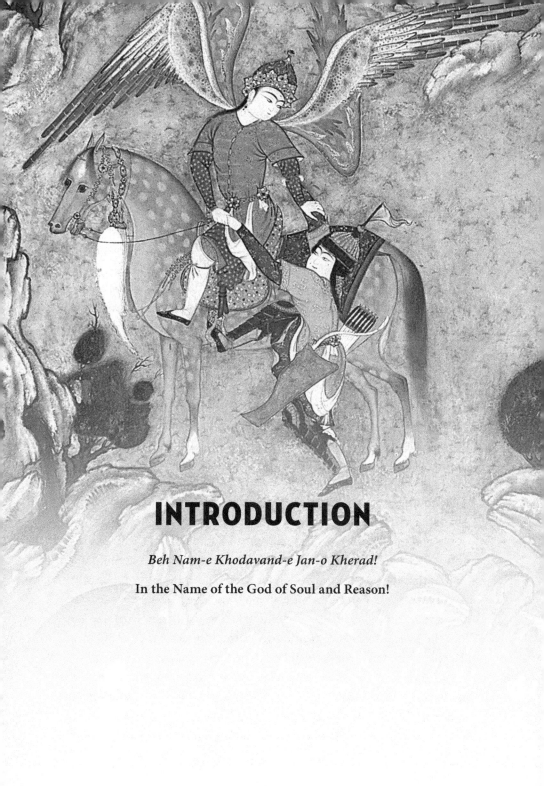

INTRODUCTION

Beh Nam-e Khodavand-e Jan-o Kherad!

In the Name of the God of Soul and Reason!

t takes certain audacity, a lofty sense of purpose, an abiding determination to do, or to have done, what is necessary, to begin a book with that kind of magisterial pronouncement and authorial power: *In the Name of the God of Soul and Reason!* And then to bring the evocation home: *For beyond this, (human) intellect cannot reach!*

Khodavand is God in Persian, the language in which this poem is composed. But the poet opts to specify what kind of God is to sit so majestically upon the commencement of his poetic edifice: the God that has given us life and reason, a soul and a sense of right and wrong, the ability to think, for beyond the invocation of the name of such a God human intellect itself cannot reach. He then goes on to specify who exactly this God is: the God that makes it possible for us to secure a good name for ourselves and ascertain a respectable standing among our peers, and the God that gives us our daily sustenance and who guides us, the God that created this vast universe and its planets, and the God who brought light to the Sun, the Moon, and Venus. The poet then confesses this God is superior to our ability to name, to identify, or to speculate about his nature, so we must think of him as an artist perhaps whose work of art is quite evident but not his own whereabouts. I keep using the gender-specific pronoun "he" or "him." But in Persian we don't have gender-specific pronouns. So this God is beyond gender and thus beyond any pronouns. So as you see you enter the commencement of these lines of poetry, and before you know it a whole different universe is opened up to you. You keep reading and going down the lines, every line a step upward and downward and sideways into the making of an edifice that the poet and you build together. The imperial world he inherited and the poetic world he built, before you know it, become your world too, the world in which you live and read and teach and learn. He gives you the line and you keep reading and fathoming what they could mean. The play is endless. The game joyous. The stage sparkles with magic.[1]

Who is the poet who wrote those words at the commencement of his monumental epic? Whence his pious vigilance, this august sobriety, this power and poise with which he commands the attention and secures the respect of any person who can read and understand Persian anywhere around the world, from the epicenter of Khorasan in northeastern Iran where the poet lived around the world into the home and habitat of any Afghan, Iranian, Tajik, or any other person who can claim Ferdowsi's mother tongue as his or her own.

Ferdowsi's *Shahnameh*. There have been many *Shahnameh*s in the course of Persian poetic history—both before and after Ferdowsi's *Shahnameh* (composed ca. 1010). But today as indeed throughout history when we say "the *Shahnameh*" we mean Ferdowsi's *Shahnameh*. "The Book of Kings": that is what "*Shahnameh*" means, for it is a book about kings, queens, and heroes. But the word "shah" does not only mean "king" but can also mean "the Best," "the Most Significant," "the Chief." *Shah-daneh* means the best seed, *Shah-tut* means the best berry, *Shah-rag* means the most important vein, *Shah-parak* means the most beautiful wings and thus a "butterfly": thus *Shahnameh* can also mean "The Best Book," "The Master Book," "The Principal Book," or simply "The Book."[2]

"The *Shahnameh* to me is what the Hebrew Bible is to an orthodox Jew." Mahmoud Omidsalar, one of a handful of eminent *Shahnameh* scholars alive today, is not usually taken by hyperbole. I still remember this phrase with his solid Isfahani accent and I wonder. Every time I come near Ferdowsi's *Shahnameh*, Omidsalar's phrase first stands between my reverential fingers and the opening page of the Persian epic. The first few lines I read still echo Omidsalar's voice, but soon Ferdowsi's magic begins to strip you of all your worldly concerns and seduces you into its poetic power, storytelling panache, wise missives, heartbreaking asides, rising crescendos of battlefields, erotic corners of his heroes' amorous adventures, and above all the triumphant defiance of his sublime gift of storytelling. You become a character, willy-nilly, in his plays. You act out, you sing along, you recite the lines out loud that demand and exact elocution.

I write this book to tell you all about the *Shahnameh*, most everything I have learned reading and teaching the Persian epic for a lifetime. But first let me tell you one of the stories of the *Shahnameh* before we go any further.

THE STORY

Once upon a time, and what a strange time it was, in a faraway land there lived a king named Merdas who had a young and handsome son named Zahhak. Zahhak was fiercely brave and blindly ambitious and very receptive when Ahriman (Satan) appeared to him as a counselor and advised him to kill his father and become the king. Zahhak did as Iblis (Satan) had told him to do (with the possible and perhaps even tacit complicity of his mother), agreed for Iblis to plot and kill his father, and became the king of his father's realm. Next the selfsame Satan appeared to Zahhak as a cook and every day prepared for him a delicious feast and eventually made him carnivorous. Grateful to his amazing cook, Zahhak ordered him one day to ask his king for a favor. Iblis said all he wanted was to kiss Zahhak's shoulders. Zahhak said fine. No sooner had Iblis kissed Zahhak's shoulders than he disappeared into the thin air and two monstrous serpents emerged from Zahhak's shoulders exactly where Iblis had kissed them. Next Iblis appeared to him as a physician and told him the only cure for his serpents, to prevent them from devouring him, was to kill two young men every day and feed the monstrous serpents their brains. Meanwhile in Iran a just and magnanimous king named Jamshid was ruling the world, and yet eventually arrogance and hubris took over him and weakened his kingdom, which is precisely the moment when Zahhak accepted the invitation of Iranian nobility to come to their capital, which he did and from where he ruled the world with terror and tyranny.

In the *Shahnameh* story of Zahhak we come across one of the earliest accounts of the father-son-mother power struggle and erotic tensions that will run consistently throughout much of the Persian epic. In this particular case, we see a son who covets his father's throne and through the intermediary function of Iblis kills him. Ferdowsi's wording of this murder suggests either a conspiracy between Zahhak and his mother to kill his father or else an allusion that the king was in fact not Zahhak's father and he was born out of wedlock to an illicit relationship between his mother and someone else.

He conspired to kill his own father—
I have heard wise men say:
That an evil son even if fierce as a lion
Will never kill his own father—
Unless in secret the story is something else:
The curious must discover the mother's secret.[3]

In either case, if Ferdowsi is merely alluding to the possibility of Zahhak's being a bastard or his mother's having shared his son's plot to murder her husband, we have a decidedly circuitous twist on the Freudian Oedipal complex, in which case Zahhak's two giant snakes become phallic symbols of an insatiable urge to kill all the other sons to prevent them from murdering Zahhak himself. This, which posits Zahhak and his mother as an archetype of the trope for the rest of the *Shahnameh*, is the first case of patricide as regicide in one of the earliest stories of the Persian epic. Zahhak's mother's possible complicity in the murder of her husband and helping her son ascend the throne can itself be read as her desire for the father-king to be replaced by the son-king. She wants the father-king to come out of her womb as a son-king, so that fathers are symbolically castrated, preempted, foreclosed. Even if we opt for the reading that Zahhak's mother did not conspire with her son to kill her husband still we have the narratively absented biological father of Zahhak, which in effect reduces the triumvirate of father-mother-son to a mother-son register.[4]

Such *Shahnameh* stories, which abound in the Persian epic, offer fresh, provocative, and at times destabilizing occasions to reflect back on psychoanalytic theories we have received from mostly European provenances. If, for example, we were to read Zahhak's story in this manner, then what the French philosopher Gilles Deleuze suggests in his *Présentation de Sacher-Masoch* (*Masochism: Coldness and Cruelty*, 1967) not only offers a partially plausible reading of the late nineteenth-century German novelist Leopold von Sacher-Masoch but also takes us much farther into a renewed understanding of *world literature*. In Deleuze's reading, the masochist subject (which he successfully decouples from the sadist) effectively dismantles the patriarchal order and reaches out for a pre-Oedipal maternal universe. In this pre- or post-Oedipal subversion of the patriarchal, the acting subject becomes always already heteronormative in his/her pansexual trajectory of desire. Zahhak's feeding his snakes with the brains of the young male subjects (Iblis had turned him into not just a carnivore but also in fact a cannibal) reflects his fear of castration and offers a powerful homoerotic urge, while his pending demise in the hands of Kaveh the Blacksmith (whose sons had been killed by the king to feed their brains to his serpents) and the restoration of Fereydun to the Iranian throne represent a pronounced return to the patriarchal order.[5]

I occasionally venture out into such speculative reflections on *Shahnameh* stories via theoretical familiarities in the European domain in order both to wet your speculative appetites and yet hold them at bay when we go back to the stories themselves. As a towering masterpiece of worldly literature, Ferdowsi's *Shahnameh* is a gold mine of such exquisite stories that are yet to be fully explored and assayed in their social and psychological implications. If you wish to learn what happened to Zahhak and his serpents at the end you need to allow me to welcome you to this magnificent epic in its entirety, so full of strange and amazing stories as it is. The first thing you will probably need to know is who the author of this epic was, when and where it was composed, in what language, for what purpose, how it survived through the ages, how it reached us, what the stories told in this epic are, how they are related, and how we might benefit from reading it today. If we are to consider it in the enticing category of "World Literature," what could that inclusion possibly mean? By focusing on one literary masterpiece definitive to an entire world of literary imagination, I place the text and its author in the larger frame of their historical contexts (in plural). I am particularly mindful of both the inner world of the Persian epic itself and the multiple imperial worldliness in which it has been put to political use. The normative and moral space in between these worlds is itself an unfolding world. By bringing a global attention to these interwoven layers of worldliness I wish to map out the hidden geography of ignorance and negligence that today passes as "World Literature."

I therefore write this book in order to facilitate your reading of the *Shahnameh*, learning about its composition, its heroes and villains, love stories and tragedies, memorable dramas and historical narratives. Imagine Shakespearean dramas and mix them with Homeric deeds, if those are the literary classics with which you are familiar, and then forget about them both, for in the *Shahnameh* you will learn a whole new spectrum of stories you probably never knew existed or were even possible before. I intend to make the foreignness of the Persian epic familiar to you, without losing its innate and irreducible meaning and significance. By the end of my book, I hope you will rush to read the *Shahnameh* in the best translation available in your mother tongue, and even if you didn't then through my book you will gain a solid and reliable command over what the book is all about and why people consider it a world-class epic, and what sorts of lessons it has to teach us even today. I will read the *Shahnameh* with you, place you in its history, tell you about its author, guide you through its illustrious labyrinth, and then we sit down together to wonder at its magic. I have wondered at its magic since I discovered myself the native speaker of the language in which the Persian epic is composed. I have marveled at the fact that Ferdowsi and I were born to the same maternal language. I have heard it recited by wandering storytellers in the streets of my hometown. I have learned its diction and prosody from my elementary and high school teachers. I have read its poetic power from the learned scholars of my homeland.

When my eldest son, Kaveh (named after a *Shahnameh* hero as you will soon discover), was a young boy I used to tell him *Shahnameh* stories. Before long he began to compose his own "*Shahnameh* stories," placing his favorite heroes of the Persian epic on various planets around the galaxy. He soon became distracted by other superheroes—Superman, Batman, and such. But something of the *Shahnameh* stayed with him and grew to give sculpted vision to his later literary taste. Kaveh is born and raised in the United States. His Persian is sufficient but hesitant. I told him *Shahnameh* stories in English. I now think the stories of the *Shahnameh* I told him and later taught my other children require and deserve a much wider readership. I write this book to share the joy of telling *Shahnameh* stories to my own children and teaching my students to a much wider audience. I believe the sheer pleasure of these stories is the surest path to their inner truth, their wider philosophical implications. In many of the existing translations in English unfortunately the segments of the *Shahnameh* in which Ferdowsi is meditative, self-reflective, and addresses profound issues his stories raise are left untranslated, for what reason I shirk from speculating. I alert you to these what I call the poetic implosions within the narrative and ask you to think with me about what they mean.

Why is this epic so important? It is impossible to exaggerate the significance of Ferdowsi's *Shahnameh* as the imperial epic of a bygone age and successive empires to which today a number of postcolonial nations such as Iran, Afghanistan, Tajikistan, Azerbaijan, and even the vaster Persianate world that includes Georgia, Armenia, Turkey, Dagestan, Pakistan, and as far as India have a legitimate claim. A long epic poem written originally in Persian and subsequently translated into countless other languages, the *Shahnameh* was composed in some fifty thousand verses between 977 and 1010, when the shape of the civilized world was much different than what we see today. It is the longest epic poem ever composed by a single poet. It is usually divided into three sections—mythical, heroic, and historical—narrating a global history of a people that Ferdowsi himself calls Iranians and their land Iran—from the creation of the world to the Arab conquest of the Sassanid Empire in 650s. What today we call Iran is only a fragment of what Ferdowsi called Iran. His was an imperial age and lexicon, ours a postcolonial. We need to reimagine ourselves back to his age before we commence our journey forward to come to ours.

When and where and why was the *Shahnameh* written? Who wrote it and for what reasons and purposes? What were the historical circumstances of its composition? Can you imagine a gifted poet spending his entire lifetime writing only one book? Just imagine the courage, the conviction, the sense of purpose and the determination. What literary tradition does it come from? Who was Ferdowsi, the single author of this epic, and what prompted him to spend a lifetime collecting the necessary written and oral material and then sit down and write it from beginning to end of this monumental work? What is the basic structural composition of the *Shahnameh* narrative, and how are these sections connected? What are some of the most important stories of the *Shahnameh*: Zahhak and his serpents on his shoulders; King Jamshid, who became immortal and arrogant; the tragedy of Rostam, who inadvertently killed his own son Sohrab; the story of innocent Seyavash, whose stepmother fell in love with him; the tragedy of Esfandiar, and Rostam's sad fate to kill him; what about the love stories of Rostam and Tahmineh, Bizhan and Manizheh; what about the stories of Anushirvan and his wise vizier, Bozorgmehr? Did you know Alexander the Great has a whole story in the *Shahnameh*?

What are these stories and how are we to read and interpret them? There is not a single volume in English or any other European language that can act as a simple and solid guide to the *Shahnameh* or what its fate was after its composition in 1010 and before modern scholars in the nineteenth and twentieth centuries began to collect all the available manuscripts they could find and prepare a critical edition of it. What was the organic link between the significance of the *Shahnameh*—both materially and symbolically—for all those Persianate empires that preserved and staged and celebrated it: the Ghaznavids, the Seljuqids, the Mongols, the Timurids, the Mughals, the Safavids, or the Ottomans? What can we learn from such an intimate structural link between the *Shahnameh* as an epic and the different empires that decidedly celebrated it?

What happened to the *Shahnameh* when these empires collapsed and eventually postcolonial nation-states emerged? How and to what particular purpose was the *Shahnameh* claimed and reclaimed by modern nation-states? How can an imperial epic be claimed and appropriated by postcolonial nation-states? Can the politics of an epic be separated from the epical politics it invokes? Ferdowsi's *Shahnameh* is no ordinary book. It breathes with a living history. It makes past present, the present palpitate with past. It shrinks time, it collapses distant spaces upon one another, it mixes facts and fantasies, it matches otherwise dissonant cognitive stages of our historical consciousness. It is written in beautiful calligraphy, it is recited eloquently, it is performed dramatically, it is painted elegantly, it is staged theatrically and cinematically. It is cited when children are born, or when revolutionaries succeed, or dynasties fall, and it is cited when national heroes die. It is the talismanic evidence of dignity and pride of place of a people, a nation, a national consciousness, scattered beyond many fictive frontiers, evident through any and all boundaries.

Having been born to the language and culture of the *Shahnameh*, and growing up with both the learned and the popular versions of the book, and after decades of studying it closely and teaching it to generations of my students, I intend to open up the evident and concealed pleasures and wisdom of one of the greatest literary masterpieces in *world literature* for a new generation of students and educated public alike. My ambition is to make the *Shahnameh* as proverbial to a global conversation about epic and poetry as the *Gilgamesh*, *Iliad*, *Odyssey*, or *Aeneid* have been, and as the *Mahabharata* should be. A classic, they say, is a book everyone cites but no one reads. I intend to make people read the *Shahnameh*.

THE POET AND HIS PATRON

The *Shahnameh* is no antiquarian relic. It is a living organism. Based on earlier sources, it was conceived at a certain point in history. It was poetically delivered by a master craftsman and born into this world with a conscious awareness of its significance. It was not canonized by changing literary historiography. It was made definitive to an imperial political culture that had given birth to it to begin with. It has gone through successive generations and gestations. It has aged gracefully. Today its aging countenance still carries its youthful disposition. As a text, it can excite and instruct at one and the same time. But that is not all that there is to its living organism. It is an imperial consciousness now embedded in multiple peoples and nations from one end of the world to the next, anywhere and everywhere that a Persian-speaking person can open it to its initial pages and read: *Beh Nam-e Khodavand-e Jan-o Kherad!*

The author of the epic is Hakim Abolqasem Ferdowsi Tusi (ca. 940–1020), one of the towering Persian poets of all time. He was born in the village of Paj near the city of Tus in the northeastern province of Khorasan to an impoverished landed gentry in the year 940. Khorasan was a rich and fertile region in the nascent Samanid Empire (819–999) that had secured a sizable territory in Central Asian domains that today encompasses Iran, Afghanistan, and Tajikistan. The little that is known about Ferdowsi's personal life portrays him as a young husband and a loving father who is grief-stricken by the death of his young son, and who makes a note of that tragedy in his *Shahnameh*. Such personal remarks are a veritable feature of the Persian epic, where we are always conscious and aware of the person and the poet behind his magnum opus.

The text of the *Shahnameh* and the authorship of Ferdowsi are intertwined in our reading of the Persian epic. The poet and his poem have become interchangeable signifiers for each other, to the point that today the mere mentioning of the name Ferdowsi also means his *Shahnameh* and *Shahnameh* also means Ferdowsi. Sultan Mahmoud of Ghazna (r. 998–1002), who would become Ferdowsi's patron, was a powerful warlord and world conqueror, the most prominent sultan in the Ghaznavid Empire (977–1186), which extended from eastern Iran into the northern Indian subcontinent. Under his reign the Ghaznavid Empire became a solid bastion of Persian language and culture, inheriting what the Samanids had already achieved and expanding it deeply from Central Asia through Iran to northern India. Though rooted in the Samanid cultural revival of the Persian culture, Ferdowsi came to full fruition under Mahmoud of Ghazna, and thus historically the poet, the patron, and the poetic legacy of the *Shahnameh* have all been intertwined. The fusion of the three is so endearing and enduring that it has spread deeply into the folkloric traditions surrounding the poet and the poem and extended to satirical remembrances of the patron who had originally commissioned the writing of the *Shahnameh*.

According to one such delightful folkloric story, when Ferdowsi finished his *Shahnameh* he offered it to Sultan Mahmoud. The powerful sultan had promised him a gold coin for every line of his poetry in the epic, which had now reached more than fifty thousand couplets. The sultan looked at that many lines and thought no way he could give the poet so many gold coins. He consulted with his viziers and offered him as many coins of silver. Ferdowsi was deeply disappointed by the sultan's reneging on his promise. "Your Majesty," he said, "I just remembered a few additional lines, and I'd like to take my manuscript back and add them to the end of the book." On his way out he gave all the silver coins to the sultan's retinue. He went straight to a mosque where the sultan used to pray and wrote a graffito on its wall somewhere Mahmoud could see it:

> Oh you Sultan Mahmoud the world conqueror:
> If you are not afraid of me be afraid of God!
> For thirty years I suffered to write the *Shahnameh*
> So that the King would appropriately reward me—
> For sure the King was born to a lowly baker,
> For he has given me the rewards enough to buy a loaf of bread!
> If the King's mother were of a noble descent,
> I would have been richly rewarded with gold and silver.

Sultan Mahmoud heard of this story and had his soldiers chase after the poet to punish him, but Ferdowsi ran away to Baghdad and sought refuge with the ruling caliph. At the end Ferdowsi returned to his homeland upon receiving the sad news his son had passed away. Sultan Mahmoud sent for Ferdowsi with the award he had initially promised him. But his delegation and their award arrived as Ferdowsi's coffin was being carried to his grave.[6]

The apocryphal nature of this folkloric story has all the plausible elements of Ferdowsi's life embedded in an implausible narrative that speaks of the truth of the fiction at the heart of the memorial manner in which generations have opted to remember Ferdowsi the poet, his patron Sultan Mahmoud, and his epic masterpiece. The fictive manner of this prose is almost entirely irrelevant to the factual evidence of a world in which people's creative imagination across centuries and through empires lends a helping hand to the most abiding truths of their cultural heritage.

THE HISTORY

Yeki bud yeki nabud gheyr az Khoda hich kas nabud! That is how in Persian we say, "Once upon a time," though literally we say, "There was one, there was no other, except for God no one else was!" The phrase is an invitation into a time immemorial. "There were those who were alive, and there were those who were yet to be born, but except for God no one ever exists anyway"—that is what the phrase really means idiomatically: transfusing a theological speculation into a story time that has the time of its own. By telling you the stories of the *Shahnameh*, I plan to make the magic of that phrase meaningful to you. The stories of the *Shahnameh* are embedded in history. There is an active fusion between the stories of the Persian epic, rooted in bygone ages, and the living ages people have experienced with the stories that Ferdowsi put into beautiful poetry for them as the trusted codex of their lived experiences. Like all other good stories, the tale of the *Shahnameh* itself is embedded in history—and it is in history that we must begin.

The Muslim conquest of Iran in the seventh century dismantled the more than four-hundred-year reign of the Sassanid Empire (224–651) and subjected its vast domain to the emerging Arab dynasties. That was a powerful empire, and this was a crushing defeat. As Iran was actively incorporated into the expanding Umayyad (656–750) and then Abbasid (750–1258) Empires, Arabic language and Islamic culture and civilization dominated the world from the Indus Valley to the Mediterranean coasts. From this fateful encounter between a dying empire and its culture and a rising imperium and its civilization, the Persian language eventually emerged with a new zest and energy. As the power of the central caliphate initially in Damascus and subsequently in Baghdad began to decline in the late ninth century, Persianate dynasties emerged in the eastern and northern provinces. The Samanid Empire (819–999), under whose rule Ferdowsi emerged as a prominent poet, was one among such dynasties. These dynasties in general, and the Samanids in particular, were politically drawn to the Persian language as the lingua franca of their expanding domains, for their subjects may have converted to Islam but their language and culture had remained mostly Persian. By culture and character their ruling monarchs were drawn to Persian heritage, including myths and legends, language and literature, prose and poetry. Beholden to the Sassanid Empire as the prototype of their own imperial ambitions, the Samanid and all other subsequent monarchs were looking favorably to those poets and prose stylists who had started gathering such ancient Persian sources. Ferdowsi was the culmination of such poets, their crowning achievement.

Like all other epics, the *Shahnameh* is an imperial narrative, the product of an imperial heritage, embedded in a crucial period in history when Iranian dynasties were actively asserting themselves against their Arab conquerors. From its completion in the year 1010, it has had an enduring significance in the life and long history of the Persianate world and successive empires that have ruled it. As a living text, it has been the cultural heritage of multiple nations within such bygone empires. As such the *Shahnameh* has functioned as the political icon of both national sovereignty and state legitimacy in subsequent postcolonial nation-states. The content and the context of the Persian epic are thus intertwined, one framing the interpretation of the other. The story of the *Shahnameh* itself, as a book, an epic, an enduring icon, is as a result intertwined with the long history of post–Arab conquest Persianate dynasties from Central Asia to the Mediterranean leading to the active formations of the postcolonial nations. While its function as a tool of "state legitimacy" may vary from a Pahlavi dynasty (1925–1979) to an Islamic Republic in our own lifetime, its centrality to the historic constitution of "national sovereignty" in a country like Iran becomes definitive.

How can this central significance of the *Shahnameh* as a text be historically documented? The enduring importance of Ferdowsi's *Shahnameh* can be assayed by the countless simple or lavishly illustrated manuscripts of its various copies that have reached our time from various royal courts and dynasties. With the rise of every new dynasty the commissioning of the writing and illustration of a copy of the Persian epic was the surest manner of laying claim on loyalty and legitimacy. In the course of postcolonial nation-states, the preparation of a critical edition of the book based on such original manuscripts became a functional equivalent of such earlier efforts and kept generations of scholars very busy, searching for the closest possible approximation to the original text of Ferdowsi. European and non-European Orientalists have also been deeply involved in preparing such critical editions. Two of the earliest such editions were prepared in 1811 by Matthew Lumsden and 1829 by T. Macan, both in India. Between 1838 and 1878, the French scholar Julius Mohl (1831–1868) prepared another critical edition that remained reliable for decades. A German scholar, J. A. Vullers, began yet another critical edition in 1877 but did not get to finish it. A Russian team of scholars led by E. E. Bertels prepared (1960–1971) a finely edited critical edition of Ferdowsi's *Shahnameh*, which became the most authoritative text for many decades. But the critical edition prepared by Djalal Khaleghi-Motlagh and his colleagues beginning in 1988 is today considered by far the most reliable version of the epic. All these critical editions are monuments to successive generations of scholarship dedicated to the enduring significance of Ferdowsi's *Shahnameh*. Throughout the ages, from courtly sponsored and lavishly illustrated manuscripts to preparing critical editions, the iconic significance of the *Shahnameh* in both empire- and nation-building projects has been paramount.

The European discovery of the *Shahnameh*, as perhaps best represented by Matthew Arnold's (1822–1888) famous poem "Tragedy of Sohrab and Rustum," but also in the admiration for it expressed by Victor Hugo and Goethe, gave it a renewed global significance far beyond its Persianate borders. The translations of the *Shahnameh* into European languages were sporadic but consistent. Louis M. Langlès translated a few episodes of the Persian epic into French in 1788. Later, in 1859, Victor Hugo, who was drawn to Persian poetry, became seriously interested in the Persian epic. Finally, Julius Mohl produced the first complete translation of the epic in French. Numerous other translations into other European languages appeared, and the first serious attention to it in the English-speaking world was by Sir William Jones (1746–1794).[7] Many other partial or complete translations were made into other languages; the version done by Dick Davis today stands as the most widely admired and justly celebrated version of the *Shahnameh* available in English.[8] The most recent illustrated version of the epic in English is the popular

Shahnameh: The Epic of the Persian Kings, translated equally compe-
tently by Ahmad Sadri and illustrated by Hamid Rahmanian. A number of interrelated factors and forces are at work throughout these
mostly European, Russian, and North American interests in the Persian
epic. The romantic aspects of the *Shahnameh* appeared to the European
Romanticists, while colonial officers like Sir William Jones were attracted
to its imperial pedigree when in the service of the British Empire.

Although the seal and signature of an imperial age are all over the
Shahnameh, its continued relevance brings its mesmerizing stories to our
own age. There are reports that during the Iran-Iraq War (1980–1988)
the former Iranian president Abolhassan Bani-Sadr referenced it in his
speeches to high-ranking Iranian officers to instill courage in them to
defend Iran against the Iraqi invasion. During the celebration of Noruz
at the time of U.S. president Obama's administration pictures of a recent
edition of the *Shahnameh* could be seen on the Haft Sin table at the
White House. The living symbolism and enduring power of the Persian
epic continue to unfold apace long after Ferdowsi first put pen to paper
and wrote, *Beh Nam-e Khodavand-e Jan-o Kherad!*

THE *SHAHNAMEH* AS AN EPIC
IN WORLD LITERATURE

What can a close familiarity with this Persian epic as I intend to provide in this book do to help us rethink the very idea of "World Literature" as we understand it today? Can the *Shahnameh* be considered part
and parcel of *world literature*, and what would such a designation actually mean? How would it affect our reading of the *Shahnameh* as we have
received it today? How would it affect our understanding of *world literature* if we bring the *Shahnameh* into our consideration? I wish to posit
Ferdowsi's *Shahnameh* not merely as a significant epic that merits being
included in that category (which many scholars have always held) but
also, and far more important, as an occasion that enables us to critically
think through the very idea of *world literature*. Other scholars (older and

younger generations) have already made persuasive arguments as to why the Persian epic richly deserves to be thus considered. But I have a far more ambitious proposal here. I wish to tell the story of the *Shahnameh*, its author, its patronage, its ancient roots, its imperial provenance, and later its varied national destinies as a constellation of parameters that enables us to see a whole different *world*, in fact multiple *worlds*, in which epic poetry and the literary imagination it has enabled had a towering presence. In this book, in other words, I intend to bring back to life a different "world" in which a vastly different conception of "word literature" was possible long before Goethe and other European and North American thinkers and scholars entertained the idea. I have already addressed the theoretical foregrounding of this argument in *The World of Persian Literary Humanism*.[9] In this book I want to deliver and map out that argument in the specific case of this epic masterpiece. We cannot simply take the notion of "World Literature" as it has been articulated by Western European and North American scholars for granted and then try to push the *Shahnameh* onto it—awaiting or expecting the theoretical generosity of "First World" theorists. We need to rethink the whole category. This objective is not merely to rescue the very idea of *world literature* from its astonishingly prolonged Eurocentric provincialism but also, conversely, to liberate the *Shahnameh* itself from generations of its abusive readings for decidedly political purposes. The Persian epic has sustained an entirely original relationship to questions of temporality, history, and empire hitherto left un- or undertheorized by its most serious readers. The next generation of scholarship needs to address that challenge. For now, the groundwork I laid in *The World of Persian Literary Humanism* I need to bring to bear on this singularly significant text to see in what particular way the Persian epic fares in the grander scheme of things.

To do so, my objective in this book is to bring *The Book of Kings* to life at the forefront of a new generation of literary consciousness by asking the simple question, how are we to understand the place of Ferdowsi's *Shahnameh* as a Persian epic and its relations to various Persianate empires it informed in the context of other studies of epic and empires?

In *Epic and Empire: Politics and Generic Form from Virgil to Milton* (1993) David Quint divides the genre of European epics into two kinds: the Virgilian epics of conquest siding with the victors (Virgil's *Aeneid*, Camões's *Lusíadas*, Tasso's *Gerusalemme liberata*) and the countervailing epic of the defeated (Lucan's *Pharsalia*, Ercilla's *Araucana*, and d'Aubigné's *Les tragiques*). Whereas the victorious Virgilian epic follows a linear, teleological narrative, the epic of the defeated follows an episodic and open-ended cycle. In an equally significant study, *Modern Epic: The World-System from Goethe to García Márquez* (1996), Franco Moretti offers a theory of "the modern epic" in which he seeks to account for such monumental works of modern fiction as *Faust*, *Moby-Dick*, *The Nibelung's Ring*, *Ulysses*, *The Cantos*, *The Waste Land*, *The Man Without Qualities*, and *One Hundred Years of Solitude*. These works of modern epics, Moretti argues, represent and naturalize the imperial and colonial European domination of the planet. In this book, I will have multiple occasions and different reasons to refer to these two significant books. In my subsequent chapters you will see me invoke the ideas of these two eminent theorists not to find fault with them but to use their crucial studies as a springboard to think the Persian epic into a renewed worldliness beyond both its nativist readings and cliché-ridden praise deprived of any critical thinking. I am not critical of these theorists because they are Eurocentric. They are European and American literary scholars. Why should they not be Eurocentric? Europe and its cultural environs are their area of scholarly interest. Their blind spots, however, are the locations where we can place worldly epics like the *Shahnameh* as we seek to rethink the notion of "World Literature." You will see me having multiple reasons in this book to dwell on this Eurocentric limitation.

These two complementary studies, both offering sweeping theorizations of Comparative and World Literature, contain significant insights into the working of European or what their authors decidedly call Western epics—and yet neither of them has anything (serious or even in passing) to say about any other (what perforce is) "non-Western epic," be it classical or modern, the *Ramayana* and *Mahabharata* or the *Shahnameh*. This is neither surprising nor indeed any fault of these distinguished scholars, who habitually talk (as they should) about their areas of competence, knowledge, and interest. But given the normative hegemony of scholarship on "Western epics," what they think and write ipso facto denaturalizes other "non-Western epics," turns them into oddities, exceptions, abnormalities. That inexorable division inevitably distorts the very assumption that we can critically think through *other* epics that have already been *othered* and therefore alienated from their own genre, their own textuality, their own history. When they write in English but effectively privilege certain epics and disregard others they seem to forget that the imperial reach of their scholarly language has already run ahead of them to put the global literary scene on the same pedestal— European and American literary theorists write in colonial languages (English or French) but retreat to their respective literary provincialism when they talk about "epic." But their imperial English is also a postcolonial English—namely, what they generically theorize, we can, with the very same English, detheorize, meaning what they universalize we must particularize, epistemically dethrone.

The task here is not to "provincialize Europe," as it is now fashionable to say following the publication of Dipesh Chakrabarty's *Provincializing Europe: Postcolonial Thought and Historical Difference* (2000), a book that in fact recentralized rather than "provincialized" Europe by positing the notion of "translation" as the modus operandi of transition to capitalist modernity.[10] We should not even "provincialize Europe," if that is what we were doing, as in cross-authenticate it but by considering the rest of the world its translations. We need to deuniversalize the self-asserted imperial hubris of Europe (and these are two vastly different projects)—and nowhere is this task more urgent than in the field of literature and the literary, where theorization is integral to reimagining vanquished and repressed civilizations and the worlds they inhabited. Provincializing Europe on the model offered by Chakrabarty assumes its innate (God-given) universalism but wishes to limit it by territorializing it. But Europe was neither a theory nor a province. It was an imperial metaphor of conquest and ravaging of the earth, and it is precisely in that domain and in those terms that it must be deuniversalized to set the world free of its epistemic violence. That deuniversalization does not occur by either aping its terms of self-universalization or through an act of epistemological ressentiment (from Søren Kierkegaard and Friedrich Nietzsche to Max Scheller and Gilles Deleuze). You deuniversalize Eurocentrism by exposing its vacuous imperial hubris, by historicizing its systemic colonization of concepts and categories, land thefts and acculturations, enabling alterities and possibilities thus it made impossible. "Europe" became a metaphor for capitalist modernity, cross-authenticated on the ravaged sites of its colonial consequences. You do not "provincialize" that global calamity. You dethrone its universal inevitability.

It is because of this false and falsifying self-universalization that today if performed in English—or any other "European language" that has so successfully repressed its colonial consequences that it can no longer realize these languages have long ceased to be "European"—works with serious theoretical contentions are always treated suspiciously and condescendingly by their prose being racially profiled. If Edward Said and Gayatri Spivak move to the English department, there to teach and write European literatures as Europeanists, they can be as theoretically mysterious in their prose as they wish, to the point that even their own colleagues in the same department consider them incomprehensible. But if a book has the adjectival Arabic, Turkish, Chinese, Persian, or Malayalam in its title, the author better behave and be just a native informer and refrain from any theoretical speculations and leave that to superior European theorists, merely offer a "close reading" of the "actual literature" so the folks in the English department can easily do their "distant reading" and theorize those literatures too. *Theorizing* by the First World about *their* "Third World" is tantamount to literary *terrorizing* underwritten with full-throttle racism in tow. The issue here is not to solicit permission to theorize from anyone who lacks the authority to issue any such permission. The issue is to mark the unfortunate circumstances of the blindfold horse in the dark and dingy mill of "World Literature."

The joy of writing about an epic like the *Shahnameh*, however, is not merely to dethrone the self-asserted primacy of "the First World" theories. The task is far more pleasant and purposeful. The findings and suggestions of these and similar scholars raise certain significant issues that if we were to present an epic like the *Shahnameh* to the larger English-speaking world, and *the world* at large beholden to *this world*, we need to wonder in what ways it would tally with the insights that Quint or Moretti proffer. I read these scholars as colleagues and comrades and happily acknowledge my intellectual debt to them. But in writing about Ferdowsi's *Shahnameh*, I too have things to say that might alter the very presumptive notions of "epic" altogether. That is the only way that "the world" of the *Shahnameh* can have a catalytic effect on the very idea of *world literature*. I do not plan to add "an Oriental example" to the idea of "World Literature" as we know it today by offering this reading of the *Shahnameh*. I intend to alter the very notion of *world literature*, the very assumption of "World Literature," as developed by scholars entirely alien to epics like the *Shahnameh* by introducing you to the multiple worlds the Persian epic has historically occupied and but which have been terra incognita to these and similar scholars. It is the "world" that these colleagues have occupied that I propose to be astonishingly provincial and is in dire need of being liberated and let loose into far wider and richer horizons.

To do so it is not enough to rethink the worlds Ferdowsi's *Shahnameh* has occupied, helped define, and in which it has lived. That is necessary but not sufficient. I therefore intend to embed the Persian epic into a renewed readership by reaching out for a far wider domain of critical thinking around it, cultivate and imagine a global audience, a transnational public sphere upon which the *Shahnameh* now needs to be read anew. The manner in which we can reflect the worldly disposition of the *Shahnameh* is not to merely invite the world into it but also to take it to the world, to prepare and present it to a new world, a globalized world, make it literarily critical to this world by assessing its worldliness, marking its literary magic, philosophical prowess, theoretical might. Very few people in the English-speaking world (which is both the imperial and the postcolonial worlds in which we now live) have even heard of the monumental Persian epic, let alone read its more than fifty thousand verses in the original or any readily available translation. Chances are the same students and educated public to whose education Homer's *Iliad* and *Odyssey* have been integral have scarcely heard of the *Shahnameh*.

Even those who may know or have been partially exposed to the famous Indian epics of the *Ramayana* and *Mahabharata* are still hard-pressed to know a single episode of the *Shahnameh*. The task is not simply to push the Persian epic on a larger reading public as a piece of antiquarian ("Oriental") curiosity. The far more pressing and important (and pleasant and joyous I might add) task is to see in what particular way this epic is pertinent, relevant, integral to the world in which we now live, and to the social and psychological issues that preoccupy it. This is how a work of poetic art from bygone ages becomes definitive to a renewed conception of *world literature*.

Why has the *Shahnameh* not been definitive to "World Literature" in the manner I propose here—what is to blame? There are partial or complete, both prose and poetic translations of the *Shahnameh* available in many European (colonial) languages, especially in English. But who has had the time or the inclination of reading through a thick and forbidding volume without any guide as to how to read it, what to look for, why this epic is so important to its original audiences and beyond, how to make head from its tail, or when and where the original Persian was written and subsequently read and interpreted through millennia and generations? It is easy to blame the public and its increasingly shortened attention span. But has the *Shahnameh* been interpreted and theorized for them in a manner that speaks to our present-day realities? Have they been told in some simple but significant ways why this masterpiece of *world literature* is so important and what it means when we call it part of *world literature*? Translating it into English or other languages is of course absolutely necessary and indispensable, but not sufficient. Like two strangers who meet for the first time, the *Shahnameh* and its new readers in this fast-changing world need to be properly introduced to each other—in a language familiar to both parties, rooted in the text but at the same time speculative in the spirit of our own age. Assimilating Ferdowsi's *Shahnameh* backward to Homer or Virgil is the last thing that must ever happen to a work of literary art systematically alienated from "World Literature" as it has been historically theorized by Western European or North American literary critics who have taken their own provincial world for the world at large. Translating the *Shahnameh* in a manner that you systematically take the profoundest moral lessons and poetic meditations Ferdowsi has to offer before, after, or during his stories, for they "try the patience of the Western reader," inevitably reduces it to a potpourri of "Oriental tales" told for entertainment and amusement the way *The Arabian Nights*, for example, have been thus read and Orientalized.

Studies such as Quint's and Moretti's have theorized "epic" in its classical and contemporary registers in the context of a conception of "World Literature" that is decidedly single-worldly, and as such it fetishizes and alienates other worlds from themselves. For them "the West" is the Hegelian end of history. Whatever came before this "West" were the infantile stages of this dialectical unfolding of the Hegelian *Geist*. "The West" is not just *a world*, it is *the world*. It is not just a particular rendition of an imperial map of the world in which we now live— but the very meaning and destination of History. From Hegelian to neo-Hegelian to Marxist, this "developmental" and "progressive" metaphor of history has no theoretical reason or room for an epic like the *Shahnameh*— except as an object of Oriental curiosity. They have delegated it to the realm of "their Orient," and if they want to learn something about it they go or refer to "their Orientalist," their European Orientalists preferably. It is this nasty alienation of a book like the *Shahnameh* that I wish to undress and dismantle. It is useless to argue that European or American theorists are Eurocentric. Of course they are. The question is that no other epic has any reason, any theoretical justification, to be in the vicinity of Homer or Virgil. It is that Hegelian reason, that theoretical impossibility, not any particularly theorist, that must be dismantled and discredited.

THE PERSIAN EPIC IN ITS IMMEDIATE HABITAT

There is a vast body of scholarship in the form of erudite books and essays on the *Shahnameh*, written by learned scholars and renowned experts, each dealing with a crucial but abstruse aspect of the Persian epic. But strange as it may seem there is not a single volume—short, succinct, reliable, inviting, and authoritative—that a college student or any other educated person can walk into a bookstore, or visit a website, and purchase for a relatively cheap price, go home, and cozy up with in a corner of the sofa with a hot cup of tea or coffee and read cover to cover and learn why it is that generations of scholars have spent their lives trying to figure out the wonder and magic of the *Shahnameh*. No one in particular is responsible for that unfortunate fact, except of course for those who are capable of writing such a book and for whatever reason have not yet done so. The Persian epic must be brought home to the corner of that sofa and made relevant to that expecting reader—relevant to her and his universe of creative and critical imagination and, right in that very corner of the sofa, to the world that gathers around it: the world of our minor and major fears and hopes, of poverty of nations and wealth of empires. There is no reading or caring to read of any epic if that distant epic does not speak to the more immediate epics ordinary heroes wage in their daily lives.

Why would anyone care about a poet who lived more than a thousand years ago in a "faraway land" and wonder what he had to say? There are numerous accounts of both Ferdowsi's life and the significance of his opus available in Persian, the original language in which the *Shahnameh* was composed. Zabihollah Safa's *Hamaseh Sura'i dar Iran* (Epic poetry in Iran, 1942) is a pioneering study in the field. Mojtaba Minovi's *Ferdowsi va She'r-e Ou* (Ferdowsi and his poetry, 1967), and M. A. Eslami Nadushan's *Zendegi va Marg-e Pahlavanan dar* Shahnameh (Life and death of heroes in the *Shahnameh*, 1969) are among the most important pieces of scholarship offered on the Persian epic. Shahrokh Meskoub's two seminal studies *Moqaddameh'i bar Rostam va Esfandiar* (An introduction to Rostam and Esfandiar, 1964) and *Sug-e Seyavash* (Mourning Seyavash, 1971) vastly popularized the *Shahnameh* to a wide reach of younger readership when they were originally published. Mahmoud Omidsalar's edited volume *Justar-ha-ye* Shahnameh *Shenasi va Mabahes-e Adabi* (Essays on the *Shahnameh* and literary topics, 2002) includes the most recent scholarly encounters with the text. One reads such deeply informed and richly competent works of scholarship and one wonders how deeply and how widely the Persian epic has been explored and yet how sadly unaware of these treasure troves is the world at large—the world in which the *Shahnameh* needs to be thought through as a work of *world literature*.

Europe has of course been deeply informed about the *Shahnameh*. But Europe is not the world. We need to rethink the world in a manner that includes Europe but is not reduced to "Europe" as a metaphoric hegemony that we need first and foremost to overcome if we are to free our minds from the shackles of mental colonialism. There is a significant body of scholarship in European languages on the *Shahnameh*, interwoven with multiple critical editions of the original Persian text prepared by both European and Iranian scholars, and numerous partial or complete, in prose or poetry, translations into many languages. T. Nöldeke's *Das iranische Nationalepos* (The Iranian national epic, 1920) is a classical study of the text, though now both too recondite in its language and dated in its scholarship. Produced decades later, Amin Banani's "Ferdowsi and the Art of Tragic Epic" (1988) represents the subsequent generation of literary scholarship. Olga Davidson's *Poet and Hero in the Persian Book of Kings* (2006) as well as her earlier book, *Comparative Literature and Classical Persian Poetics: Seven Essays* (1999), represent a younger generation of significant scholarship, as does Dick Davis's *Epic and Sedition: A Case of Ferdowsi's Shahnameh* (2006). A recent issue of the journal *Iranian Studies* (2015) has been dedicated to various scholarly treatments by multiple scholars on the notion of "The *Shahnameh* of Ferdowsi as World Literature." Mahmoud Omidsalar's work in English, his *Poetics and Politics of Iran's National Epic* (2011) as well as his *Iran's Epic and America's Empire* (2012) are deeply informed polemical responses to works of scholarship done in Europe and the United States. Meanwhile A. Shapur Shahbazi's *Ferdowsi: A Critical Biography* (1991) remains a solid biographical account of the poet. No study of the *Shahnameh* is possible without due respect, acknowledgment, and awareness of these crucial works of scholarship on the Persian epic—and yet none of these books and essays has reached the wider readership they richly deserve. They have been increasingly drawn into the contested domains of equally competent scholars debating significant but arcane issues, crucial for our understanding of the *Shahnameh* and yet tangential to its articulation outside the existing frames of literary scholarship by self-referential academics.

Despite their impressive scholarship, none of these sources facilitates a fresh reading of the Persian epic for a wider readership or enables a new generation of students, teachers, and other educated readers to have a solid, reliable, hassle-free, pleasant, and engaging introduction to the entirety of the *Shahnameh* and its literary and worldly significance. Throughout the English-speaking world (and I would venture to say beyond) there is not a single volume that addresses all the historic, textual, and poetic dimensions of Ferdowsi's *Shahnameh* in a simple, accessible, and comprehensive volume that college students and their professors can pick up and start reading cover to cover and even share with their friends and families beyond any course requirements. The *Shahnameh* needs to be made integral to an educated global public, made meaningful to their daily encounters with such simple questions as, what does it mean to be human, to face adversities, to triumph against all odds, to be ennobled by an innate sense of tragic loss at the heart of any vainglory?

After a lifetime of intimate familiarity and subsequent scholarly engagements with the *Shahnameh* in both Persian and English I began teaching it to my undergraduate and graduate students in a yearly seminar at Columbia University, where I teach. Year after year I have witnessed the sparkle of joy and discovery as I have led my students into the obvious and hidden treasures of the text. It is that joy of first-time encounter with the *Shahnameh* that I now wish to share with a much larger audience in this book: to make it worldly to their lived experiences, the only legitimate way that a piece of poetry from a distant past can become integral to *world literature* through and beyond the manners in which it has been definitive to multiple worlds it has encountered in its long and glorious history.

I have placed Ferdowsi's *Shahnameh* in front of generations of American and non-American students in my classes on epics and empires and asked them to read it and wonder. American students had come from a variety of backgrounds, native to this land or else distant and more recent immigrants to its shores—white, black, brown, men, women, young or old. Sitting next to them were Asian, African, European, and Latin American students, all of them students at Columbia University in the city of New York, an oasis of learning beyond the reaches of time and space. The text created a rare tabula rasa for them, upon which they began to rewrite their own histories anew, as their reading provoked new meaning for me in a book I had known since my childhood. None of them knew anything except perhaps had heard the name of the Persian text—and now the Persian poet began to speak to them from across the ages. They began to read it, cover to cover, story after story, like explorers upon a distant shore. Their initial hesitation to pronounce the Persian names of heroes they had not even known before eventually yielded to a far more confident encounter with the substance of the stories. They soon began to analyze, synthesize, theorize the intricacies of the text. Before the term had ended the *Shahnameh* had become integral to their moral imagination, to their political consciousness, to their understanding of where in the world they were standing. They remained who they were—American, European, Asian, or African—but now Ferdowsi's *Shahnameh* had entered their poetic consciousness. I began writing this book on the *Shahnameh* with their sense of wonder in me.

I recall the sense of joyous amazement in one of my students when he began to understand the enormity of the phrase "In the Name of God of Soul and Wisdom" with which Ferdowsi begins his *Shahnameh*. What does the word *Jan* (Soul) mean, he wondered, and what does Ferdowsi mean when he says *Kherad* (Reason) in eleventh-century Khorasan? I remember the sense of joy in another student when she came to read of the heroism of the female warrior Gordafarid in her battle with Sohrab. How could that be, she asked with excitement—that changes everything! I have an active memory of a Mexican student who wrote an utterly wonderful essay on the politics of enmity and friendship in the *Shahnameh*. I remember an African-American student who wanted to jump-cut on every passage in the *Shahnameh* in which we have color codifications of power. I had a Native American student once whose reading of the Persian epic she constantly compared with stories she had heard from her grandmother. Ferdowsi's *Book of Kings* has found a home in North America on my university campus. I write this book on the *Shahnameh* conscious of that renewed awareness in a land far from its poet's imagination.

A NEW STORY OF AN OLD BOOK

How are we to tell the story of Ferdowsi's *Shahnameh* today in a manner that is true to its historic significance and yet speaks to vastly altering realities of a contemporary learned reader. This is an old book but full of wondrous stories, and their eternal truths continue to resonate with the inner core of our humanity, and may even give it renewed meaning and significance. Ferdowsi and his *Shahnameh* have been subjects of the most vigorous contemporary scholarship and the centerpiece of a vast body of visual and performing arts. The Persian epic is like a river, now quiet, now thunderous, upon which people have sailed in different vessels of differing speeds. I intend to write my book in a very simple and widely accessible prose for colleagues, students, and other educated readers alike, inviting them to enter this amazing book and find their own whereabouts in the bosom of its wonders. To facilitate the widest possible reach of my book I intend to follow a simple progression of chapters in a straightforward roadmap. The complicated emotions and deeply dramatic events will do the trick themselves.

In chapter 1, "The Persian Epic," I offer a genealogy of the Persian epic, introduce the whole genre of *hamaseh sura'i* and its pre-Islamic origin until we get to the eleventh century and the writing of Ferdowsi's *Shahnameh*, and then carry the history forward to what happens even after this landmark epic was composed. The *Shahnameh* of Ferdowsi, composed single-handedly by the poet, is based on both written and oral sources available to the poet at the time of his composition. The now-lost prose *Shahnameh* to which Ferdowsi had access was based on the Pahlavi (Middle Persian) source of the *Khvatay-namak* (Book of Lords), the early prototype of Ferdowsi's opus. Before Ferdowsi began the composition of his version, another Persian poet, Abu Mansur Muhammad ibn Ahmad Daqiqi Tusi (ca. 942–980), had begun rendering it into a poetic narrative but was murdered before he could finish his book, a clear indication that Ferdowsi was not the first or the last but certainly the best poet to turn his attention to the Persian epic. Ferdowsi had access to this early attempt at versification of the Persian epic and with due acknowledgment incorporated those verses into his *Shahnameh*. In this chapter I give a detailed account of the social and intellectual context of this period in which Ferdowsi composed his epic, with equal attention to its mythic, heroic, and historical components.

In chapter 2, "Ferdowsi the Poet," I provide a biography of Ferdowsi and describe the historical context in which he set upon himself the monumental task of giving the Persian epic its final and most enduring form. At the center of this epic undertaking is the steadfast and singular determination of a young poet from a modest background committed to the truth and power of an architectonic narrative that resurrects the forgotten myths, the neglected heroes, and the scattered histories of a people, made a people precisely by the accumulated drama of these stories. The landed gentry, or the Dehghan, from which background Ferdowsi emerged, dated its origin back to the last pre-Islamic Iranian dynasty of the Sassanids and tucked away in the Khorasan region, which was known for its learned families' penchant for ancient Iranian mythologies, heroic narratives, and histories. Times were now out of joint. A massive Arab invasion had dismantled an ancient order of things. The power, eloquence, and beauty of the Arabic language were intertwined with the divine message of the Muslim Holy Book, the Qur'an. A new culture and a monumental civilization were dawning and Iranians as millions of other Muslims were integral to it. Iranians had abandoned their ancient Zoroastrian faith and were converting to Islam. Here in this context, it was the power of Ferdowsi's imaginative gift as a poet that retrieved forgotten stories and gave them a beautiful twist and an enduring significance. Ferdowsi did not just preserve the Persian language with this epic undertaking. He in effect crafted that language and made it possible. Who was he, what animated his urge to write the *Shahnameh*, what were the political and social circumstances of his rise as an epic poet, who else before him had tried to do the same but failed? These and many other related questions will place the writing of the *Shahnameh* in its historic context and reveal the manner in which the Persian language developed as a marker of ethnicity (*ethnos*; *nezhad*) to a marker of poetic eloquence (*logos*; *sokhan*), preparing for the future emergence of the language as a marker of ethical conduct (*ethos*; *hanjar*).

In chapter 3, "The Book of Kings," I break down the *Shahnameh* into its three main components (the mythical, heroic, and historical) and then discuss its most famous and powerful stories, such as Zahhak the Tyrant, Rostam and Sohrab, Seyavash and Sudabeh, Bizhan and Manizheh, Rostam and Esfandiar, and offer the central significance of each story. My intention in this chapter is to provide a critical inroad into how to read these stories, so that when contemporary readers pick up a story of the *Shahnameh* to read they will know what themes, clues, ideas, and characters they should look for and how to understand them. The most exciting and rewarding parts of the *Shahnameh* are its first two parts, its mythical and heroic components, full of amazing stories: how the world was first created, who invented writing and why, how civilization began and social classes were formed. We have stories of just kings who lose their divine gift of grace and become tyrants, tyrant conquerors who grow serpents on their shoulders, albino sons abandoned to the wilderness by their parents to be raised by wild but civilizing birds, heroes born via "C-section" because they were too enormous for natural birth. Fathers deny their sons their kingdom, as other fathers inadvertently kill their own sons, while young stepmothers covet their handsome stepsons. There is an endless succession of exquisite stories, extraordinary deeds, amazing friendships, deadly rivalries, exemplary chivalries, and nasty treacheries. I wish to tell these stories in a manner that will make my own book an exciting read, a taste that will send a new generation of readers to the Persian epic itself but with a set of alerted receptive antennae, sharpened consciousness, informed and critical awareness. I wish to alert my readers to the question of time and narrative: what happens when mythic, heroic, and historical times are woven seamlessly together?

In chapter 4, "Epics and Empires," I trace the history of the *Shahnameh* in its immediate Samanids (819–999) and Ghaznavid (977–1186) and all the subsequent empires up to and including the Mughals

(1526–1857), the Safavids (1501–1736), and the Ottomans (1299–1923) in which the Persian epic was identically important. Even before these almost simultaneous Muslim empires, the *Shahnameh* was centrally significant during the Seljuqid (1037–1194), Mongol (1206–1368), and Timurid (1370–1507) Empires, judged by the many illustrated manuscripts of the epic from these periods, it offered political legitimacy to these Persianate empires. Here I explore the link between the commissioning of illustrated manuscripts in the royal atelier of these courts and the evident legitimacy the gesture toward the *Shahnameh* offered them. What would such a central role of the Persian epic in successive empires tell us about the link between epics and empires, when at the most triumphant point of their ascendency these dynasties are drawn toward the *Shahnameh*? I also tell the fascinating story of the Shah Tahmasp (aka Houghton) *Shahnameh* that was produced during the Safavid period and then given as a gift to the Ottoman sultan Selim II (r. 1566–1574) and eventually reached the American collector Arthur Houghton Jr., who gave Harvard its Houghton Library and who also presided as chairman of the Metropolitan Museum of Art and the New York Philharmonic. Houghton tore this Shah Tahmasp *Shahnameh* to pieces and sold each folio for millions of dollars, although fortunately it was carefully studied and published in two large-scale facsimiles in a limited and expensive edition by the distinguished Harvard curator Cary Welch and Martin B. Dickson of Princeton before its destruction. More recently Sheila Canby painstakingly traced all the pages of that *Shahnameh* and published a complete copy of it in a handsome edition.

In chapter 5, "Empires Fall, Nations Rise," I discuss the later history of the text and its political uses and abuses for nation-building projects in Iran and elsewhere in the Persianate world. Here I consider the history of the *Shahnameh* along two extended lines: its imperial origin and its postcolonial destination in the traumatic heat of nation building. When in 1934 the first Pahlavi monarch, Reza Shah (r. 1925–1941), launched a major millennial celebration of Ferdowsi's *Shahnameh*, the Persian epic was put to use for the founder of the newly established dynasty to overcome the revolutionary upheaval of the constitutional period (1906–1911), the collapse of the Qajar dynasty (1789–1925), and the chaos of the recently occupied Iran to seek to link his reign back to ancient Persian empires. How did the *Shahnameh* fare in this transition from empire building to nation building? The Persian epic was a product of an imperial age and not a text pertinent to a postcolonial nation-state. The transition was, however, inevitable, perhaps, given the genealogy of the epic and the manner in which it had been historically appropriated. The appropriation, however, was not entirely successful or one-sided; soon contemporary Persian poets and literati began appropriating the *Shahnameh* and its heroes for their own oppositional and militant purposes—and Ferdowsi and his *Shahnameh* were there to oblige. Heroes such as Kaveh the Blacksmith became proverbial to a new generation of the Iranian left appropriating his rebellion against an unjust king to their own political purposes. Poets like Mehdi Akhavan-e Sales and Seyavash Kasra'i, novelists like Simin Daneshvar and Sadegh Chubak, and scholars like Mehrdad Bahar and Shahrokh Meskoub soon emerged as leading public intellectuals appropriating the figures of the *Shahnameh* for their own progressive causes. But despite all these uses and abuses, the more enduring question to ask in this period is, how exactly did the encounter of the Persianate world from India to Iran with European colonialism affect the narrative cohesion of the *Shahnameh* from mythic to heroic to historical? It is upon that traumatic experience that we need to rethink the parameters of what it means today to place the *Shahnameh* in the domain of *world literature*.

In the conclusion, I bring all these chapters together through a discussion of the *Shahnameh* as integral to the idea of *world literature*, once it is liberated from its incurably Eurocentric provenance. Predicated on its historical and textual experiences, the Persian epic must today be placed in its contemporary worldly context with its worldly disposition reasserted and theorized. We have received this epic as the embodiment of successive *worlds* it has encountered and now remembers. Today the text encounters a different world, but it has never been placed inside this world to make it integral to a *worldly literature*, which idea remains central to my arguments in this book. How has the *Shahnameh* been used in its contemporary history? It has been used and abused for a variety of purposes, including postcolonial nation building by successive abusive states. It has been loved and admired by generations of Iranians claiming it all to themselves, and then it has even been maligned by leading poets like Ahmad Shamlou. People name their children after its heroes, use and abuse it for jingoistic purposes, claim it exclusively for themselves for nationalistic purposes, disregarding its transnational imperial pedigree. Artists make movies, authors write children's stories, playwrights stage plays, and directors stage operas based on its stories. People adopt it into modernist poetry, as the leading Iranian poet Mehdi Akhavan-e Sales did. As they do all these things they have made it worldly to their particular anxieties, hopes, and aspirations. The learned scholars prepare critical editions of it and debate every single word of it in passionate debates. Competent bilingual literati translate it, filmmakers make films based on its stories, poets write new poetries, women's rights' activists renarrate its heroines, as court and popular painters have depicted its most heroic episodes and as *naqqal* (troubadour storytellers) narrate its stories. Critical thinkers like Shahrokh Meskoub and Mostafa Rahimi consider it for deeper occasions of reflections on its dramatic stories. All these engagements with the *Shahnameh* make it worldly to their immediate and palpable worlds. The *Shahnameh* is today inhabiting a vastly different world and occupies a prominent space in a transnational public sphere that includes Iranians and non-Iranians alike. That is what is worldly about the Persian epic. How would that fact score with the notion of "World Literature" as deliberated by leading literary scholars like David Damrosch, Emily Apter, or Gayatri Spivak considering the issue in various theoretical contexts? My conclusion is the occasion for me to bring home the notion that the *Shahnameh* is integral to a liberated and renewed conception of *world literature* that its rich and empowering history will enable us to redefine and reimagine.

ONE
THE PERSIAN EPIC

Konun razm-e Sohrab-o Rostam Sheno
Degar-ha Shanidasti inham sheno:
Yeki dastan ast por ab-e chashm,
Del-e nazok az Rostam ayad beh khashm.

Come now: Listen to the battle of Sohrab and Rostam
You have heard all the others: now come and hear
this one too—
It's a story full of tears and agony,
The sensitive heart will be angry with Rostam.

C all him Rostam. One fine morning in the prime of his fame and fortune the towering hero of Iran woke up from a restless night and having little or nothing to entertain and tickle his finicky fancies he felt gloomy and bored; with nothing particular to interest him in his immediate whereabouts he thought of taking his legendary horse Rakhsh for a ride and going hunting on the border of Iran and its eternal nemesis Turan to see what if anything fortune would bring him.[1]

Little did he know.

In the woods near Samangan, border citadel between Iran and Turan, he chanced upon a thick woods and a pack of zebras. He had a splendid time chasing and hunting a few of them. Then he took a whole mighty-looking zebra and skinned and skewered it, ate it, and fell fast asleep. A gang of Turanian soldiers were passing by and saw Rostam and his Rakhsh and decided to capture his noble steed. Rakhsh, true to his name, put up a splendid resistance and managed to kill two of the soldiers, but finally fell into their trap and was captured. They left Rostam there in slumber and stole his horse. Rostam woke up and realized his horse was gone. Furious, he walked toward Samangan, hoping to find his horse. The king of Samangan heard that Rostam was approaching his castle on foot. He rushed to welcome the legendary hero and wondered where his Rakhsh was. "Some bastards have stolen it," Rostam said in anger, "and you better help me find it," he further threatened the king. "No problem," said the king of Samangan, "you come here inside the castle, rest and relax, and partake in our royal hospitality, and we will find your horse for you." Rostam accepted the invitation, enjoyed the banquet in his honor, and went to his private quarters to rest and sleep. Just as he was about to fall asleep, the door to his chamber opens and a beautiful young princess and her chamber maid walk in, and the Persian hero and the beautiful princess make love. The young princess is Tahmineh, and from this one night of passion soon a valiant son will be born.

The following day bright and early the good news arrived that Rakhsh had been found. Rostam mounted his horse and said good-bye to Tahmineh, giving her an amulet to put onto the hair of their child if she is a girl and around the arm if he is a son. Off Rostam went back to Iran to keep the world safe for the Iranian monarchy. Nine months later

Tahmineh gave birth to a magnificent son she named Sohrab. Sohrab grew up to become a valiant young man and soon demanded from his young mother to know who his father was. "Your father is none other than the great Rostam," Tahmineh told her son proudly. "Fine," the young Sohrab said, "I'll lead an army to Iran, find my father, defeat the bastard kings Key Kavous and Afrasiab together, the emperors of Iran and Turan, respectively, unify Iran and Turan, and put my father on the throne. With him as my father and me as his son, we will conquer the world." With this pronouncement of Sohrab we are drawn deeply into the dynastic rivalries between Iranians and Turanians and the geopolitics of their regions.

So far so good: but why did Ferdowsi warn us at the very beginning that this would be a sad story? What has the old poet in mind?

SHALL WE CALL IT JUSTICE OR TYRANNY?

The story of Rostam and Sohrab is perhaps the most famous episode of the *Shahnameh* in and out of the Persian-speaking world. The English poet and cultural critic Matthew Arnold's "Sohrab and Rustum" (1853) was widely read and admired in Victorian England. Loris Tjeknavorian and Uzeyir Hajibeyov turned it into an opera, one version in the original Persian the other in Azeri. Agha Hashar Kashmiri turned it into a play in Urdu. *Rustom and Sohrab* (1963) was an Indian Hindi-language film starring Prithviraj, Premnath, Suraiyya, and Mumtaz, and Benyamin Kimyagarov made yet another film based on Ferdowsi's account in Tajikistan. In Iran and other Persian-speaking parts of the world, children are named after Rostam or Sohrab, parents read the story to their children, young adults study it in high school, wandering storytellers (*naqqal*) recite it in coffeehouses, dramatists stage it with powerful dramaturgical effect, while cultural critics publish learned books and critical psychoanalytic essays examining various aspects of it. I still remember the street corner in my hometown in southern Iran where as a small child I watched a *naqqal* tell us the story off his frightfully exiting illustrated canvas. Why this widespread appeal, whence this dramatic attraction, what is in this or any other *Shahnameh* story that has made them so widely popular with the learned and the uneducated alike?

Before we turn to this or other stories of Ferdowsi's *Shahnameh* we need to have a more detailed account of the imperial, social, and intellectual context of the period in which he composed his epic, with equal attention to its mythic, heroic, and historical components, as it has been usually divided. A narrative genealogy of Ferdowsi's *Shahnameh* points to a long history of the Persian epic before and after that momentous text. That genealogy links the composition of the *Shahnameh* in the Islamic period to its pre-Islamic origins. There is a whole genre of *hamaseh sura'i* (epic poetry), with its pre-Islamic origins, that comes to full fruition in the writing of Ferdowsi's *Shahnameh*. That genre has certain normative particularities and technical components, which Ferdowsi mastered and surpassed. As a landmark epic, the *Shahnameh* of Ferdowsi is based on existing sources available to him at the time of this composition. This fact both gives his epic narrative an aura of authenticity and predicates his poetic gift of uplifting the genre to unsurpassed levels. The written *Shahnameh* to which Ferdowsi had access was based on the Pahlavi (Middle Persian) source of the *Khvatay-namak* (Book of lords), the early prototype of Ferdowsi's opus. Before Ferdowsi, Abu Mansur Muhammad ibn Ahmad Daqiqi Tusi (ca. 942–980) had begun his own poetic composition of a *Shahnameh*, but he met a tragic death before he had a chance to finish what he had started. Ferdowsi was not the first or the last poet to try his hand at the composition of the *Shahnameh*, but he was certainly the best to turn his attention to the Persian epic. He had access to this early attempt at versification of the epic and with due acknowledgment in fact incorporated those verses into his *Shahnameh*.

With all its poetic majesty and literary elegance, Ferdowsi's *Shahnameh* is the beneficiary of this long and enduring tradition of epic poetry. A genealogy of the Persian epic takes us back to the whole genre of *Khvatay-namak* before we get to the time of Ferdowsi and his original composition of the *Shahnameh*.[2] Both the oral and the literary traditions of the epic continue apace way beyond Ferdowsi's time and reach far into the colonial and postcolonial periods. As late as the early nineteenth century Fath Ali Khan Kashani "Saba" (ca. 1765–1822), the Qajar court poet, composed a *Shahanshah-nameh* on the model of Ferdowsi's epic for the ruling monarch, Fath Ali Shah (r. 1797–1834). Ferdowsi tells us early in his introductory passages that before he began composing his *Shahnameh*, Daqiqi had started doing so but left it unfinished at the time of his early and tragic death. The fact that Ferdowsi incorporates this earlier version of the epic composition into his *Shahnameh* shows that the writing of the Persian epic was something dominant among the court poets of the time, with an obvious rivalry among them to outshine one another. The sustained history of writing the *Shahnameh* from before the time of Ferdowsi, through his time, and then way beyond his age reveals a continuous spectrum of variation on the theme of elaborating on the Persian epic that holds a sweeping vista of historical consciousness way beyond any pre-Islamic, Islamic, colonial, or postcolonial periods.

What was the social and intellectual context of the period in which Ferdowsi composed his epic? Who commissioned it and why? How did it survive the test of time?

THE IMPERIAL CONTEXT

Ferdowsi composed his *Shahnameh* around the year 1000 in the Christian calendar in the eastern part of the Muslim empire, at which time the Iranian world was quite ancient in its memorial remembrances of itself—in both the written and oral consciousness of its distant and recent history, successive dynasties, and imperial conquests. The Arab conquest of Iran occurred in the mid-seventh century, with the decisive battle of Qadisiyyah in 636 marking the definitive defeat of the Sassanid Empire (224–651), which had ruled over the Iranian plateau and confronted the Byzantine Empire (ca. 330–1453) to the east. But the historical memory of Ferdowsi and his generation of court poets and literati went much deeper than the Sassanid period and reached deep into what later historians have identified as the Arsacid Empire (the Persian Ashkanian,

250 B.C.E.–226 C.E.), the Seleucid Empire (312–63 B.C.E.), and all the way back to the Achaemenids (550–330 B.C.E.). From these bygone empires, two bodies of literature, one Avestan and the other Pahlavi, had come down to Ferdowsi and his generation, and all of which inform the deep historical foregrounding of his *Shahnameh* as both a historical and a poetic document.

This particular chronology of successive empires has been established and consolidated based on archaeological, numismatic, and written sources by later scholarship. But a mythic, heroic, and historical fusion of it was available to Ferdowsi and his contemporaries as the narrative foregrounding of the writing of the *Shahnameh*. What we know now is the chronological order of successive empires, from the Achaemenids to their defeat by Alexander the Great in 331 B.C.E., to the establishment of the Seleucids by his generals, followed by the Arsacids, and then the rise of the Sassanids, before their collapse under the force of the Arab conquest of Iran in the mid-seventh century. That imperial history was integral to Ferdowsi's epic consciousness when he sat down to write his *Shahnameh*. He was, to be more exact, conscious of this history, but in his epic he transcended it in decidedly poetic terms, of which fact I speak in more detail throughout this book.

The sudden shock of the Arab conquest initially under the Four Rightly Guided Caliphs (632–650) extended into the Umayyad dynasty (656–750) and eventually led to the formation of the Abbasid Empire (750–1258). On the easternmost frontiers of the Muslim lands, the eventual rise of the Saffarids, the Samanids, and the Ghaznavids carved out a major territorial domain for the rise and eventual ascendency of a Persianate world at once Iranian in its consciousness and yet Muslim in its cultural affinities. The Persian language as we know it now, achieving a powerful linguistic register for new modes, manners, and spectrums of knowledge production, took shape at this period. This is the historical domain of the birth and upbringing of Ferdowsi and the writing of his *Shahnameh*.

An even fuller recognition of this world requires the crucial understanding that Islam as a mighty metaphysical force now had an expansive claim on the emerging imperial territories of both Arab and Persian domains. A new revelation had descended upon the Arabs, and their Prophet rose from the heart of Arabia to give them cause and momentum for a vastly expansive claim on the fate of humanity. The Prophet of Islam, Muhammad, was born in 570 and died in 632, and in the course of the last two decades of his life he brought his people, and through them humanity at large, a solid claim on being purposefully in this world through a divinely ordained message. He died having consolidated his power over Arabia and bequeathed to his followers a Divine Revelation called the Qur'an they believed to be the salvation of the earth. Soon after his death Muslims began spreading his message with increasing knowledge and a corresponding and unrelenting power. The two mighty empires of the Sassanids and the Byzantines began to crumble under the feet of small but effective Muslim armies. In the battle of Qadisiyyah and that of Nahavand, known to Muslims as Fath al-Futuh (The Victory above All Others, 642), the Sassanids yielded to the Arab generals. The Umayyads rose to power, and soon they yielded to the Abbasids, who laid an expansive claim on a vast imperial territory. But soon the Saffarids under Ya'qub Layth Saffari rose in revolt against their Arab conquerors and founded the Saffarid dynasty (861–1003), and thus began a succession of Iranian or Persianate dynasties in the east, where the Persian language and court poetry now began to have royal patronage. As these developments were happening in the battle of swords, in the field of ideas emerged the Shu'ubiyyah movement, a pervasive cosmopolitan intellectual movement that turned Baghdad of the Abbasid Caliphate into a major urban site of revolt against retrograde Arab tribalism, replacing it with an embracing literary consciousness that eventually elevated the Arabic and Persian languages into the two towering lingua franca of an entire civilization.

By now the expanded Muslim empire had created its own contradictions in both political and social terms. The rise of the Abbasids in the middle of the eighth century was concomitant with two contradictory consequences: wealth and power at the top, misery and revolt at the bottom. Revolts against the central caliphate assumed many forms: sectarian outbreaks like the Shi'ites and Kharijites within Islam, theological disputations like the Mu'tazilites and Ash'arites in its doctrinal foundations, non-Islamist revolts by the impoverished peasantry and the urban poor like the proto-Zoroastrian uprisings in eastern Iranian domains, urban intellectual movements like the Shu'ubiyyah against tribal Arabism of the Umayyads, and dynastic revolts like the Saffarids against the Abbasids. While Islamic scholasticism was consolidating itself in the form of juridical schools and theological and philosophical divergences, a corresponding literary humanism (*adab*) emerged in conjunction with the increased cosmopolitanism of the Abbasid period in Arab and Persian domains.

By the time Ferdowsi began writing his *Shahnameh* in the last quarter of the tenth century, Persian literary humanism and Persian poetry had reached their classical height. Pahlavi sources were either preserved or translated into Persian. A creative adaptation of the Arabic alphabet had liberated the Persian language from its archaic entrapments within the limited courtly readership in the Sassanid period. Soon the rise of Persianate dynasties like the Saffarids and Samanids began to occasion the rise of Persian court poets like Hanzaleh Badghisi and Abu Salik Gorkani, and above them all Rudaki (ca. 858–941) and Daghighi (ca. 935–980), whose work on the *Shahnameh* Ferdowsi knew and whose initial compositions he borrowed and incorporated into his composition of the *Shahnameh*. Equally developed by this time was a robust Persian prose—among its earliest texts were the Persian translations of the *History* of al-Tabari, known as *Tarikh Bal'ami*, a Persian translation of his Quranic commentary, the composition of the *Hedayat al-Mutu'allemin* on medicine, as well as *Hudud al-Alam* on geography, and a prose introduction to the *Shahnameh* that is also evidenced in Ferdowsi's composition.

The *Shahnameh* emerged on this fertile ground and endured all subsequent historical vicissitudes, and its numerous extant manuscripts are the clearest indication that it commanded the towering attention of dynasties and empires to the east and west of Muslim lands. Of hundreds of existing copies of the Persian epic, Djalal Khaleghi-Motlagh, the eminent *Shahnameh* scholar of our time, has identified about four dozen copies as most noteworthy in preparation of his and his colleagues' critical edition of the book.[3] The oldest manuscripts of the *Shahnameh* he identifies are from the thirteenth century, from which we have two copies in Florence (1217) and London (1276). From the fourteenth century are nine copies now in libraries in Istanbul (1330, 1371), Leningrad (1333), Dublin (1340, another undated), Cairo (1341, 1394, a third undated), and Mumbai (undated). From the fifteenth century thirty-four copies are scattered in libraries in Istanbul (1400, 1464, 1482, 1486, 1490, 1494, two dated 1495, two dated 1496, 1497, 1498, and two dated only fifteenth century), Leiden (1437), London (1438, 1486), Cambridge (1438, another dated only fifteenth century), Paris (1438, 1444, 1490), the Vatican (1444), Leningrad (1445, another dated only fifteenth century), Oxford (1448, 1494), Bengal (1478), Vienna (1478), Dublin (two dated 1480), Berlin (1489), Madrid (1496), and Munich (1497). The meandering map of these manuscripts reveals the long and labyrinthine history of the *Shahnameh* through the imperial and colonial ages when these copies were written and where they are now held. The genealogy of these manuscripts and the critical editions Russian, European, Indian, and Iranian scholars have prepared on the base of their evidence and made available to a global readership links our generation of readers of the *Shahnameh* to those of time immemorial. When today we pick up a copy of the *Shahnameh* and start reading it, every word, every stanza, and every story of it resonates with the tonal chord of a history so distant, so remote, so archaic that time and space are humbled in its presence.

These extant *Shahnameh* manuscripts point to the favorable historical circumstances of its enduring reception, celebration, and canonization. We must imagine the time when Muslim conquerors had the Qur'an and the words of their Prophet as their unifying force and abiding convictions, and when Iranian and Persianate dynasties saw in the *Shahnameh* narratives the modus operandi of their own imperial legitimacy. But the *Shahnameh* spoke of both thriving nations and crumbling empires, of expansive myth and tragic history, of noble heroes and corrupt kings. Its narrative was and remained dialogical; no monarchy or empire could claim one side without the other. The deep-rooted ancient origins of the *Shahnameh* stories spoke of an alternative metaphysics of historical continuity and political leadership.[4] The mythic dimensions of Ferdowsi's *Shahnameh* are a clear indication of its origin in time immemorial, pointing to an Indo-Iranian universe rooted in both Vedic and Avestan sources. Names of kings like Houshang, Jamshid, Zahhak, and Fereydun all appear in the Yashts parts of the Zoroastrian sacred text *Avesta*, and they eventually reach the Sassanid Pahlavi sources, from which they trickle down to the *Shahnameh*. The Achaemenid emperor Cyrus the Great, for example, has occasionally been identified with Key Khosrow in the *Shahnameh*.

As an imperial epic narrative composed in the *Motaghareb* metric system of classical Persian prosody, Ferdowsi's *Shahnameh* was composed at a time when panegyric poetry was paramount at both the Samanid and the Ghaznavid courts. Later lyrical and meditative forms of poetry became integral to Persian poetic varieties and were competing for courtly readership. While epic poetry was known to Ferdowsi's generation, his lifelong achievement became the singular achievement of the genre. While composing his *Shahnameh*, Ferdowsi was fully conscious of the historical roots of his epic, and throughout his book he exudes a sense of obsessive responsibility to finish a task he had set for himself. The transition from the Samanids to the Ghaznavids was a crucial historical juncture when Ferdowsi's epic performed a crucial narrative task for and at the royal court of his Persianate patrons. Most of the stories Ferdowsi had gathered and composed in his *Shahnameh* were widely known, but his singular composition dovetailed with the imperial age of its composition. He does not invent these stories. Based on the *Shahnameh* of Abu Mansuri at his immediate disposal, he elaborates and dramatizes them. But there is a sense of historical urgency about his composition of the *Shahnameh*.

As the Iranian, Persianate, and Islamic worlds go through successive imperial and dynastic gestations—from the Samanids to the Ghaznavids, the Seljuqids, the Mongols, the Timurdis, the Mughals, the Safavids, and the Ottomans—whatever other sources of the *Shahnameh* may have existed increasingly fade from collective memories. Throughout these millennia and generations Ferdowsi's *Shahnameh* provides a singularly cohesive and coherent narrative to the Persianate world and a sense of historical self-consciousness of bygone ages and a pride of place. From the time of its composition to this day Ferdowsi's *Shahnameh* has been an available source of consistent historical awareness and confidence initially within the royal court circles but increasingly reaching out to a wider public readership, until we get into the nineteenth and twentieth centuries and the exponential expansion of a public sphere that is identified as *vatan* (homeland).

As I have argued in detail in my *Persophilia*, the interest on the part of European bourgeois intellectuals, scholars, and literati in the *Shahnameh* in the course of the nineteenth century was instrumental in its renewed canonization at the crucial periods leading to the constitutional revolution of 1906–1911.[5] The *Shahnameh* in other words becomes recanonized in the European public sphere and for a variety of social and political reasons before the colonial extensions of that imperial public sphere reached Iran or elsewhere and brought back the Persian epic to Iranians as a people, a nation now forming a postcolonial nation-state beyond its dynastic histories, imperial pedigrees, and royal courts. At this stage the *Shahnameh* does not just receive its widest-ever readership in history but also in fact becomes definitive to the formation of the public sphere Iranians now occupied and called *Vatan*. Here I make a crucial distinction between the significance of the *Shahnameh* in the formative organicity of the idea of *national sovereignty* rooted in a robust public sphere (on the one hand) and the uses and abuses to which it has been put aggressively for *state legitimacy* (on the other). The very idea of *Vatan*, which I have proposed as the functional equivalent of *public sphere*, is in fact predicated mostly on the poetic antecedent of Ferdowsi's *Shahnameh*, despite the fact that in the epic itself the word *Vatan* does not appear, but words like *Keshvar, Iran-zamin*, or *Mihan* do. *Vatan* as a site of the homeland is an almost entirely recent vintage rooted in the tumultuous events of the constitutional period of 1906–1911. Upon this fertile ground, the recanonization of the *Shahnameh* in the bourgeois public sphere in Europe returns to Iran with renewed synergy. In this final phase, the *Shahnameh* is still very much read in an imperial context, but this imperium is decidedly European and no longer Iranian, Persianate, or Islamic in its character and disposition. From the transnational public sphere contingent on European empires emerges a renewed reading of the Persian epic that now extends into Iran and the Persianate world at large, with the full paradoxical synergy of an epic that at once sustains and dismantles any and all empires that come close to it. This central textual paradox of the *Shahnameh* will remain definitive to its contextual history. As its royal form, ceremonious decorum, manuscript commissions, and priceless illustrations and therefore symbolic aura were employed to give emblematic legitimacy to dynasties that came close to celebrating it, its actual stories, its unrelenting dramas of the rise and fall of empires, of megalomaniac monarchs and their murderous plots against their own children, and other courtly intrigues dismantled them. The *Shahnameh* is not the story of just one empire. It is a miasmatic *longue durée* account of multiple empires, their rise and fall, arrogance and eventual demise. It embraces any single dynasty that comes close to it just to humble and historicize it.

The idea of the *Shahnameh* as the cornerstone of *Vatan* I propose here is decidedly predicated on a conception of "the nation" not as a racial category but as the site of a *collective consciousness* predicated on a *shared memory* accumulated over a sustained and renewed course of history. People are members of a nation not by virtue of any fictive claim to a singular race but by virtue of gathering around a public sphere (to which a renewed reading of the *Shahnameh* has been definitive) and there and then generating, sustaining, and accumulating a shared memory to which they continue to contribute through the thick and thin of their history. The idea of "the nation" based on a common race is as ludicrous as predicated on a single gender or a single class. Racialized ideas of the nation are therefore categorically masculinist, misogynist, colonial, and bourgeois in their origin, culture, and disposition. This notion of nation as a racialized category was in fact European in origin and colonial in its nomenclature. It was colonially imposed on other nations and readily appropriated by bourgeois nationalisms around the colonized world. Therefore, I make a categorical distinction between the colonially manufactured idea of racialized nationalism and the idea of anticolonial national consciousness predicated on shared anticolonial struggles of multiple communities within a postcolonial nation-state.[6]

It is, moreover, crucial to keep in mind that when Ferdowsi or, after him, other poets like Asadi Tusi in *Garshasp-nameh*, or Farrokhi in his poetry refer to "Iran" in their poetry, this is to Iran as an *empire* and not as a *nation* in the sense I propose here. Up until the Safavid period in the sixteenth century still *Iran* is an imperial category in contradistinction to the Mughals to its east and the Ottomans to its west. The idea of "Iran" as a *Vatan* will not emerge until later during the anticolonial and antimonarchic struggles gathering momentum around the constitutional revolution of 1906–1911. This conception of *Vatan* as homeland is also not to be confused with any Islamic or Islamized idea of "nation" that stands for *ummah* and as such is a community of the faithful and not a community of shared national experiences, especially when Muslims were fighting against one another along class or sectarian divides. Ferdowsi's *Shahnameh*, therefore, must be seen as the textual evidence of connecting the fate of the Iranian and Persianate world from its postcolonial predicament back into the deepest recesses of mythic and historical memories.

SOURCES OF THE PERSIAN EPIC

What does it mean when we say the *Shahnameh* is the summation of time immemorial, rooted in mythic, heroic, and historical narratives few scarcely remember any longer except through and because of the Persian epic?

It has taken generations of painstaking scholarship to piece together the textual evidence of the materials available to Ferdowsi and his generation before he put pen to paper and began composing his *Shahnameh*.[7] Those materials were available to Ferdowsi during the thirty-odd years he spent composing the Persian epic until he finished it before his death. Some scholars believe these materials were of two different provenances: (1) the literary sources available at the royal courts and to their Zoroastrian priesthood or literary circles and scribes and (2) oral traditions available to urban and rural storytellers (known as *gosan*, or "minstrels").[8] But others, with overwhelming evidence, are absolutely convinced that Ferdowsi's *Shahnameh* is based entirely on written sources, more specifically on the prose *Shahnameh* written by

Abu Mansur.[9] Either way, what is incontrovertible is the fact that Ferdowsi's *Shahnameh* is the poetic summation of an epic consciousness that predates him by centuries.

Among the pre-Islamic sources of Ferdowsi's *Shahnameh*, rooting it in a much earlier history, is *Ayadgar-e Zareran* (Memorial of Zarir), the only surviving example of ancient Iranian epic poetry in the Pahlavi language. It is the story of Zarir, brother to Wishtasp, who has converted to Zoroastrianism and whose authority for precisely that reason is challenged by a rival warlord, Arjasp. In the battle Zarir fights heroically but is killed, soon to be revenged and mourned by his son Bastwar. Some scholars of the period consider *Memorial of Zarir* to be "a heroic poem, a Sasanian adaptation of an Arsacid original. . . . The tale became part of the materials amassed by Persian priests for the Sasanian royal chronicle, the *Khvatay-namak* [Book of lords]; and partly on the basis of that work, partly perhaps from a still living oral tradition in north-eastern Iran, Daqiqi turned it into rhymed verse in the tenth century A.D. His poem was incorporated by Ferdowsi in his *Shahnameh*."[10] Other scholars contest this linkage.

Among other sources at the deep roots of the *Shahnameh* is *Kar-Namag-e Ardashir-e Pabagan*, a Pahlavi prose narrative describing the life of the Sassanid king Ardashir I (180–242) and his rise to power and the establishment of the Sassanid dynasty. The sole existing manuscript of this text dates back to 1322 in Gujarat. Scholars of this text believe that "there can be no doubt that the contents of the text draw from more ancient Iranian lore, since some traits of Ardašīr's life as narrated in this work reflect themes known from the legend of Cyrus the Great. Moreover, in all probability a telling of the life of the founder of the Sasanian dynasty close to what is found in the *Kār-nāmag* existed at least as early as late Sasanian times."[11] The historical roots of these emperors, monarchs, their dynasties, and conquests give additional historical significance to the heroic and mythic dimensions of the Persian epic. What is crucial is the manner in which these components of diverse sources assume unified, consistent, and dramatic dimensions in Ferdowsi's rendition, no doubt in part because of their common "heroic pattern."

Another major pre-Islamic source that is at the root of Ferdowsi's *Shahnameh* was *Khvatay-namak*, a Sassanid imperial history, though there is no indication that Ferdowsi himself knew Pahlavi. The writing of this book, which except for references to it in Arabic and Persian sources of the later periods now no longer exists, was ordered by the mighty Sassanid emperor Khosrow I (aka Anushirvan the Just, r. 531–579) in order "to learn statesmanship better."[12] In this book, its royal compilers "described the Iranian past, from the creation and the appearance of the first man, in four dynastic periods." The existing accounts of this book indicate how it had influenced the writing of the *Shahnameh*: "The mythical figures of the Indo-Iranian antiquity were represented as 'the first kings,' the Pišdāds . . . and a coherent historical narrative (derived from various traditions and anachronistic historiography) was concocted for them. They were described as establishers of political institutions, promoters of urban and agricultural developments, inventors of skills and crafts, originators of laws and social classes, and defenders of Iranian people."[13] Based on such bodies of historical speculations, some scholars now believe "by the end of the 6th century, a national history of Iran existed in the royal archive at Ctesiphon."[14] The text of Ferdowsi's *Shahnameh* as we read it today is perhaps reminiscent of all these bygone ages and yet transcends them all by virtue of its unsurpassed dramaturgical power.

What can we conclude about the nature and function of Iranian historiography at the time Ferdowsi composed the *Shahnameh*? Based on these sources, scholars of the period have concluded that

Iranian historiography was moralistic, providential, apocalyptic, rather particularistic, and utilitarian . . . which assigned man a significant place in the universe by making him a partner with the Creator Ahura Mazda in the cosmic fight against Ahriman and his emissaries. Man's actions were thus part of a cosmic plan, hence memorable. This memory was to serve future generations as a guide, a device for maintaining and promoting national and moral ideals of the state. . . . God had created man as His active partner for bringing about, within a limited time, the final annihilation of evil, when a Savior would restore the cosmic order on earth. The course of history exhibited a series of conflicts between the forces of good, usually Iranians, and the destructive powers, usually associated with non-Iranians . . . thus historiographer, far from being an impartial investigator of facts, was an upholder and promoter of the social, political, and moral values cherished by the Sasanian élite.[15]

Although much of this description can equally apply to Ferdowsi's *Shahnameh*, the text itself has historically assumed a poetic significance and a dramatic force that place it in a unique literary position above and beyond such historiographical description. The *Shahnameh* will ultimately have to be considered as a poetic text sui generis, though solidly rooted in such normative historiographical foregrounding.

This history brings us to a number of previous *Shahnameh*s composed just before Ferdowsi's. One is a composition by Abu al-Moayyad Balkhi, a Samanid poet who was evidently deeply interested in ancient history.[16] Abu Ali Muhammad ibn Ahmad al-Balkhi is the next poet who had composed a detailed *Shahnameh* just before Ferdowsi did.[17] Finally, there is a prose *Shahnameh* that was compiled by the order of Abu Mansur Muhammad ibn Abd al-Razzaq, a prominent aristocrat from the famed Dehqan class of the landed gentry in Tus.[18] Although the actual text of this prose *Shahnameh* is now lost, its introduction has survived. Ferdowsi in his own *Shahnameh* refers to this book. Like a towering cypress tree rising from fertile ground, Ferdowsi's *Shahnameh* remains a landmark sign of an entire political and literary history that had anticipated it.

CANONIZATION OF FERDOWSI'S *SHAHNAMEH*

Both contemporary with Ferdowsi and long after him epic poetry continued to attract many gifted poets. This includes books like *Garshaspnameh* (1063) of Asadi Tusi, *Bahman-nameh* (126), attributed to Hakim

Iranshah ibn Abi al-Khayr, or, in the same tradition, also *Faramarz-nameh, Kushnameh, Banu Goshasp-nameh, Borzu-nameh, Shahryar-nameh, Bizhan-nameh, Lohrasp-nameh, Sawsan-nameh.*[19] Other poets attended to the historical components of the *Shahnameh*, such as *Iskandar-nameh, Shahanshah-nameh, Zafar-nameh, Bahman-nameh.* An equally important genre of religious epics attending to Muslim saints and heroes soon joined this rank, among them *Khavaran-nameh, Sahebqiran-nameh, Mokhtar-nameh.*[20]

What is particularly important about these minor and tangential genres of the *Shahnameh* is the manner in which in effect they have paradoxically helped centralize and canonize Ferdowsi's *Shahnameh*. Based on the singular and overriding evidence of successive royal patronage of the writing of the lavishly illustrated copies of the *Shahnameh* and its systematic and consistent canonization internal to the Persianate world from the Mughal to and through the Safavid to the Ottoman Empires in the most recent stages we can argue that Ferdowsi's epic has had two basic functions, one iconic and the other substantive. Iconically it has been chief among the paraphernalia of legitimacy, while substantively it has offered the royal dynasties with a sustained body of stories as admonitory lessons in kingship.[21] Through such functions the *Shahnameh* has sustained its systemic course of self-canonizing itself throughout the ages.

The canonization of Ferdowsi's *Shahnameh* extends from the royal court and its illustrated manuscripts to court and noncourt poets and literati who used and referred to it as a model of eloquence, or else prepared selections from it, or tried to imitate it, or even more extensively expanded upon one of its stories and developed it in ever more florid directions. Later in Iranian history, the *Shahnameh* exits the royal courts and enters what we can now call the public domain, the public sphere, and through the popular storytelling practices of the *naqqal* in coffee-houses and other public spaces the Persian epic reaches a much wider audience and readership. These *naqqal* did for the *Shahnameh* what the Muslim (Shi'i) clerical order did for the Qur'an, Shi'i saints popularizing it far beyond the limited court audiences or the madrassa system. A cosmic order of the universe was contingent on these stories that was made subterranean to the Persian-speaking world that extended from the Indian subcontinent through Central Asia and Iran all the way to Asia Minor.

EPICS AND EMPIRES

In what way can we talk about the *Shahnameh* as an epic? The Persian and Arabic term we ordinarily use for "epic" is *hamaseh*, and epic poetry becomes *hamaseh-sura'i*. Another bifurcation in Persian poetic traditions divides court-related poetry into *razm* (battle) and *bazm* (banquet), with romance corresponding to *bazm* and epic to *razm*. The simplest frame of reference is to see the *Shahnameh* as an epic in the tradition of *Hamaseh-sura'i* and *razm* in the imperial contexts of its production and canonization. Ferdowsi's *Shahnameh* was produced in an imperial courtly context, and until much later it continued its survival as a court-related document. It certainly has a gradual and eventual transition into a colonial and postcolonial nation-building context in the aftermath of the collapse of the last three Muslim empires of the Mughals, the Safavids, and the Ottomans. But from its conception during the Samanid and Ghaznavid dynasties, predicated on its written and oral sources in the pre-Islamic imperial contexts going back from the Sassanids to the Achaemenids, both the genre of writing the *Shahnameh* and Ferdowsi's specific *Shahnameh* are imperial products, and as such warrant the designation of "epic" in a very generic sense of the term. If so, if we consider Ferdowsi's *Shahnameh* in the more universal context of epic poetry, the next question is, how does it fare in comparison with other epic traditions, extending from the Indian texts of the *Ramayana* and *Mahabharata* to European genres of epic poetry from Homer's *Iliad* (ca. 1194–1184 B.C.E.) to Virgil's *Aeneid* (29–19 B.C.E.) and beyond?

In the introduction I briefly referred to David Quint's *Epic and Empire: Politics and Generic Form from Virgil to Milton* (1993) by way of an example of how the active theorization of the genre of epic in its European context effectively alienates an epic like the *Shahnameh* from itself by

taking the specific world in which the Greek or Roman epics are produced as *the universal world* in which those epics are naturalized. The
study of the *Shahnameh* is thereafter delegated to the realm of Orientalist specialization, and thus that alienation is epistemically consolidated.
To reverse and alter that premise I wish to play Ferdowsi's *Book of Kings*
against the grain of Quint's theorization of epic to see how the two sides
of the theoretical disequilibrium fare in the interface. My purpose here
is not to dismiss Quint as irrelevant to the *Shahnameh* but to mark the
boundaries of the literary provinces within which Eurocentric theorization operates. The task at hand is not to mark anyone's provincialism
but to map out the multiple worlds outside the blindfolded geography
of "World Literature."

In his *Epic and Empire*, David Quint offers a thorough examination of
the relationship between epic poetry and the political dynamics of empire
building in Europe and the manner in which ancient Romans, for example, were inspired by Virgil's *Aeneid* in pursuit of their imperialism.[22] In
Quint's estimation there are basically two trajectories in epic poetry in
their European domain: the triumphant epic of the winners and the
defeatist epic of the losers. As early as Homer's *Iliad* (triumphalist, linear,
teleological, and deterministic) and *Odyssey* (contemplative, redemptive,
repetitive, and circular) this dichotomy, he believes, is evident, but it later
becomes narratively codified in Virgil's *Aeneid*. The link between political context and epic poetry therefore leads Quint to a generic distinction
between the Virgilian epic of conquest and empire building and what he
terms the epic of the defeated. If the *Aeneid*, Luís de Camões's *Lusíadas*,
and Torquato Tasso's *Gerusalemme liberata* are the examples of the former, then Lucan's *Pharsalia*, Ercilla's *Araucana*, and d'Aubigné's *Les
tragiques* are examples of the latter. For the victorious epic, Quint detects
a linear, teleological narrative and for the defeated an episodic and open-
ended narrative.

Quint proposes that this binary is essential for an understanding of
the historical contexts of epics and their sustained political implications.
In effect both the winners and the losers have their respective form of
epic poetry, one beating its chest triumphantly, the other is lamenting
in defeat. While in the first part of his book Quint traces the history of

Virgil's epic, in the second part he examines the more recent cases of Tasso and Milton. The epics of winners, he proposes, issue from the vantage point of the victors through a linear narrative, but the epics of losers narrate from the defeated perspective in an episodic and circular motion. While the former equates power with the power to tell its story, the latter doubts that cohesion, defies a linear teleology, questions power as reasonable, and negates the possibility of superimposing cohesion on an otherwise interrupted history. The ideologically charged confidence of the former is questioned by the fragmented fact of the latter. The former is triumphantly masculinist, unitary, and identitarian condemning the latter to be feminine, chaotic, and foreign.

If we were to place Ferdowsi's *Shahnameh* on this scale of epics as examined by David Quint and divided between the epic of winners and the epic of losers, where would it sit? Is the *Shahnameh* an epic of conquest or an epic of defeat? Actually neither of the two. It is simply astonishing how radically different the *Shahnameh* is from both sides of this Manichaean binary Quint detects in European epics. Quint's theorization is entirely tangential to Ferdowsi's epic, and yet precisely for that reason quite helpful in guiding us to make a few comparative observations. Quint's persuasive and elegant theorization is partially helpful in guiding us to ask similar but decidedly different questions. Ferdowsi wrote his *Shahnameh* not ex nihilo but in fact based on a consistently imperial pedigree of the Iranian dynastic heritage, from time immemorial down to the collapse of the Sassanid Empire. So the dominant dialectic of his epic is one of loyalty to his sources and creativity with his dramatization. This makes of his epic a judiciously balanced temperament. Moreover, the Sassanid Empire, from which much of the written and oral foregrounding of the *Shahnameh* emerges, was in fact the prototype of all other triumphant empires that came after it, whether Arab, Persian, Indian, or Ottoman, and in fact arguably even into European empires. Though the Sassanids were defeated by the invading Muslim armies, once Muslims became the leaders of a new empire of their own they had nowhere to turn for a model of how to run a vast territory but to the Sassanid model for their own imperial administration. The Barmecides (Barmakids)—an influential Iranian family, originally

Buddhist, who became highly powerful under the Abbasid dynasty—
were a significant link between the Abbasids and their Sassanid predecessors, offering them generations of competent viziers to run their
empire. Even the Byzantines were arguably modeled on the Persian
prototype of the Achaemenids ever since the canonical significance of
Xenophon's *Cyropaedia* (370 B.C.E.), which was evidently a favorite of
Alexander the Great's and Julius Caesar's and competed with Plato's
Republic for classical attention, a fact completely (and surprisingly)
absent from Quint's analysis of the relationship between epics and
empires.

Ferdowsi therefore wrote his *Shahnameh* during a victorious dynasty
(the Samanids), leading to another victorious empire (the Ghaznavids),
and his epic was canonized by all the subsequent empires at the prime
moment of their victory when they commissioned the luxurious preparation of a new *Shahnameh*. The *Shahnameh* is moreover both teleological and linear and yet also episodic and contemplative at one and the
same time. It contains both epic (centered around the chief hero, Rostam) and romance (in stories of Bizhan and Manizheh, Zal and Rudabeh,
etc.). So it entirely disregards Quint's binary and in fact against it posits
an entirely different way of looking at the genre. The *Shahnameh* is neither this nor that, neither triumphalist nor defeatist, neither exclusively
linear nor entirely episodic. Instead it has an abiding sense of archetypal
awareness, rooted in the two crucial factors of its antiquity and its
poetic eloquence and dramatic storytelling. It has both triumph and
defeat, celebrates victories, teaches from defeat, but both these traits are
squarely at the service of uplifting it into a realm of a metahistorical
intuition of transcendence. It is triumphalist and defeatist at one and the
same time. In victory it anticipates defeat, and in defeat it remembers
victory. Therefore, it transcends them both. Its linearity goes through
mythic, heroic, and historical phases, so it transfuses spatial and historical chronology, its episodic focal points (Rostam and Sohrab, Seyavash
and Sudabeh, Bizhan and Manizheh, etc.) are archetypal not admonitory. This is the reason why its admonitions keep being repeated (which
even its best translator, Dick Davis, alas considers boring and thus does
not translate them for his "Western reader.")[23] Quint is able to ask some

very good questions indeed, but his theory fails in understanding Ferdowsi's epic, for it completely confuses his categories. There are implications therefore to be drawn from this comparison between the *Shahnameh* and the epics Quint studies. Quint is triumphalist in theorization and the *Shahnameh* cosmic in its narrative confidence.

The most helpful chart that David Quint offers summarizing his theory is figure 1, "Virgil's Actium,"[24] where he divides the binary he has constructed between two columns of "West" and "East." While "West" is identified with "One, Male, Control, and Cosmic Order," "the East" is contrapuntally identified with "Many, Female, Loss of Control, and Chaos." "The West" thus becomes identified with "Olympian Gods" as "the East" with "Monster Gods," and "Egyptians, Indians, Arabs" panic at the sight of Apollo, Apollo is favorably disposed to "Mars, Dirae, Discordia, and Bellona." "The West" is blessed with "Permanence and Reason," "the East" with "Flux, Nature, and Loss of Identity," and as such marked by "Suicide, and Death Wish"; "the West" with "Order," "the East" with "Disorder"; "the West" with "One, the Imperial Unity out of many, conquering nations, and Empire without end," as "the East" is marked by "many, with indigent Araxes, the Parthian hordes, and the End of Empire." He prefaces this binary opposition by saying,

> The struggle between Augustus and Anthony pits the forces of the West against those of the East, continuing the pattern of epic confrontation that Virgil found in the *Iliad*. This pattern would be subsequently repeated in those Renaissance epics that portray an expansionist Europe conquering the people and territories of Asia, Africa, and the recently discovered New World: Ariosto's knights vanquish an Islamic army collected from Spain, North Africa, Samarkand, India, and Cathay; Tasso's paladins deliver Jerusalem from the Syrians, Egyptians, and Turks; Camões' Portuguese seamen lay the foundation for a commercial empire in Mozambique, India and the Far East; Alonso de Ercilla's Spanish conquistadors attempt to wipe out the resistance of the Araucanian Indians of Chile, Indians who speak surprisingly in the Latinate accents of Virgil's Turnus and Mazentius. . . . Milton's

God wrests his "eternal empire" from the realm of Night, the darkest of dark continents, and Satan is described as a "sultan" whose palace in Pandemonium, built by diabolic art from the most precious materials in nature, far outdoes the wealth and splendor of an oriental despot, "where the gorgeous East with richest hands / Showers on her kings barbaric pearl and gold."[25]

What in effect Quint is here theorizing, based on his detailed reading of an entire tradition of European epics, is a poetics and even a metaphysics of imperial conquest, through and by virtue of which Europe is destined to wipe out the entire world of its existing histories, worldliness, cultures, and communities of sensibilities and pacify them all for a European global conquest. Fortunately, Ferdowsi's *Shahnameh* has no room in these racist ideologies of epic proportions. With all its dramatic detailing of mythic heroes and historical conquests, the *Shahnameh* is ultimately about human frailty, the very fragility of historical existence. In the *Shahnameh* we meet a poet with a full consciousness of human follies, not an ideologue for world conquest. In that respect, Ferdowsi is much closer to Shakespeare than to Homer or Virgil.

Consider the story of Kaveh the Blacksmith, central to the political culture of the *Shahnameh*. Zahhak triumphs over Jamshid because of Jamshid's hubris and arrogance, which ultimately cause his divine grace to abandon him. Zahhak rules with unsurpassed cruelty, killing young men and feeding their brains to his two serpents. Many of Kaveh's sons were thus murdered and their brains fed to Zahhak's serpents. It is against this cruelty that Kaveh revolts, topples Zahhak, and reinstalls Fereydun to the throne. The moral outrage of Kaveh is definitive to the entire course of the *Shahnameh* stories. The most significant ethical voice of the *Shahnameh* is Ferdowsi himself and the moral conclusions he draws from the various stories he tells. The moral edifice of the *Shahnameh* is not geared toward triumphant conquest or lamentations from defeat. It pivots toward a sense of reason and sanity against the cruelty of fate. In mapping out that spectrum, Ferdowsi has no political agenda, to promote or denounce the Persian monarchy; he is the defiant voice of what at the very outset of his epic he calls *sokhan*, reasonable, righteous, logical, and wise words. The entire *Shahnameh* might in fact be read as an epic celebration of this *sokhan*.

Toward the end of his book, when he examines the Russian filmmaker Sergey Eisenstein's work, Quint concludes by suggesting, "If we return to the ideological dichotomies of the shield of Aeneas—West victorious over East, Male over Female, Reason over Nature, the unified one over the disorganized Many, Permanence over Flux, *Alexander Nevsky* can be seen to reverse the entire Virgilian imperialist pattern."[26] The supposition of this reversal in effect corroborates the historic mission of the European imperial epic to conquer the world and make it safe for the manifest destiny of its European conquerors. Nothing could be further from the very soul of the *Shahnameh*. What in effect the *Shahnameh* does is precisely not to fit this imperialist epic narrative, though it was symbolically the epic definitive to many successive empires, and by refusing to fit in, with elegance and gentility it dismantles the whole project— dismantling not by opposing it, not by showing the binary to be false and violent, but by offering an entirely different world that the Virgilian epic condemns as confused and demonic, chaotic and monstrous, suicidal and afflicted with lamentations. Ferdowsi in his *Shahnameh* in effect laughs at this grotesque ignorance of the world it has to share with the Virgilian world. Reading through the *Shahnameh* is the most civilized, composed, graceful dismantling of this entire metaphysics of delusional fantasies that have sustained the myth of "the West" for so many successive imperial thuggeries. In the Virgilian epic, as Quint theorizes it, we see Parthians as hordes, and Egyptians, Indians, and Arabs as panicking in wild despair at the sight of Apollo. Not so in the *Shahnameh*, where even the Macedonian general Alexander is domesticated to its narrative and thereby civilized.[27]

There is a reason that none of these European classical, medieval, or Renaissance epics survive from their immediate imperial contexts and disposable usefulness into the capitalist imperialism of the post–French Revolution, and as Franco Moretti argues in his *Modern Epic* a whole different set of fictions needed to emerge to correspond to the later stages of the European claim to global conquest. The *Shahnameh*, on the other hand, aged gracefully and transitioned well into the tumultuous post-colonial nation building and tolerated the abuse of the Pahlavi monar-chy as it endures the official neglect of the Islamic Republic to dwell where it ultimately belongs—with the fate of a people to whom it has been the source of solace and solidarity. So no, the world did not have to wait for Sergey Eisenstein's *Alexander Nevsky* (1938) to dismantle that imperialist delusion. The world was already thriving, living, being, cel-ebrating in alternative epics such as the *Shahnameh, Mahabharata*, and others with an entirely different genealogy of morals to the very fabric of their epic narratives.

So one more time: Why would we say all of this about the *Shahnameh*? In what way do we relate to it as an imperial epic? The *Shahnameh* is an epic unlike the manner in which the *Iliad, Odyssey*, or *Aeneid* are epics for a very simple and compelling reason. Ferdowsi wrote the *Shahnameh* neither at the end nor at the beginning of any imperial formation but smack at the center of two successive intersections of world empires, empires that happen before him and empires that were unfolding beyond him. The problem therefore with the very normative idea of "World Lit-erature" is that its theorists are decidedly located and rooted in a very limited (however rich and diverse) conception of literary productions like epic and sit royally on the throne of their theories asking epics out-side their playing field to explain themselves. That imperial arrogance must be dismantled.

FILICIDE, OEDIPAL, SOHRABANEH

Afrasiab the king of Turan hears of Sohrab's plan to invade Iran, takes advantage of the opportunity, and sends an army to help him in his cam-paign and charges two of his trusted advisers with the mission to make sure Rostam and Sohrab do not recognize each other, for if they did the fate of both the Turanian and Iranian monarchies would be sealed. They had to keep them hostile and to destroy them both and thereafter con-quer Iran.

Meanwhile Sohrab leads his army toward Iran, comes near a major fortress held by some leading generals of the Iranian empire. He charges against the fortress and is confronted by a valiant knight named Gordafarid (imagine her as Brienne of Tarth if you are a *Game of Thrones* fan), disguising herself as a man. They battle fiercely, and finally Sohrab is victorious and realizes his nemesis is an attractive woman. She seduces Sohrab to let her go. She runs back to the fortress. Overnight a message is sent to the Iranian monarch Key Kavous informing him of the invading army headed by this young valiant hero Sohrab. Key Kavous as usual sends Give, one of his trusted generals, to summon Rostam. Rostam is busy partying and frolicking and spends days and nights with Give drinking and enjoying himself, disregarding the king's urgent request. They finally get to the court. Key Kavous is furious with him for being late. But Rostam tells him to be quiet for he is nothing without him and leaves the court in anger. Other heroes at the court go after him, bring him to the court, where the king apologizes and asks him to help out with this new menace to his empire. Rostam is clueless that his own valiant son is leading the enemy's army. Sohrab, however, is desperate to find out who among the enemy's knights is his father. But divine destiny and man's folly and political treachery all come together for the father and son not to recognize each other.

To make a long story short, Rostam and Sohrab face each other in battle over many days fighting forcefully, and at one fateful moment Rostam finally overcomes Sohrab, draws his dagger, and . . . at just about this instant, Ferdowsi pauses his narrative, takes a snapshot of the scene of Rostam sitting on his son's chest and about to bring down his dagger and kill him, and, in a frozen second, wonders how come these two did not recognize each other.[28] Fish in the sea, he says, and birds in the sky recognize their children and parents. What is man, "this quintessence of dust," as Omar Khayyam and William Shakespeare will add generations later, that his greed and folly prevent him from recognizing his own parents and offspring? The deeply saddened poet then unfreezes the frame, and Rostam brings down his dagger and kills his own son.

The story of Rostam and Sohrab offers us a crucial occasion to reflect on the nature of the father-son relationship in the *Shahnameh*. The story initially happens in a liminal space, neither in Iran nor in Turan. Rostam goes to a remissive space, Samangan, located somewhere between the two opposing empires. His soon-to-be wife and mother of his valiant son Sohrab, Tahmineh, is from this remissive space, a liminal location where the parameters of the two opposing camps can be remapped. Rostam's losing his Rakhsh is a premonition of suspending his manhood and masculinity, both of which Tahmineh will soon restore by returning his horse before giving him a son. Upon his return to Iran and soon after Sohrab's invasion, Rostam's reluctance to come to the king's court and his rushed anger to leave that court are all signs of his fear of the encounter with Sohrab and the prospect of his own mortality—for the mere mention of his son reminds him of his lost horse/manhood. Sohrab's onslaught is threatening not just the Iranian empire but the place of his father as a kingmaker. Sohrab in effect wants to overcome and replace his father. Sohrab's encounter with Gordafarid is the substitutional moment of his lifelong accompaniment of his mother, Tahmineh. That encounter at one and the same time emasculates Sohrab and restores his manhood. Sohrab's towering ambition is turning his father into a useless king and replacing him as the looming hero of the two empires, which is precisely what troubles the patriarchal order. His dalliance with Gordafarid is a moment of generational alliance against the father figures of the empire, as her disguise marks the transgender eroticism that amplifies the erotic violence of their first encounter. The story of Rostam and Sohrab might therefore be read as the Oedipal in reverse, a "Sohrabaneh" in full gear, the story of a father who kills his own son to prevent him from replacing him as a kingmaker. Sohrab is the product of a night of desire, and his murder marks the paramount example of filicide. But Sohrab too seeks his father "to kill" and replace him as the kingmaker and thus to foreclose the father figure he had never seen, to fold the figure of the father that has cast a long but useless shadow between him and his mother all his life.

Stories like Zahhak's being instrumental in killing his father or Rostam's unknowingly killing his son are central and transfigurative in the making of the *Shahnameh* as an epic. What sustains the course of the epic are these repeated patterns of generational encounters between aging fathers and their ambitious sons. Ferdowsi is not to persuade you of one thing or another, of fathers over sons, or sons over fathers. He just uses these stories to wonder about the nature of human folly. His poetic voice is paramount over and above the stories he shares. If Zahhak's mother is suspected of vicious compliance in the murder of her husband, like Gertrude in *Hamlet*, Sohrab's mother, Tahmineh, is the picture of chastity whose single night of pleasure with Rostam is predicated on a proper marital vow, after which she remains a loyal wife and a devout mother. But in both cases the ambitious sons compete for the love of their respective mothers by seeking to overcome the towering figures of their respective fathers. The triangulation of the mother-son-father in these and other such cases sustains the synergy of the epic from the familial to the imperial. This makes the *Shahnameh* an epic of human frailty as the *conditia sine qua non* of history.

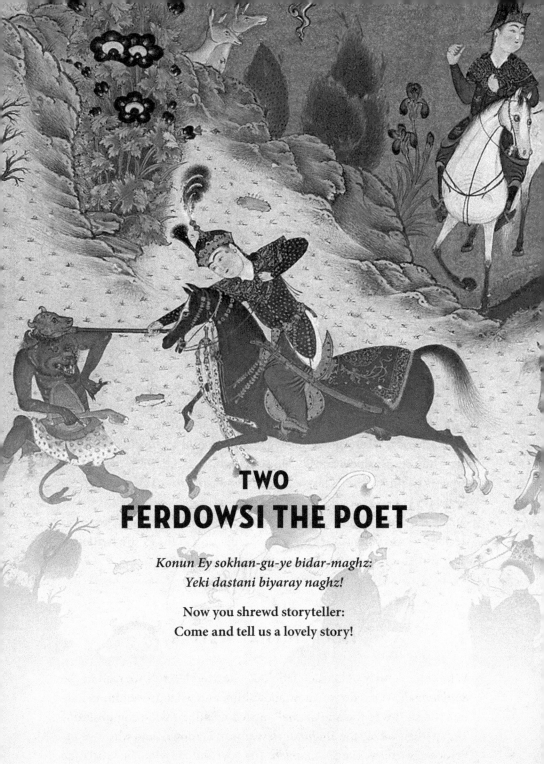

TWO
FERDOWSI THE POET

Konun Ey sokhan-gu-ye bidar-maghz:
Yeki dastani biyaray naghz!

Now you shrewd storyteller:
Come and tell us a lovely story!

ranian knights were one day out hunting and having fun. They came across a beautiful woman lost in the woods. Unable to decide which one should have the young woman, they take her to their king, Key Kavous, to decide for them. The king keeps the young woman for himself, and soon a son is born from their casual union. They name the boy Seyavash and soon give him to Rostam to raise and train as a valiant prince. Under the care of Rostam, Seyavash grows up to become a noble warrior. It is now time for the young prince to go back to his father's court and prove his worth. Seyavash returns to Key Kavous's court, and everyone is mesmerized by his valiance, elegance, and beauty of body and soul—women of the royal court in particular, and even more particularly his own stepmother, Sudabeh, who falls madly in love with him, burning with a consuming erotic desire for the young prince. Sudabeh summons Seyavash to her court, tries to seduce him, promises him her total loyalty and an assurance of his father's throne. But Seyavash refuses her repeated advances. She finally gets infuriated with Seyavash and goes to her husband, Seyavash's royal father, King Key Kavous, and accuses the young Seyavash of unwanted sexual advances toward her, which she says has resulted in her aborting a child of the king's she was carrying. Seyavash declares his innocence and in order to prove it volunteers to ride with his horse through a blazing fire. The king agrees. Seyavash rides through the fire and emerges safely, proving his innocence. Disappointed by the treacheries at his father's court, Seyavash decides to leave his royal realm altogether and rides to the border of Iran and Turan, heartbroken at the treacheries of his fate.

THE PEN THAT WRITES

Who is the author of all such fabulous tales and legends we read in the *Shahnameh*? What do we know about him, and what drove him to narrate the stories of the *Shahnameh* in a compelling poetic composition? Today when we say the *Shahnameh* we mean Ferdowsi, and when we say Ferdowsi we mean the *Shahnameh*. The poet and his poem have become intertwined. He came to this world to write that epic, and the legacy of that epic from time immemorial was waiting for him to immortalize.

We can think of Ferdowsi's biography, his poetic person, his authorial persona, and social significance and character in multiple ways. One of course is as the man who was born around the year 940 on the Christian calendar in Tus, in the northeastern region of contemporary Iran, and grew up to become a magnificent poet and, after he completed his magnum opus the *Shahnameh*, died in the year 1025 according to the same calendar. Those are certainly the most basic facts about his life that we can know given the scarcity of sources. But there are other, equally if not even more important ways in which we need to have an understanding of his life and character. A literary history of the rise of Persian poets as definitive to the courtly culture predates the emergence of Ferdowsi and embraces him within its social context. The social function of poets in those bygone cultures foregrounds the writing of the *Shahnameh*. The actual biography of Ferdowsi must therefore be located in this context. But most important, we need to come to grips with his poetic voice, with the manner in which he speaks in his poetic persona when introducing a story, beyond the voice of the omniscient narrator he assumes when telling those stories. In such occasions, Ferdowsi has a biographical voice, a consciously self-referential voice, a meditative voice, a voice of poetically plotting his stories, a voice of moral meditation. All these voices constitute the person and the persona we today call Ferdowsi.

When we put all these voices together what emerges is a polyvocal poet as a participant observer in his real and imaginative world, in the world he has inherited and his masterpiece embodies, animating the moral imagination that occupies and informs that world. The world into which Ferdowsi was born and raised was worldly, meaning fully aware and conscious of itself, materially robust with its own place in an already rich history. That world is violently deworlded, robbed of its self-consciousness when the readers of Ferdowsi are today divided between "the natives" and the "nonnatives," between a fictive "Western reader" and the rest of the world that might come to read the *Shahnameh*.[1] Thus deworlding the world of the *Shahnameh*, depriving it of its innate worldliness, bars it from becoming worldly in a new world by making it falsely Eurocentric. The task of positing the *Shahnameh* as a literary work in *world literature* must first and foremost begin by de-Europeanizing its reception, restoring to it its own world and other worlds it can occupy. An English or French translation of the *Shahnameh* is not for "the Western reader" only, whoever that fictive creature might be. It is for the world at large, the world the English and French languages have conquered and subjected to their cultural hegemony. Those languages have been confiscated and repossessed by people from India to Africa. Once we thus distort the *Shahnameh*, rob it of its universe, it no longer matters what world the *Shahnameh* has occupied, it no longer matters what world the *Shahnameh* can occupy today. What matters is what "the Western reader," a figment of a colonial imagination, has made of the *Shahnameh*. Equally damaging to the full respect and recognition for the world the *Shahnameh* embodies are the multiple voices its author speaks, the worlds those voices had occupied, and the future worlds it has continued to engender and occupy. Entirely subversive of these worlds is the false binary presumed between "a medieval audience" and a modern "general reader."[2] Iranian historiography has its own inner logic and has nothing to do with the European periodization of its history into "ancient," "medieval," and "modern." We do not have such historical periods anywhere except in Europe—perhaps perfectly logical for European history (though many contemporary historians of Europe have in fact challenged such periodizations), but they have absolutely nothing to do with the inner logic of historical epochs, or the very assumption of such epochs, in India, China, Africa, Latin America, the Islamic or Iranian worlds. The violent superimposition of these temporal and spatial categories distorts the realities of these worlds, deworlds and forces them into an obedient servitude to European historiography. There can never be any conception of *world literature* before the very idea of "world" and how it is inhabited is liberated from its quintessentially Eurocentric gestations.

In coming close to Ferdowsi's biographical life, social significance, and poetic persona we need to keep this overcoming of distorting forces paramount in mind and seek to retrieve and reconceptualize his person and persona in a manner definitive to our understanding of his enduring masterpiece. First and foremost, Ferdowsi was and remains the author of his *Shahnameh*, and the *Shahnameh* foregrounds our understanding of its author. It is in the productive domain of that dialectic that we need to locate the author and the text. Any biography of the poet that compromises the literary primacy of his work, or, alternatively, any reading of the text that compromises the world in which its author lived, will do irreparable damage to our understanding of who Ferdowsi was and what the significance of his epic masterpiece is.

BEING BORN POETICALLY

Before Abu a-Qasem Ferdowsi Tusi (ca. 940–1025) was born in person he was born poetically—the literary imagination of the world into which he was born willed and gave birth to him. The world of Persian literary humanism anticipated and "gave birth" to him. By the time Ferdowsi was born in Tus and raised in Khorasan, where he reached his professional maturity as a poet, the category of "Persian poet" at the royal court was a fully functional component of the accoutrements of power in the eastern parts of the Muslim empires. By the time Nezami Aruzi, a prominent literary critic and one of the earliest biographers of Ferdowsi, wrote his seminal book, *Chahar Maqaleh* (Four treatises, 1156), the crucial craft of a Persian court poet was well placed next to the crafts of astronomer, physician, and scribe (the four subjects of this book) as most essential to a royal court. Ferdowsi was among the seminal figures definitive and integral to that prototype at its most nascent historical moments. A dialectic of reciprocity was therefore formed between the prototype of a court poet and the figure of Ferdowsi that defined and foregrounded the task of writing the Persian epic.

A number of prominent court poets had emerged and consolidated their profession long before Ferdowsi entered the scene to define the very prototype of the "court poet." Abu Abdollah Ja'far ibn Mohammad Rudaki (ca. 858–941) is usually referred to as "the Adam of poets" for being the prototypical court poet who inaugurated the type that would last for centuries. The rising reputation of Rudaki eventually reached the eminent Samanid prince Amir Nasr ibn Ahmad Samani, who summoned him to his court, where he amassed a sizable fortune and reached great prominence.[3] Rudaki was evidently born blind, and among his compositions was a versed version of "Kelilah and Dimnah." He is reported to have become a very rich man as a court poet. Other prominent poets like Abu Mansur Muhammad ibn Ahmad Daqiqi Tusi (ca. 942–980) were in fact contemporaries of Ferdowsi's. The apocryphal story of Ferdowsi's encounter with the three court poets Farrokhi (ca. 980–1038), Onsori (d. ca. 1040), and Asjadi (d. 1040) speaks to the dominance of court poets in this era and Ferdowsi's dramatic entry into that scene.[4] The rise of Manuchehri Damghani (d. 1040) to prominence in this era marks the height of panegyrical poetry as the modus operandi of royal propaganda—so much so that poets like Manuchehri in fact received their noms de plume from the patron prince they served.[5] These poets were integral to the calculus of power and propaganda, and the dominant genre particularly favored among them was panegyrical poetry, although attraction to epic poetry was evident among some other poets before Ferdowsi became totally identified with the genre. The monumental figure of Abu Sa'id Abi al-Khayr (967–1049) in this era, however, marks the significant presence of non-court-affiliated poetry cultivated by Sufi masters of Khorasan.[6] The towering presence of Ferdowsi in this environment speaks of a cultural and political context where Persian poetry, both of a panegyrical and epic vintage, pushed the significance of the composition of the *Shahnameh* to a historic stage.

Ferdowsi was therefore born into a character type that existed before him, for the circumstances of Iranian dynasties farthest removed from the central Abbasid Caliphate in Baghdad had politically demanded and culturally produced it. A biography of Ferdowsi will therefore have to be placed in the context of this larger social history into which he was born as a poet. The historical context in which Ferdowsi set upon himself the monumental task of giving the Persian epic its final and most enduring form was predicated on the active formation of a poetic prototype that was politically foregrounded on a social construction of

literary genres. At the center of the *Shahnameh* dwells the singular determination of a young poet from a modest background committed to the
truth and power of an architectonic resurrection of forgotten myths,
neglected heroes, and scattered histories of a people to whom Ferdowsi
felt he belonged. Iranians of his and previous generations knew these stories and had transmitted them orally and in written form long before
Ferdowsi, but after Ferdowsi these stories assumed a sustained dramatic
narrative never before achieved. After every recitation of these stories
before and after Ferdowsi, the ideas of these people of themselves were
ever more intensified and poetically sublated. Ferdowsi's biography is
therefore also the biography of an imperial epic, consistently reclaimed
by generations of Persian-speaking peoples.

The family background of Ferdowsi, of the mostly impoverished
landed gentry, or the Dehghans, from which he emerged had exposed
him to the ancient stories and the heroic deeds of earliest Iranian dynasties long before the Arab invasion and the Muslim conquest of Iran. But
a general familiarity with the Persian epic narrative was not limited to
any particular class. As the politically dominant narrative of Muslim culture ruled and thrived supreme in former Sassanid domains, so did an
element of cultural and linguistic resistance to it. By and large Iranians
had converted and perforce joined the new religion, and in their scholarship and even literary preferences and achievements they had opted
for Islam and Arabic. Ferdowsi's task of putting into a singular poetic
narrative these ancient stories had therefore an urgent political purpose.
Here we need to keep in mind that the monumental work of Ferdowsi's
epic did not just preserve but in fact also helped to reinvent the new Persian language for posterity. This reinvention, done over centuries and
by myriad poets, historians, scientists, and Qur'anic scholars, in turn
gave a new birth to the very person of a Persian poet (both before and
after Ferdowsi), now charged with a towering historical task. In his life
and lifetime achievement, Ferdowsi in effect created a new mandate for
the Persian poet. While the younger generation that had come before
Ferdowsi and had resisted the total hegemony of the Arabic language
and Islamic culture had used the Persian language as a marker of ethnicity (*ethnos*; *nezhad*), Ferdowsi had single-handedly changed that

ethnocentricity to a marker of poetic eloquence (*logos*; *sokhan*), preparing for the future emergence of the language as a marker of ethical conduct (*ethos*; *hanjar*).[7]

Because of this singular significance of his poetic achievement, far more than his mortal life it is his life as a poet that underlies his enduring relevance in the history of Persian letters and a liberated conception of *world literature*. In that sense, we need to heed his own conception of his life and immortality. At one point toward the end of the *Shahnameh* he turns to his autobiographical voice and says he is now seventy-one years old, and his old age is dawning on him with illness and pain. He says he needed to write a history of kings, as he thanks two local dignitaries who had helped him. He praises the ruling sultan Mahmoud before turning to himself and boasting about his epic and then adds,

> *Az an pas Namiram keh man zendeh-am*
> *Keh tokhm-e sokhan man parakande'am*

> Thenceforth I will never die for I am alive
> For I have spread the seeds of eloquence.[8]

This self-assertion puts the whole notion of "the death of the author" under a whole new perspective. Ferdowsi, in his own words, dwells in his poetic voice, thrives in his poetic birth, an immortality he knows, and rightly so, he has secured for himself in the very quintessence of his existence: the *Shahnameh*.

"I WILL NEVER DIE FOR I AM ALIVE"

His name was either Mansur or Hassan or Ahmad. His father's name was Hassan, Ahmad, or Ali. His grandfather's name was Sharafshah. His patronymic name was Abu al-Qasem, his nom de plume Ferdowsi. He was also known by the name of the city in which he was born, and thus al-Tusi. Why was he called by the sobriquet Ferdowsi? Perhaps because his patron, Sultan Mahmoud, first called him that, meaning the man from Ferdowsi, the man from Paradise. He was born circa 940 to a family of landed gentry in the village of Bazh in the Tabaran district near the major city of Tus in Khorasan. As a class, this landed gentry had converted to Islam while safeguarding its deeper roots in the local, regional, and imperial lore of the Sassanid Empire (226–651).[9]

Ferdowsi began composing the *Shahnameh* in the year 977, when he was in his midthirties and at which time he was a married man and the father of a seven-year-old boy. There is no factual evidence as to who his wife was—her name, her background, nothing. We know that initially he had intended to travel to the Samanid capital, Bokhara, where a manuscript of the prose *Shahnameh* of Abu Mansur ibn Abd al-Razzaq was held in the royal library, but he changed his mind and remained in Tus when a friend made available to him another copy of the same text. From Tus, however, he was supported by the Samanid nobleman Mansur ibn Abd al-Razzaq, whom he praises posthumously. Ferdowsi was evidently quite attached to this patron. The year 987, in which Mansur was arrested in Nishpur and taken to Bokhara, where he was then executed, was a turning point in Ferdowsi's life: "From this moment onward," Djalal Khaleghi-Motlagh reports, "there is no mention of anything to indicate either physical comfort or peace of mind, rather we find frequent complaints concerning his old age, poverty, and anxiety."[10] Indications therefore are that he happily began the composition of the *Shahnameh* under the patronage of the Samanids and had his happiest years while protected and rewarded by them. The latter part of his life and thus composition of the *Shahnameh* were not as happy.

Did Ferdowsi compose any poem other than his *Shahnameh*? The attribution of the narrative poem "Yusuf and Zuleika" (Joseph and Potiphar's wife) and many other shorter pieces are certainly apocryphal. Legends attribute the "Joseph and Potiphar's Wife" poem to a younger brother of Ferdowsi's named Mas'ud or Hossein.[11] The towering accomplishment of the *Shahnameh* overshadows any other poetic composition he may have produced. Ferdowsi finished the first draft of the *Shahnameh* in the year 994 but continued to work on it well into Sultan Mahmoud's reign, until 997, and then by 999 he began working on the reign of Anushirvan in the historical part of the epic, while periodically complaining of old age and his failing health in his epic. Nevertheless, by the year 1000 he had finished most of the story of Anushirvan. Subsequent parts of the historical period were composed by 1002. In 1006, when the poet was sixty-seven, a deeply troubling tragedy befell him, and he lost his son and recorded the incident while continuing to work on his opus. On March 8, 1010, he is believed to have finally finished the *Shahnameh*.[12] He therefore spent approximately thirty years of his life composing his epic.

Perhaps the most traumatic tragedy in Ferdowsi's life was the death of his young son, for which he interrupts the flow of his narrative in the course of the reign of Khosrow Parviz in the historical part of the *Shahnameh* to mourn and reflect on its untimely occurrence. He says he is sixty-five years old when this tragedy befell him. It would be unbecoming of him, he says, to think of worldly riches after this tragedy. Then he says he must heed his own admonition and think of his young son's death.

> It was my turn but my young son is gone,
> Leaving my lifeless body in pain—
> I rush forth to catch up with him
> And when I do will I scold him, saying,
> "It was my time to leave,
> Why without my permission,
> Did you leave and take my peace with you?
> You were my support in times of trouble,
> Why did you leave the company of an old man?
> Did you find younger companions?
> Is that why you left me in a rush?"
> My young son was only thirty-seven
> Did not find this world to his liking and left,
> He was always contentious with me,
> So suddenly he became angry and left.
> He left, but his pain is here with me—
> My heart and my eyes are drowning in tearful blood.

Now he has joined the light,
To find a place for his father.
A long time has thus passed, and none of my fellow travelers
[who passed away] has ever returned.
Now he is waiting for me impatiently
He is angry that I linger behind.
He was thirty-seven and I was sixty-seven—
He did not worry about me and left.
He was in a rush and I hesitant,
What we will gain of our deeds, we shall see.
May your soul the Creator keep in light!
And may He make of reason an armor around your soul!
The only thing I ask from God Almighty—
Who sustains us openly and in secret:
To forgive all my sins,
And enlighten my darkened abode.[13]

Based on his references in the *Shahnameh* biographers of Ferdowsi have concluded that he lived in relative poverty much of his life, and Sultan Mahmoud was not forthcoming in providing for him, while copyists and reciters of his poetry were being rewarded by various courtiers during his lifetime. Based on the earliest sources, however, his biographers believe that by the year 1010 Ferdowsi's manuscript was already in the capable hands of both copyists. But the royal acknowledgment of his achievement was not forthcoming. Legend has it that he was paid much less than he was promised and that he "was extremely upset by this and went to a bathhouse; upon leaving the bathhouse he drank some beer and divided the king's present between the beer seller and the bath attendant. Then, fearing punishment by Mahmud, he fled from Ghazna by night."[14] Much of these latter parts of his biography, especially his hostility with Mahmud and the satirical poems about him, are entirely apocryphal and hagiographic with little factual evidence. The dramatic narratives of these events are in fact further proof of their fictive character. "Later . . . Mahmud regretted his behavior toward the poet and . . . had camel loads of indigo to the value of 20,000 dinars sent to Ferdowsi, but as the camels were entering Tus by the Rudbar gate Ferdowsi's corpse was being borne out of the city by the Razan gate."[15] The dramatic story does not end there: "In the cemetery the preacher of Tabaran prevented his being buried in the Muslim cemetery on the grounds that Ferdowsi was a Shi'ite, and so there was no choice but to bury the poet in his own orchard. . . . Ferdowsi left only one daughter, and the poet had wanted the king's payment as a dowry for her. But after the poet's death, his daughter would not accept the payment."[16]

All these dramatic stories, with a grain of historical truth to them, perhaps point to the immense popularity of Ferdowsi's character to his ordinary audiences. His date of death is given as either 1020 at the age of eighty-two or 1025, at the age of eighty-seven.

The fundamental problem with any attempt in reconstructing Ferdowsi's biography is the fact that there are no contemporary sources, and much of the rest is in fact apocryphal and hagiographical—information that is of course of immense importance in its own right but not sufficient or reliable for us to re-create a solid, consistent, and detailed biography. The result of venturing into his *Shahnameh* to extrapolate information about his personal life, if it is not done very judiciously, is the fact that before we know it we will have perpetrated systemic violence on Ferdowsi's poetic poise and persona to extrapolate biographical information from it. Djalal Khaleghi-Motlagh, one of the most eminent *Shahnameh* scholars of our time, chief among many others, uses Ferdowsi's poetic persona to extrapolate his "mood" and "disposition," far beyond simple biographical facts. This is a very dubious exercise. To use autobiographical passages to guess at Ferdowsi's age, for example, or mark the point when he is mourning the death of his son is one thing, but to use the introduction to the magnificent story of Bizhan and Manizheh to surmise Ferdowsi's personal life,[17] the social status of his wife, and so on is entirely speculative, unreliable, and in fact does epistemic violence to his poetic voice—plus the fact that such speculations introduce serious contradictions in guessing at Ferdowsi's "mood."

Another major issue giving rise to spurious speculations about Ferdowsi's life as a court poet is his troubled relationship with Sultan Mahmoud, leading to his lampooning of the Ghaznavid monarch, which, again, has to be understood in the context of a popular poetic imagination appropriating the poet for itself and away from the royal court of both the Samanids and the Ghaznavids over many centuries and epochs. In this respect, Ferdowsi in effect becomes the figurative replica of his own chief hero in the *Shahnameh*, Rostam, whose presence in the royal court is always tension ridden, as, for example, when Key Kavous summons him to fight Sohrab and he takes his sweet time partying with his fellow hero Give and does not show up at the royal court, and when he does finally come to the court and Key Kavous admonishes him for being late, he denounces the king and leaves his court in anger. It is that prototype, we can surmise, that the popular imagination has borrowed and followed to distance Ferdowsi from the Ghaznavid court. Some scholars have questioned even the validity of the satire Ferdowsi presumably wrote against Sultan Mahmoud; others believe it existed but that some of its lines are spurious.[18] But the whole supposition of Ferdowsi satirizing Mahmoud can also be understood in the context of successive generations of later poets, scribes, and their audiences wresting the towering Persian poet away from the royal court and claiming him for themselves. This possibility opens a whole new perspective on the organic presence of the *Shahnameh* among its readers far beyond the dubious speculations about a historically founded hostility between the poet and his patron to the point of producing an entire satirical poem by Ferdowsi against Sultan Mahmoud.

An equally contentious point of exaggeration concerns the raising of issues of "religion in the *Shahnameh*," wondering about his relationship with Zoroastrians, followed by the presumed sectarian hostilities between Ferdowsi and his patron.[19] The attribution of this sectarian animus by Sunni authorities close to Mahmoud toward Ferdowsi's Shi'ism might indeed have an element of truth to it, but it does not completely account for the effervescence of popular poetic appropriation of Ferdowsi away from the royal court, as evident in subsequent manuscript compilations. It is dynastic power versus the popular poetic imagination that is at work here rather than a cliché-ridden and even ahistorical Sunni-Shi'i rivalry. The Khorasani Isma'ili poet and philosopher Nasser Khosrow (1004–1088) is reported to have seen "a large caravansary and was told that this had been built with the money from the gift that Mahmud had sent to the poet, which, since he had already died, his heir refused to accept."[20] Such accounts, if proven trustworthy, indicate that the effervescent popular imagination about Ferdowsi, based on scant facts, had arisen to legendary proportions very soon after his passing in Khorasan. Much of Ferdowsi's praise for Sultan Mahmoud (though not all) is either spurious and inauthentic or insincere and hyperbolic in comparison with his praise for the Samanid prince Mansur.[21] All indications are that Ferdowsi was not sufficiently rewarded for his lifetime achievement by Sultan Mahmoud. Satirizing Mahmoud when he was assured no reward would be forthcoming is the clearest indication that this confrontation between the poet and the patron would feed into future popular sentiments.

Both Ferdowsi and his *Shahnameh* are also too enthusiastically and ahistorically assimilated into the presumed "cultural resistances of Iranians" to the Arab conquest of the mid-seventh century. The political, linguistic, and cultural resistance to Arab conquest was perfectly evident in the northeastern region of Khorasan from proto-Zoroastrian revolutionary uprisings like those of Babak Khorramdin (ca. 795–838), Ustadh Sis (fl. 767), and Al-Muqanna (d. ca. 783) in the eighth and ninth centuries to dynastic formations like those of the Saffarids (861–1003) and the Samanids (819–999) in the ninth, tenth, and eleventh centuries. These developments should not, however, be so broadly racialized, for along with the rise of the Shu'ubiyyah movement from Baghdad itself they offer a glimpse at the transregional social and political changes and imperial expansions in which Ferdowsi was born and raised. At the heart of his *Shahnameh*, however, is the archetypal articulation of an imperial pedigree that transcends his own particular history and reaches out for a far deeper conception of history. Too much undue attention to these historical circumstances by much later Iranian nationalist historiography has in fact paradoxically diminished the epic, dramatic, and above all archetypal dimensions of his masterpiece. There can be little doubt that Ferdowsi was very much a product of the political circumstances of his time. But reducing the poetic, literary, and dramatic dimensions of the *Shahnameh* to such factors does irreparable epistemic violence to something beyond, beneath, and above these circumstances. They can potentially blind us to the literary idiomaticity of the text itself, the manner in which it reveals and stages its own inner poetic logic and rhetoric.

Along the same lines, much speculation has also been made about Ferdowsi's "education," again at the expense of compromising the evidence of his exquisite erudition and poetic gift of grace in his masterpiece.[22] In the absence of any relevant and reliable biographical data, the proof is in the pudding. It is the *Shahnameh* itself that stages a deeply perceptive poet missing no occasion in his vast and varied gifts of storytelling to muse and reflect on the nature of human folly and destiny. Did he or did he not know Arabic and Pahlavi? This is like asking if Shakespeare or Dante or Goethe knew Greek and Latin. Perhaps they did, perhaps they did not. How does that probable knowledge or ignorance add or subtract from the force and elegance of their respective poetry or gift of storytelling? These are biographical questions that might occasion some convoluted scholarly debates but add very little, if anything at all, to our understanding of Ferdowsi's poetry. Potentially in fact they can exacerbate that epistemic violence on his poetry every time we go near it to extrapolate one or another useless biographical datum from it. Ferdowsi's possible knowledge of Arabic or Pahlavi is a diversionary question almost entirely irrelevant to any understanding of the substance of his poetry, which is delivered entirely in a sublime poetic Persian.

The same is true about the endless and useless discussions about Ferdowsi being a Shi'i, what kind of Shi'i, or a Sunni, or even having Zoroastrian sentiments.[23] The fact is solidly established that he was a Twelver Shi'i. But that fact adds or subtracts nothing from our reading of his magnum opus and again might in fact cast a wrong shadow on over- or underinterpreting him in entirely extratextual ways. A literary masterpiece like the *Shahnameh* generates and sustains its own moral universe and ethical idiomaticity. It is ludicrous to reduce that universe to a theological systematicity outside that text. A perfect example of the confounding of Ferdowsi's Shi'ism with an Iranian ultranationalist reading of Ferdowsi is when the two aspects are conflated to suggest that Ferdowsi's Shi'ism had to do with his Iranian nationalism.[24] Even deducing theological positions from Ferdowsi's poetic speculations are suspect, for they are in fact occasioned by various story lines. We cannot conclude any such position when we read Plato's dialogues, for example, as to what Plato's "theology" was. Ferdowsi is a poet not a theologian, as Plato was a philosopher and not a mystic. It is the dialogical disposition of such positions that matter, and not any conclusion about Ferdowsi's personal sectarian or theological preferences, or even affinity with pre-Islamic Zoroastrian thought. All such misguided speculations occur when we do not pay closer attention to the moral and ethical speculations that arise from the stories themselves. Ferdowsi was a Muslim, a Shi'a, an Iranian of very proud and self-confident descent, all of which are evident in his lifetime achievement, the greatest Persian epic poem ever composed in this language. He does not teach by admonition but by dramatic reenactment of stories, by the judicious, periodic, and polyvocal introduction of his poetic voices. It is a fundamentally flawed hermeneutics to take any one line of his epic and interpret it as an indication that Ferdowsi as a person said this, that, or the other thing. This is a violation of the poetic disposition of his work and does irreparable damage to his dramatic narratives. The nationalist abuse of the *Shahnameh* has turned him into an anti-Arab, anti-Turk "patriot," all at the unconscionable expense of damaging his poetic dramatization of history.

The study of the *Shahnameh* in fact needs to progress exactly in the opposite direction, not taxing it to squeeze nonexistent biographical data about Ferdowsi (more than is possible and trustworthy) but toward a renewed attempt at coming to terms with the work's literary character, its poetic disposition, and above all its dramatic idiomaticity. It is true that, as major scholars of the *Shahnameh* have duly noted, Ferdowsi's masterpiece "has not received its rightful attention in works written in Persian on the art of poetry . . . which works consider eloquence and poetic style largely as a matter of particular figures of speech."[25] It is also true that "in discussing Ferdowsi's achievement one must consider, on the one hand, the totality of the *Shahnameh* as a whole and, on the other, his artistry as a storyteller."[26] But precisely such legitimate concerns and projects are conceptually subverted by extracting dubious biographical material from the selfsame text. A remarkable feature of Ferdowsi's epic narrative, for example, is his exquisite "cinematic" techniques: the manner in which he "cuts" and edits a scene. In that regard, his characterizations of his dramatis personae, too, exude polyvocality, intimacy, and confidence. The manner in which Khaleghi-Motlagh aptly describes Ferdowsi's character development must remain central to our reading of his masterpiece:

> Many of the narrative poets who followed Ferdowsi were more interested in the construction of individual lines than of their stories as a whole. In such narrative poems, the poet himself speaks much more than the characters of his poem, and even where there is dialogue, there is little difference between the attitudes of the various characters of the story, so that the speaker is still the author, who at one moment speaks in the role of one character and the next moment speaks in the role of another. The result is that in such poems . . . the characters in the story are less individuals than types. In contrast, the dialogues in the *Shahnameh* are realistic and frequently argumentative, and the poet uses them to good effect as a means of portraying the inner life of his characters.[27]

To do as Khaleghi-Motlagh rightly suggests, the task of producing a biography of Ferdowsi must not task the text in abusive and violent ways. "Ferdowsi was also a master as a lyric poet," he tells us, "such moments in the *Shahnameh* distinguish it from other epics of the world . . . due to their simplicity and brevity, however, they do not harm the epic spirit of the poem, rather they give it a certain musicality and tenderness; in particular, due to the descriptions of love in the poem, these lyric moments take it beyond the world of primary epic."[28] This is an apt and incisive observation. To allow this lyricism of the epic to reveal itself we need to pay particular attention to the *poetic persona* of the epic narrator and see how Ferdowsi actually stages it. Let us now turn to one specific such case in the *Shahnameh* and see how it works.

ONE POET IN THREE PERSONAE

Let us look at one such opening gambit of a story of the *Shahnameh* and see how Ferdowsi's narrative voice (the poetic summation of his "biography") sets up the plot.[29] For this story, "Bizhan and Manizheh," we have an utterly exquisite translation of the opening lines, though alas only partial. But it is still long enough to help us find our way back into the original. Dick Davis's beautiful translation captures the soul of the original:

> A night as black as coal bedaubed with pitch,
> A night of ebony, a night on which
> Mars, Mercury, and Saturn would not rise.
> Even the moon seemed fearful of the skies:
> Her face was three-fourths dimmed, and all the night
> Looked gray and dusty in her pallid light.[30]

The sense of the original, perfectly captured here, is a deeply dark night, marked by no star except a thin sliver of moon, that in fact demarcates the pitch-darkness surrounding the narrator, a witness to the standing still of the universe: absolute, utter, frightening darkness.[31]

> On plain and mountainside dark henchmen laid
> Night's raven carpet, shade on blacker shade;
> The heavens seemed rusted iron, as if each star
> Were blotted out by tenebrous, thick tar;
> Dark Ahriman appeared on every side
> Like a huge snake whose jaws gape open wide.[32]

The only crucial point lost in this otherwise perfect translation is when Ferdowsi suddenly and subtly in the original introduces his own voice and says *nemudam*, "to me appeared," where Davis opts for the passive voice "appeared." That first-person pronoun *-m* is critical to our detection of how Ferdowsi's poetic voice gets introduced and articulated in the rest of the opening stanza. For it is to the poetic voice of Ferdowsi himself that "dark Ahriman appears on every side / Like a huge snake whose jaws gape open wide." Fortunately (and cleverly), Davis recaptures that personal pronoun in the following section:

> The garden and the stream by which I lay
> Became a sea of pitch; it seemed that day
> Would never come, the skies no longer turned,
> The weakened sun no longer moved or burned.
> Fear gripped the world and utter silence fell,
> Stilling the clamor of the watchman's bell,
> Silencing all the myriad cries and calls
> Of everything that flies or walks or crawls.[33]

The only point I would add here is where Davis says "Fear gripped the world" in the original and more closely we have *Jahan-ra del az khishtan por haras*, "the world was filled with fear of itself." It is imperative for us to see the source of fear in the world is not external but internal to it. This adds to the sense of fright and despair Ferdowsi generates. From here on the poetic voice of Ferdowsi becomes more pronounced:

> I started up, bewildered, terrified;
> My fear awoke the woman at my side.
> I called for her to bring torches, light;
> She fetched bright candles to dispel the night
> And laid a little feast on which to dine,
> Red pomegranates, citrons, quinces, wine,
> Together with a polished goblet fit
> For kings and emperors to drink from it.[34]

Here we need a bit more crucial specification. There is no "woman" at the poet's side. The narrator simply says when he jumps from his bed in fear and despair, *yeki mehrban budam andar saray*, "There was a kind person with me at home." To be sure, Davis is taking a perfectly plausible poetic license here from his own heterosexual perspective—nor indeed do we have any indication that Ferdowsi's narrator did not mean a female companion by that "kind person."[35] It could be a male, a female, or just a figment of Ferdowsi's poetic imagination, or what I propose to be simply a narratological trope. By falsely gendering it we rob the metaphor of its poetic potency. The fact is in Persian we do not have gender-specific pronouns, so we don't know if this person is a he or a she (though, again, it is perfectly plausible to assume, as Davis does, that it is a she, though others, like the much earlier Arabic translator of the poem, Bundari, thought it was a young man). But keep in mind that Ferdowsi's poetic persona simply says "at home" and not "at my side." I insist on this difference because anachronistically projecting the liberal bourgeois morality implied in the image of a husband's waking up next to his wife in twenty-first-century North America back to the time and texture of Ferdowsi and his poem is a bit forced on the poor poetic voice invoked in this line, and we need to be aware of it. All we know is from the commotion that the poet's voice generates a kind person in the same house wakes up. There are other subtle differences. Where Davis says "I called," in the original we have *khorushidam*, which is more like "I screamed" or "I moaned," indicating the poet's degree of fear and despair. The rest of the incident is captured perfectly fine by Davis but alas much abbreviated.

> "But why do you need candles now?" she said.
> "Has sleep refused to visit your soft bed?
> Drink up your wine and—as you do so—I
> Will tell a story from the days gone by,
> A story full of love and trickery,
> Whose hero lived for war and chivalry."
> "Sweet moon," I said, "my cypress, my delight,
> Tell me this tale to while away the night."
> "First listen well," she said, "and when you've heard
> The story through, record it word for word."[36]

The fuller account of this mise-en-scène in the original is here sacrificed to this utterly beautiful but much-abbreviated rendition. Let us now leave

Davis with much gratitude behind and turn to Ferdowsi himself and see what happens next.

A more literal translation of this introductory passage (based on Julius Mohl's edition) informs us that Ferdowsi's narrator was frightened by all these apparitions and the darkness surrounding him. The kind companion he has is awakened and "comes to the garden," presumably where the poet was sleeping in the open air, where in fact he could make all those astronomical observations about the sky and the moon and stars, and thus presumably the kind companion was sleeping somewhere else. He or she asks the poet why is he upset, why he needs a candle, and why he cannot sleep. "I told him/her," the poet says, "I cannot sleep, please bring me a candle bright like the sun / Put it next to me and play music for me, bring the lute and some wine too." The kind companion leaves the garden and brings a candle and a light as the poet wants, as well as some wine, and a few pomegranates, oranges, and quinces. So, while a mini banquet is prepared for the frightened and disconcerted poet, the companion starts drinking and playing beautiful, magical music. The companion satisfies the poet's every whim and turns the dark night bright as day. There is a festive and warming and even erotic scene clearly suggested here, an eroticism that is neither homo- nor hetero-erotic, could easily be either, but the ambiguity makes the scene ever more potent.

Now the poetic voice does something quite crucial (again based on Mohl's edition) that seriously changes the entire mise-en- scène before the story begins and introduces a new dramatis persona. The narrator turns to us and tells us, "Listen to what this kind companion said to me, soon after we began drinking together." So now "we" enter the scene, we the readers of these lines, and we become integral to the scene via this direct evocation by the poetic voice. That lovely companion prays for the poet and wishes him all the best luck. "Drink your wine," the companion says, "while I read you a story from the Ancient Book, and when you hear what I have to tell you, you will wonder about the nature of this universe." The companion proceeds to tell the poet how strange and adventuresome is this story. The poet asks his companion to tell him the story right away and teach him a lesson about the nature of this life. At this point the companion says fine, I tell you this story from a book in Pahlavi, but you must turn it into Persian poetry. The poet assures the companion that he will do precisely that, for his own poetic impulses have now been provoked. "Since you are telling me a concealed secret," the poet assures his companion, "my uncouth poetic disposition will be much refined." He then assures his companion that he will compose the poem precisely and point by point as the companion tells him the story. "I will gratefully turn the story into a poem," he assures the companion. Then he again turns to us and informs us, "That lovely companion recited the story to me, which was written in time immemorial, now listen to my poem, let your reason be alert and your heart wakened."[37]

There is not one but three dramatis personae in this prolegomena to the story of Bizhan and Manizheh—the poet, his companion, and us. The triangulated mise-en-scène is central to our reading of the drama that unfolds. There is no biographical "I" here in this as indeed in many other crucial moments of the *Shahnameh*. Literary respect for such passages means not to violate their poetic disposition and ask them to respond to mundane and quite bizarre questions as to the social status of Ferdowsi's wife!

THE MAN REDEEMING MANKIND

Ferdowsi's *Shahnameh* reads on the porous borderlines of myth, heroism, and history—all brought together into a seamless epic narrative. It is precisely on the fluidity of those lines forming and feeding on one another that his life and lifetime achievement need to be read. "A chronicler who recites events without distinguishing between major and minor ones," wrote Walter Benjamin in "Theses on the Philosophy of History," "acts in accordance with the following truth: nothing that has ever happened should be regarded as lost for history. To be sure, only a *redeemed mankind* receives the fullness of its past—which is to say, only for a *redeemed mankind* has its past become citable in all its moments. Each moment it has lived becomes a *citation à l'ordre du jour*—and that day is Judgment Day."[38]

What is a "redeemed mankind" that is solely deserving of a fullness of history? In what way has this "redeemed mankind" merited "fullness of its past . . . citable in all its moments"? A "redeemed mankind," for both Benjamin and beyond, is humanity fully conscious of itself, not of every minutia of its existence but in possession of a historical consciousness that allows for such a consciousness. To become a *"citation à l'ordre du jour"* means to be deserving of such a citation, again not merely in the details of the action reported but far more pointedly in the full historical consciousness that allows for such reporting to be registered, made meaningful and significant. Benjamin sums up the occasion of all such moments and suspends them on "Judgement Day." "Judgement Day," as Ferdowsi understood it, is the day of return, when we return to our point of origin and revisit our creator and try to answer in the affirmative the question He put to us just before he created us that He is our Lord. Benjamin suspends that totality on the fragmented moments of the history that we, and with us the whole world, have lived. Ferdowsi's archetypal narrative is the practice of that universality, gathering together what Benjamin saw scattered around, the occasion of the worldliness we live. The salvation Benjamin sought in imagining a whole different history, in his case in messianic Judaism, was to fuse a sacred certitude with his dialectical materialism. The fusion had an entirely different archaic gestation embedded in Ferdowsi's gift of storytelling, with the metaphysics of his universe rooted in the poetic intuition he had invested in his epic.

A *redeemed mankind* is rooted, fully flowering, from its imagined and poetically documented past to its unforeseen future. In that sense Ferdowsi's *Shahnameh* is both history and philosophy of history, a manner of historiography that has successfully fused its own mythic and heroic dimensions into its historical consciousness. That transfusion of fact, myth, and heroism provokes an intuition of transcendence rooted in the *Shahnameh* narrative itself. The abusive manhandling of the text to extract useless and misguided assumptions as to what Ferdowsi's "religion," "nationalism," or marital status were misses this metaphysics of the epic altogether. Ferdowsi's poetic metaphysics is always cosmic, proverbial, invoking the power of reason and reasoning, of existential being there, and the necessity of righteousness, none of which is reducible to any known or institutional religion. Reducing that cosmogony that is first and foremost poetically produced to Islam, or Shi'ism, or Zoroastrianism is as violent and abusive as trying to project a Ptolemaic or Copernican astrophysics from his astrological references. Let us dwell on one such metaphysical moment more closely:

> In the Name of God of the Sun and the Moon,
> For in His Name Reason has shown the Path:
> The Lord of Being and the Lord of Righteousness
> Who does not expect from you waywardness or shortcoming:
> The God of Saturn, Mars, and the Sun—
> The One who has given me the good tidings, and in Whom I
>   Trust.
> I cannot praise Him,
> Thinking of him casts my soul into despair.
> He created Time and Space,
> The trace of a tiny ant points to his Existence.
> From the turning sun to the dark soil,
> From fiery stars to pure water:
> They all testify to the existence of the Lord
> Acquainting your soul with Him.
> Towards that Creator who is free of want—
> You will not find any path: Do not waste your time!
> He is not in need of any ministers, or any Treasurer, Crown, or
>   Throne,
> He will not be lessened or increased, beyond good or bad
>   fortune.
> He is entirely Needless and we his servants,
> Standing in reverence of his command and wish.
> The soul and reason without a doubt,
> Can figure out the firmament and stars.
> Call no one but him Almighty God,
> For He is the source of our happiness and him we need.
> He created the day, the night, and the turning firmament,
> He created hunger, sleep, anger, and love.

This is how this fast-moving heaven is built,
It brings pain sometimes and at other times solace.
There is much wonder about Rostam,
Many people have many stories of him in their heart.
He is the towering source of chivalry and war,
He is the standard of wisdom, knowledge, and dignity.
Like an elephant in land and a serpent in sea,
A wise hero and a man of war.
Let me now tell you the story of Kamus,
Transforming it from [old] books into my poetry.
Let us now rerun to the narrative of Dehghan:
Let's see what the wise man has to say.[39]

This is the metaphysical sum total of the *Shahnameh* itself, the inner dynamics of its moral imagination, the ethical subconscious of its text made poetically self-conscious. The proverbial expressions Ferdowsi uses may sound familiar to a Persianate world, but they become idiomatic to his own epic universe. This metaphysics makes sense only in the aftermath or just before or while reading his stories. If you surgically remove them when you translate the *Shahnameh* into another language, or if you consider them repetitive, boring, or samples of "moral sententiae" you need to go back to learn the *Shahnameh* anew. The epistemic damage done to the text by trying to extract a known religious position from such references is predicated on yet another structural violence that disregards the ways in which these poetic implosions point to speculations embedded in the stories themselves. Without coming to terms with the inner world of the *Shahnameh* itself there is no placing it onto the spectrum of something we can legitimately consider *world literature*.

THE WEST AND THE REST

The inner world of the *Shahnameh* and its innate literary worldliness, pivoted toward its poetics of transcendence, correspond to the changing world around it. If the two worlds are not allowed to converse, the inner worldliness of the Persian epic and the outer worlds that have embraced it, the *Shahnameh* will be reduced to a bizarre object of curiosity for the natives and their Western interlocutors. In his fine study of the Persian epic, *Epic and Sedition*, Dick Davis begins with a casual division of various interpretations of the *Shahnameh* into "Western" and "Iranian": while "Western" receptions have been rather "grudging," Iranians have been laudatory and expressive of their "amour propre."[40] Though he proceeds to dismiss many of the non-Iranian criticisms of the epic, Davis's binary ends up positing a hermeneutic bifurcation that deworlds the *Shahnameh* by making it the subject of an Orientalist and object of a nativist curiosity—thereby disallowing the text itself the possibilities of a sustained historical unfolding. In between these two worlds—"Western" and "Iranian"—there is another world, the world itself, that engulfs both these and any other readings that might approach the *Shahnameh*. Then there is the world of the Persian epic itself, with a sustained disposition of prolonged self-revelation. In and of itself, therefore, this binary disallows the possibility of someone's reading the *Shahnameh* and not falling into the "Western" and "Iranian" camps—as I have had for decades reading it with Asian, African, and Latin American students, lately using Davis's excellent translation. Suppose someone in Senegal wants to read the Persian epic, someone in Argentina, someone in India, someone in Cairo, someone in Tokyo—and they by and large read it through its English translation. Are these potential readers "Iranian" or "Western"? Neither. This deworlding of the text, denying it a world readership, forcing it into a false binary, and therefore denying it a worldly hermeneutic circle beyond "the West and the Rest" is at the heart of the ways in which the *Shahnameh* is prevented from reclaiming its place in literary worldliness, indeed in *world literature*.

The spirit of such a systematic alienation of the *Shahnameh* from itself and from becoming a worldly part of literature is still very much informed by the Virgilian belligerence that persists in Dick Davis's manufactured binary between the natives and the Westerners. It is from Virgil that the world of epics had been divided into two opposing camps of enemies, one by "cosmic order" and the other by "chaos."[41] That spirit is entirely against the very grain of the Alexander Romance that was generated in Persian in the Iranian world, chief among which is in Ferdowsi's *Shahnameh*, and worked precisely in the opposite direction of that Virgilian division of the world between "the West and the Rest" and in fact became the far more inclusive conception of *world literature*. The historical adventures of Alexander the Great (356–323 B.C.E.) became the material of expansive legends in and out of Europe. From its Greek origin in the Pseudo-Callisthenes version, the Alexander Romance eventually spread far and wide into Latin, Armenian, Syriac, Hebrew, and most medieval European vernaculars. Through its Syriac rendition it also reached Arabic (including the Qur'an), Persian, Ottoman Turkish, and found one of its most potent renditions in Ferdowsi's *Shahnameh*.[42] What is remarkable about the Alexander Romance and its widespread reception is how it gave multiple nations an opportunity to claim it into their own literary worldliness. I propose this inclusive, pluralistic, and open-ended tradition of the Alexander Romance as exactly the opposite of the Virgilian tradition and its pernicious impact on dividing the world to conquer it better. Precisely through the world-conquering figure of Alexander, but entirely in the opposite direction of the Virgilian epic, the Alexander Romance, in which Ferdowsi's *Shahnameh* has a towering presence, is a far superior site of rethinking *world literature* than the vindictive site of the *Aeneid* still evident in the proverbial assumptions of literary scholars who keep dividing the reception of the *Shahnameh* between Iranians and non-Iranians, or "the West and the Rest."

MOTHERS AND SONS

After yet another dispute with his father—following Seyavash's refusing to kill hostages he had captured on the border between Iran and Turan—Seyavash finally defects to Turan and hopes to resume a more peaceful life in the land of the enemy. The Turanian king Afrasiab receives him lovingly, and Piran, his trusted vizier, becomes Seyavash's close confidant. Seyavash marries two princesses in Turan, one Jari-reh, the daughter of Piran, and the other Farigis, the daughter of Afra-siab, and becomes close and very dear to his royal father-in-law. This eventually provokes the jealousy of some powerful men at Afrasiab's court, chief among them Garsivaz, the brother of Afrasiab, who plots to set Seyavash and Afrasiab against each other and once and for all get rid of the Persian prince. Afrasiab mobilizes an army against Sey-avash, defeats him, and orders his execution, while his wife, Farigis, and his young son Key Khosrow eventually return to Iran.

The tragic fate of Seyavash is interwoven with the story of a city he had built while in exile from his homeland. He, we must remember, is the child of a marriage between his royal father, Key Kavous, and his Turanian mother, whom he loses upon his birth. He becomes a tragic figure from the moment of his birth, when astrologers foretell a tragic end for him, and he is entrusted to Rostam to bring him up with moral and physical rectitude and courage. From this point forward Key Kavous consistently sends his son away, perhaps for fear of his tragic ending affecting him. Soon after the Sudabeh scandal, Seyavash leaves Iran for the border with Turan, with Rostam in his company. After a fearful dream, Afrasiab refuses to fight him and asks for peace. Seyavash agrees and sends Rostam with the great news of victory to his father. Key Kavous gets angry with him and orders him to kill the hostages he had taken from the Turanian army and invade Turan. Seyavash refuses to renege on his peace treaty with the Turanians, writes a letter to Afrasiab, and asks for safe passage through his kingdom to go somewhere beyond to build a city. The city of Seyavashgard that Seyavash establishes and where he and his wife, Farigis, lived shortly together is the idyllic utopia of the Persian prince's tragic ending. The presence of Afrasiab's brother, the treacherous Garsivaz, is the diabolic force of evil that mars this uto-pian moment. What particularly angers the Turanian leadership and causes their suspicion and anger is Seyavash's introduction of Iranian figures as a fresco on buildings he had ordered constructed in this city. In telling the stories of these Persian figures and designs Ferdowsi's account is replete with nostalgia and homesickness. The idea of a home, where the tragic hero is born and raised, chases after Seyavash from one land to another and stabilizes and anchors all and every notion of imperial conquest in the case of this most tragic hero of the *Shahnameh*. To achieve that sense of home and homeliness in the midst of a massive imperial epic is the singular achievement of Ferdowsi in his *Shahnameh*.

Legend has it that from the spot where Seyavash's blood drops when he was killed a plant grows that is eventually called Par-e Seyavashan, around which name a ritual of remembrance emerges. The traumatic event has a lasting impact on the Persian poetic and literary imagination. Hafez has a poem remembering the tragedy of Seyavash:

> The Turkic king hears the words of those who badmouth
>   others:
> Shame on him for the blood of Seyavash he spilt.

Generations later, the eminent novelist Simin Daneshvar's *Suvashun* (1969) emerged as the most widely popular literary articulation of Seyavash's legend, set against the backdrop of the British occupation of Shiraz during World War II. The traumatic life and tragic death of Seyavash has fascinated generations of poets, novelists, dramatists, and literary scholars. Something innocent, something tragic, something irretrievably sad remains at the heart of the story of Seyavash. But a close reading of his encounter with his stepmother, Sudabeh, as Ferdowsi describes it in detail, reveals something beyond a mere illicit love affair. She is not as diabolic as you might think, nor is he as innocent if we understand Ferdowsi's luscious description of their erotic encounter at least in part from the young prince's perspective. Seyavash and Sudabeh represent two provocative characters whose proximity becomes erotically charged and politically combustive and therefore threatens the whole patriarchal culture of the *Shahnameh*. Here we encounter a mother figure who wishes to conspire with a son figure to overcome the father and place the son king over the father king. But the son refuses and ends up going through hellfire. Seyavash's refusal is much less moral than political, all his moral protests in fact a clear indication of "protesting too much." He already sees himself on his father's throne and does not wish to compromise that eventuality by engaging in a court intrigue.

Ferdowsi's description of Seyavash's entry into Sudabeh's private quarters and marking of his nervous trepidations allows for an interpretative space where we can see him enticed by this encounter. But he refuses to have anything to do with Sudabeh ostensibly on moral grounds but also for fear of compromising his political ambitions. Seyavash never forgives his father and thus becomes a tragic hero and by substituting his own body for the body of his father and by inflicting pain on himself seeks revenge on his father. So in him we have a peculiar case of regicide by proxy, regicide via suicide as parricide. The result, his final sacrifice, is parricide through filicide, homicide via suicide, murder of the self for the father by proxy. He goes to Turan and, by submitting his body to his father's mortal enemy, "kills" his father by being killed in his chief enemy's hands. From that mortal body's union with his father's enemy's daughter Farigis a son is born, Key Kavous, who will go back to rule Iran. The psychodrama between the father and the son here becomes substitutional, and therefore the murder of Seyavash is the final regicide within the patriarchal order of the Persian epic.

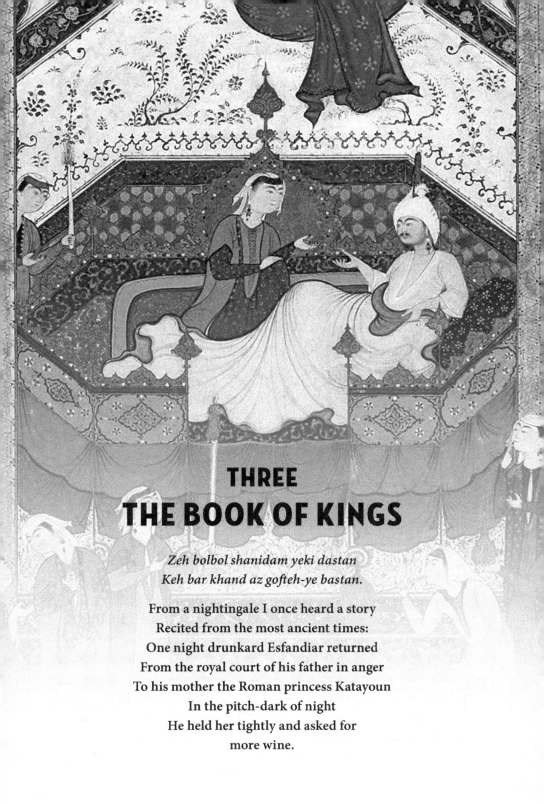

THREE
THE BOOK OF KINGS

Zeh bolbol shanidam yeki dastan
Keh bar khand az gofteh-ye bastan.

From a nightingale I once heard a story
Recited from the most ancient times:
One night drunkard Esfandiar returned
From the royal court of his father in anger
To his mother the Roman princess Katayoun
In the pitch-dark of night
He held her tightly and asked for
more wine.

sfandiar was a divinely ordained Persian prince who championed the prophetic cause of the ancient sage Zoroaster and promoted his new vision of the world. Esfandiar was invincible, triumphant, valiant, and destined to greatness, if only his father, Goshtasp, were to deliver on his promise to abdicate in his favor. Goshtasp would dispatch his fearless son to one dangerous and impossible mission after another. The valiant prince would perform all his father's commands, and on top of them venture into other heroic deeds—slaying monstrous wolves, man-eating lions, a dragon, a wicked enchantress, mythical birds—while braving storms and crossing deadly deserts. The Persian prince performs all these heroic deeds, rescues his sisters from bondage, returning to his father's court hoping to ascend his throne in due course. But the father refuses to do as he promised and decides to send his son on one more deadly mission, knowing full well he will not return from this last task alive.

EPIC AND THE WORLD

How are we to read the *Shahnameh* and its fantastic stories today? Over the years that I have taught the Persian epic at Columbia University in New York to generations of my students from around the globe I have grappled with a central question: how can I make this book as exciting to them and their diverse backgrounds as it has been to me? This succession of students from Asia, Africa, Latin America, as well as from North America and Europe, has taught me a singularly significant lesson: the *Shahnameh* has been hitherto trapped inside a false and falsifying binary—the assumption that it has an Iranian versus a "Western" reader. First and foremost, the Persian epic needs to be liberated from this distorting entrapment. The only way the *Shahnameh* can be restored to its worldly character and discussed as integral to *world literature* (beyond the provincial limitations of the discipline as it is practiced today) is first to place it in its own worldly context, the imperial habitat in which it was first crafted, and, second, to map out and theorize its own poetic worldliness, and, third, to allow it to unfold in the wide world in which it now finds itself. Read this way, the English translation of the Persian epic does not belong exclusively to English people, or even to that delusional abstraction called "the Western reader." It belongs to anyone anywhere physically or culturally subjected to British colonialism and who now therefore has a legitimate claim upon the English language and whatever is produced in it—anywhere from South Africa to Canada, from India through Africa to Mexico down to Argentina. It belongs to anyone who reads Persian from Central Asia to South Asia to Iran and beyond, as it belongs to anyone who can read it in any European language to which non-Europeans have perforce found a colonial inroad.

On the Columbia University campus the Persian epic has spoken in our common English language of instruction. New York, where my students and I read the *Shahnameh* on the Columbia campus, is a bilingual (English and Spanish) or indeed multilingual city. We pride ourselves that there are hundreds of restaurants in our city offering local cuisines from around the globe, and then with justified pride we add that you can order your food in those languages. My own younger children go to a local public school, where my wife and I regularly go to teach their classmates about the stories of the *Shahnameh* on various occasions, such as the Persian New Year of Noruz, where we tell them the stories of the mythical king Jamshid, during whose reign this festivity was inaugurated. From elementary public schools to classrooms in a major Ivy League university we are witness to the resurrection of the Persian epic in languages and climes not dreamed of in Ferdowsi's wildest imaginings. Both English and Spanish are colonial languages; their "Western" provenance was globalized from Asia and Africa to Latin America by a planetary imperialism that has now proved to be a two-edged sword—we have appropriated the language of our colonizers and speak back to them in their (now our) own languages. In the *Shahnameh* former colonies of these languages have found their own epic.

In addition to the world in which it was initially produced, and the world in which the Persian epic now finds itself, there is another world, a third world, the world of the *Shahnameh* itself, the inner dynamics of its textual coherence, the manner in which its stories come together and make a dramatic theater of the human condition. The *Shahnameh* is usually divided into three major components: the mythical, the heroic, and the historical, each seamlessly connected to the other by a singular and singularly self-conscious poet, creating a narrative cohesion entirely rooted in its dramatic thrust. Its most famous and powerful stories—such as of Zahhak the serpent shouldered; Rostam and Sohrab; Seyavash and Sudabeh; Bizhan and Manizheh; Rostam and Esfandiar—are all from its mythic and heroic parts, loved, admired, recited, and performed around the world. The central significance of each story holds the Persian epic together, gives it dramatic continuity, and offers a share of sustained moral continuity to the epic.

How are these three components of the *Shahnameh* connected to one another and how do they gel to make its world coherent? How are we to read the stories each section entails, and how can a reader today pick up a story of the *Shahnameh* and relate to it? In the first two parts of the *Shahnameh* we come to understand its most universal thematic: how the world was first created, who invented writing and why, or how civilization began and social classes were formed. The *Shahnameh* is full of amazing stories of just kings who lose their divine gift of grace and become tyrants, tyrant conquerors who grow serpents on their shoulders, white-haired sons abandoned to the wilderness by their parents to be raised by wild but civilizing birds, heroes born via "C-section" because they are too enormous for natural birth. But why are these stories important—beyond a mere antiquarian interest in a very old book and the even older stories it relates? In the *Shahnameh* we come to know fathers who deny their sons their kingdom, and other fathers who inadvertently kill their own sons. We read about young stepmothers who covet their handsome stepsons. The *Shahnameh* is full of extraordinary deeds, amazing friendships, deadly rivalries, exemplary chivalries, and also very nasty treacheries. As we read these stories we need to ask ourselves, what happens when mythic, heroic, and historical times are woven seamlessly into one another? What happens to the force of time and the power of narrative when mythic, heroic, and historical epochs are all integral to one another, pointing to a whole different spatial and temporal domain.

These three worlds—the world of the poet, the world of the poem, and the world in which we live and read the Persian epic—come together to make the *Shahnameh* command a worldly presence beyond which no conception of *world literature* has any claim to legitimacy; it is in fact childish and juvenile. It is simply astonishing how long this world has gone without realizing its own vacuity. Only an imperial hubris could have so sustained it. Today the Eurocentric world has theorized itself into universal nullity. It is clueless about other worlds it has not just ignored but also in fact concealed. Perhaps the most important lesson for me after teaching the *Shahnameh* year after year has been this extraordinary sense of wonder when my students do not quite know the contours of the this-worldly and otherworldly domains of the Persian epic they were experiencing. The multilayered temporality of the *Shahnameh*, and the fusion of multiple worlds it contains and maps out, is initially vertiginous and then exhilarating for students. Intentionally, I never taught only a segment of the *Shahnameh*. I insisted on the totality of the experience. The result was an initially formidable fear of the total at the beginning eventually yielding to the pleasure of discovery. The world of the authorial voice of the poet yields to the world of the mythic universe he crafts, before reaching its zenith in the heroic world of its chief protagonists and then descending upon our own time with gentility and grace. The movements from one world to another were organic, imperceptive, transpositional—the effect transformative. "To tell you the truth, Professor Dabashi," one well-read sophomore student once told me, "I shiver with excitement and bewilderment—how is it that I did not know this book even existed?"

THE TRIALS AND TRIBULATIONS OF LITERARY NATIONALISM

As we move to place the *Shahnameh* into its new global context and read it as an epic integral to an expanded revised conception of *world literature*, we need to be equally aware of its false and forced "nationalization" into a nativist corner in the course of postcolonial state building. The *Shahnameh* is not a "national epic." That forced nationalization of the Persian epic is a key element toward a literary nativism that in and of itself precludes the Persian epic from being read in the domain of "World Literature," as it is understood today. Though markedly different from Virgil's *Aeneid* (29–19 B.C.E.) in its imperialist projections, the *Shahnameh* is equally definitive to a particularly poignant moment in the formation of Muslim empires. It therefore belongs to a decidedly imperial age, and yet as such it has been subjected to a massive epistemic violence to "nationalize" it. We need to mark this epistemic violence and overcome it if the *Shahnameh* is to find its rightful place in *world literature* in terms domestic to its own literary prowess.

With the commencement of the European Enlightenment in earnest late in the eighteenth century and its subsequent colonial extension into the four corners of the globe, both colonial and anticolonial nationalist movements undertook extended projects of linguistic and literary nationalism. A national language, a nationalized literature, culture, and heritage, and thereafter the official commissioning of an encyclopedia, a demarcated map, a colorful flag, an airline, a rousing anthem, and soon a film festival became chief among a whole accoutrement of symbolic suggestions that were to hold the new state together and force it to forget its recent vintage, imagining a history and a continuity for itself since time immemorial and thus ad infinitum. The aggressive nationalization of a singular and official language and literature became the principal ideological project of colonial modernity for the making of a "nation-state," an entirely colonial product. Nations were violently tagged along these forced state-building projects. The active canonization of a language and a corresponding literature was achieved at great expense to both subnationalized and supranational languages and literatures. In the case of Persian, a patently imperial and supranational language, any number of subnationalized languages and literatures—Kurdish, Baluchi, Gilaki, Azari, and so forth—were aggressively suppressed under Reza Shah's state-building ideology, as was neglected the supranational fact of the spoken and written Persian in non-Iranian contexts such as in Central and South Asian territories. Persian was the lingua franca of successive empires, from the Samanids through the Mongols and beyond. That language was subsequently integral to three simultaneous empires of the Mughals, the Safavids, and even the Ottomans, including major regions of the Russian Empire. All that historical reality was overshadowed in the course of the fateful encounter with European colonial modernity when Persian eventually emerged as the official language of a single postcolonial state, Iran, disregarding its presence far beyond the colonially drawn Iranian borders in its neighbors, including but not limited to Afghanistan and Tajikistan.

The fact that Arabic was the lingua franca of much of an intellectual history to which Iranians were historically a party, the fact that the official Tehrani dialect was not the spoken and written Persian of much of the newly consolidated nation-state, the fact that the overwhelming majority of Iranians spoke their Persian in a slightly or drastically different accent and dialect from that of the Reza Shah central administration, and ultimately the fact that people from the Mediterranean shores to the walls of China spoke and wrote Persian without being "Iranian" in the newly coined postcolonial sense of the term did not bother the officiated project of linguistic and literary nationalism as a state ideology that was brought to brutal exactitude during the reign of Reza Shah and his state-building project—forcing the language of an imperial civilization into the tight narrows of a postcolonial state. Contingent on this manufactured project of linguistic and literary nationalism as a state ideology was a concomitant sense of "racial purity" that—odd as it may seem in a geographical hybridity that had Iranian, Turkish, Mongol, Arab, African, and Indian heritages running through its history—inevitably collapsed to bigoted depth during the flirtations of the Pahlavis with the racist sentiments of Nazi Germany. Ferdowsi's masterpiece was dragged into the nasty domain of such suspect state-building projects with jingoistic nationalism as its dominant ideology borrowed and expanded from Nazi Germany.

The orchestral canonization of the masterpieces of Persian literature into a fabricated linguistic and literary state-sponsored nationalism soon led to their iconic adaptation as the soaring symbolics of state building, elemental to a politics of postcolonial identity that ultimately detextualized these works of art and caused the pacification of their internal poetic tensions—tensions that at once constituted these texts and yet by pulling them in contradictory directions sustained their immortality. Literary historiography, whether by competent Orientalists like Carl Hermann Ethé, Jan Rypka, and E. G. Browne or by the patristic generation of modern Persian literati like Mohammad Qazvini, Badi' al-Zaman Foruzanfar, and Zabihollah Safa, became the principal mode of operation in a concerted effort to canonize the masterpieces of Persian literary imagination into the iconic signposts of its historical continuity. These discursive constitutions of linguistic and literary nationalism as state ideology in turn became the towering markers of a politics of identity that both the colonial nationalism of the Pahlavis and the anticolonial nationalism opposing it partook in unhealthy doses. Ideologically canonized, symbolically iconicized, and massively instrumentalized at the service of a state-building project, these texts were forced to repress their characteristic and definitive moments of narrative poetics, their paradoxical self-contradictions as they moved from a decidedly imperial to a national context, their innate nonnational politics, their in fact antinational sentiments ("national" in the postcolonial sense of the term), their countercanonical aesthetics, their multifaceted hermeneutics, and ultimately their richly multifaceted semiotics. The result was the violent deworlding of the world of the *Shahnameh*, robbing it of its patently imperial pedigree, as a particularly susceptible text to such abuses.

In the making of a long literary historiography that fit state-sponsored nationalism, masters of poetic imagination like Nezami Ganjavi (1141–1209) were placed next to any number of old versifiers simply to narrate the continuity of a literary history. Iconoclastic rebels like Omar Khayyam Nishapuri (1048–1131) were either pacified for a cliché romanticized reading or canonized for the sake of a consistent quietism. Cosmogonic visionaries like Maulana Jalal al-Din Rumi (1207–1273) were foregrounded to anticipate their later and lighter versions like Abd al-Rahman Jami (1414–1492). Sa'di and Hafez lost their universal differences and became iconic choices without substantive alterities. The inner dialectics constitutional to the making of any literary work of art were therefore perforce repressed in a concerted effort to manhandle these texts to violate their definitive characters as works of art and appropriated them into a militarily regimented project of textual state building. Ferdowsi's *Shahnameh* was caught in the snare of this forced manufacturing of a singularly national history for entire traditions of multiple imperial pedigree. The result was the systemic subversion of a literary tradition wrested away from its historical habitat and placed at the service of colonial and postcolonial state building. This violent epistemic distortion has categorically prefigured Persian literary historiography.[1]

Yet as all other forms of suppression, these politically punctuated textual repressions have continued to agitate in the subconscious of the texts, as the blinded and unread subtexts of the Persian epic, and await future critical attention. No other text in the history of Persian literary masterpieces has been so consistently used and abused in the services of state-sponsored linguistic and literary nationalism as has the *Shahnameh*. Ferdowsi's hemistich *Ajam zendeh kardam bedin Parsi* (I revived Iranians with this Persian) and his poetic rendition of the letter of Rostam Farrokhzad at the Battle of Qadisiyyah have been systematically abused to turn him into the very father of modern Persian linguistic and literary nationalism as a potent state ideology. In an anachronistic misreading of the early Islamic history in Iran, literary historians began to place Ferdowsi in the line of a succession of poets like Mas'udi Marvazi (896–956) and then Daqiqi, who had sought to collect and versify old Iranian epics in order to preserve the pre-Islamic Iranian heritage.[2] In this ultranationalist agenda to legitimize the Pahlavi dynasty, Ferdowsi's *Shahnameh* lost any narrative complexity constitutional to its text that did not add up to serve that abusive overriding project. The poetic elegance of Ferdowsi's diction and the magisterial composition of his *Shahnameh* were in no need of casting the Persian epic against Arabs, Turks, or any other people. But it was precisely in such extratextual terms that Ferdowsi's masterpiece was now read, abused, and canonized.

The fact that the first major translation of the *Shahnameh* was made in the thirteenth century into Arabic by Qawam al-Din Fath ibn Ali ibn Muhammad al-Bundari (of Kurdish origin) for an Arab prince, a translation that even today is one of the major sources for preparing a critical edition of the original text, and the fact that the second extant translation of the *Shahnameh* was made into Turkish by Ali Afandi early in the sixteenth century, did not prevent such ideologically foregrounded literary nationalism from racially abusing what it scornfully labeled "the Arabs and the Turks." The literary significance of the actual text of the *Shahnameh* in its immediate and distant neighborhoods, its repeated translations in prose and poetry and then subsequent scholarship in Arabic and Turkish, in the Ottoman and Mughal Empires, are all further testimonies to the postcolonial manufacturing of literary nationalism as a critical component of the colonial project of state-sponsored nationalism in which Iranian, Arab, and Turkish variations of the theme have competed against one another. No literary masterpiece—Arabic, Persian, or Turkish—can ever retrieve its worldly origin in such a nasty colonial context in which they are to plead to European or American literary theorists for recognition.

In its colonial context, Iranian nationalism as a potent state ideology is worse than Arab nationalism, and they are both worse than Turkish nationalism and vice versa, ad infinitum, ad absurdum, and ad nauseam: all of them systematically distorting the content and context of their literary masterpieces to manufacture a colonially conditioned sense of selfhood. Colonial nationalism, whether in conjunction with or in opposition against colonialism (and in both cases as a state-building project), has been a persistent plague at the colonial ends of capitalist modernity, systematically distorting the cultural heritage of peoples. Specific forms of colonial nationalism—Arab, Iranian, Turkish, and so on—represent the classic case of divide and rule, where the Arabs are pitted against the Persians, the Persians against the Turks, and then each one of them against the rest. Colonial nationalism in effect, and in the most self-denigrating manner possible, partakes in a deadly dose of white identification, where Iranians in fact denigrate the Arabs, the Arabs the Iranians, both the Turks, and the Turks the rest, precisely in terms articulated for them by their moral and material colonizers. Subnationalized cultures—such as the Kurds, the Baluchis, the Berbers, the Copts, or the Turkmens—are particularly short-circuited in this global project of colonial nationalism. The result is not just the most pernicious forms of self-lowering tribalism with terrifying political consequences, all to the benefit of those in the position of power. Equally damaged in the process is the literary and artistic heritage of these cultures that are trapped in a deadly cycle of empty self-aggrandizement and iconic ossifications, categorically distanced from their creative effervescence and emancipatory potentials. In the specific case of the *Shahnameh*, this literary nationalism has perpetrated lasting epistemic violence on the Persian epic, deworlded its enduring worldliness, and weakened its poetic power and rightful place in any meaningful understanding of *world literature*.

HOW ELSE TO READ THE *SHAHNAMEH*?

The state-sponsored nationalization of literature and the blindness and insights it simultaneously occasioned in the reading of the masterpieces of *world literature* have now exhausted their epistemic energies. Today texts such as the *Shahnameh* no longer yield themselves to merely iconic adaptations for outdated state-building projects. As literary works of art they have survived the uses and abuses to which they were subjected in the course of linguistic and literary nationalism. What I now cautiously propose here is a preliminary attempt at retrieving the hitherto unnoticed and decidedly unresolved, in equal terms imperceptible and irresolvable, paradox at the heart of the *Shahnameh* as an epic narrative—namely, the tension between its politics and its poetics, or between Ferdowsi as a *storyteller* and Ferdowsi as a *history teller*. My principal proposal is that there is a narrative tension, a poetic paradox, in the text of the *Shahnameh*, a discursive dialogue, as it were, between its *political narrative* and its *poetic discourse*, between the historical matters it evidently reports and the storytelling manners it deliberately purports. The *Shahnameh* is a book of stories composed in poetry: that fact in and of itself constitutes a combustive narrative tension in the text and agitation of its poetic registers. My argument is that Ferdowsi's poetry formally revolts against the content of the stories it records. In the disguise of telling the history, Ferdowsi's poetry in effect subverts it and liberates the hidden *story* from the hideout of that *history*. The playful storyteller in the *Shahnameh* is up against all the subsequent serious historians who come to abuse the text, as the *story* plays itself against any and all sober histories.

As we know, Ferdowsi inherited all these stories and reported them faithfully, but my contention is that in his poetic rendition, in the manner he reports these stories, he contrapuntally subverts them. The question is, what does it mean to say that these stories existed before and that Ferdowsi put them into poetry? Before Ferdowsi, we know that Mas'udi Marvazi and Daqiqi Tusi are also reported to have put parts of the Persian epic into poetry. What is this urge to rewrite history as poetry? What happens to prose when it becomes poetry? Ferdowsi deliberately sets himself the task of turning these stories into poetry. The enduring poetry dismantles the politics of its prosaic intention, as the storyteller negates the history teller it carries along. The text of the *Shahnameh* is thus against it context. Story after story, the text against the context, the poet against the politics, the story against the history, the *Shahnameh* undermines its own task, and yet in that very self-negating act of undermining, the Persian epic effectively defines its ulterior task—the task of poetry. To be noble in the *Shahnameh* is to be against nobility, to be civil is to be against the normative power of civilization—and that is the poetic paradox at the heart of the *Shahnameh*. Ferdowsi reports the story of Rostam and Sohrab, but as tragedy. He narrates the innocence of Seyavash, but his judiciously staged mise-en-scène leaves little doubt that Seyavash is tempted by Sudabeh. The point of this argument is to see how the poetics of the *Shahnameh* undermines and agitates its politics, or how Ferdowsi the *storyteller* undermines Ferdowsi the *history teller*, or how the manner of the *Shahnameh* cuts through its matter, or how its *ideal* subverts its *real* and then keeps up the hope of a constellation of sentiments it thus generates. The *Shahnameh* is thus at one and the same time a political *diagnosis* of a disease and the aesthetic *prognosis* of a release. As a work of art, the *Shahnameh* does not commence from an *ideality* but from a *reality*, which it then subverts into and through an emancipatory aesthetics. The *Shahnameh* reports of political atrocities of all sorts but then assures its readers of an emancipatory release, embedded in its own poetic disposition. The *Shahnameh* explicates a political culture as the predicament of a people and then implicates an emancipatory way out. Without coming to terms with that animating paradox of the *Shahnameh*, we will fail to read it. In this sense, we might even suggest that the *Shahnameh* has the Qur'an as its narrative prototype. While the Qur'an narrates biblical stories in order to push them forward toward new metaphysical and moral conclusions, the *Shahnameh*, too, reports of ancient stories in order to sublate them toward superior poetic, aesthetic, and moral reflections.

To make this point clear, it is useful to compare the poetic composition of Ferdowsi's *Shahnameh* early in the eleventh century with the political disposition of Nezam al-Molk's *Siyasatnameh* later in that same century.[3] If the *Siyasatnameh* is a diagnosis of a disease, the *Shahnameh* is the prognosis of a cure. In the *Siyasatnameh*, stories that the eminent Saljuqid vizier and political theorist has gathered are subservient to the political purpose of the prose, while in the *Shahnameh* exactly the opposite takes place, and the political purpose of the composition is subservient to the poetic it privileges. In the *Siyasatnameh*, Nezam al-Molk sets his discourse by first postulating a theoretical proposition on the art and craft of statesmanship, or guidelines for princely behavior, and then by way of demonstration of his point he narrates a story. The confinements of the story are so tightly controlled, so hermetically sealed, that their agitating energies can scarcely escape their straitjacket detention and disturb the deadly peace of the treatise. In the *Shahnameh*, on the contrary, that peace is perpetually disturbed, melodiously meandered, and the poetically emancipated stories—pagan kids let loose from a long day's incarceration in a Catholic school—roam the streets and alleys of the narrative in their rambunctious roaring toward freedom and emancipation of the whole universe they create, washing their innocent memories clean of every and all sad sagas they were just taught.

Ferdowsi achieves this dialectic through his poetic diction: the *Shahnameh* is the defining moment of its language as an act of worldly civility. What the Persian-speaking worlds have done to and with the *Shahnameh* suggests the civilizing panorama of their literary culture. In the cherished tradition of *adab*, which ranges across a number of languages and literatures in the context of Islamic empires, the Persian version of the movement has historically celebrated the very fact of the written language as the supreme art that marks and distinguishes a civilized human being. First and foremost, the defining moment of the *Shahnameh* is its language, its *logos*, its *sokhan*, with the praise of which it in fact begins. There are devoutly literate Persians who treat the text of the *Shahnameh* the same way an Orthodox Jew treats the text of the Torah, a Christian the Gospels, or a Muslim the Qur'an. During the heyday of linguistic and literary nationalism, the *Shahnameh* was elevated to the canonical text of the nation. But long before that, the *Shahnameh* had been celebrated as the very measure and model of Persian diction and poetic sublimity. Immediately related to the centrality of language in the *Shahnameh* is its poetic elegance, the crowning achievement of Persian poetry. What we read in the *Shahnameh* is the celebration of the poetic occasion when language delivers all its hidden promises, and then more. Ferdowsi's poetry is the very measure of where the lyrical and the epical collapse into a singular act of poetic confirmation of moral agency. Then comes the performative aspect of the *Shahnameh* in stagings in public recitations by the *naqqal*. Immediately related to the narrative performance of the *Shahnameh* is its calligraphic performance in manuscripts. The calligraphic performance of the *Shahnameh* is immediately linked to painting, or manuscript illustration. The *Shahnameh* is a single, sustained act of creative ingenuity—from the manner in which it is composed to the ways it is recited, written, and illustrated. The *Shahnameh* is a singular site of all such creative occasions, in its entirety the poetic composition of one historical person, a poet, Hakim Abolqasem Mansur ibn Hasan ibn Sharafshah Ferdowsi (ca. 940–1020), born, raised, and ultimately buried in the Bazh village in the Tabaran province of Tus in Khorasan. As a storyteller, Ferdowsi mobilizes the earned nobility of his characters over the routinized nobility of the caste into or against which they are born, the civility of the sole individual personas he narrates against the categorical institution of monarchy into which they are located. The name *Shahnameh* today is the embodiment of all such sentiments. Reading the *Shahnameh* must begin with this hermeneutic site of its effective history.

To read Ferdowsi as a storyteller requires a closer examination of the text of the *Shahnameh* and its habitual division into three sections: the mythological, the heroic, and the historical.[4] The mythological section begins from the commencement of the reign of Kiyumars to the uprising of Kaveh on behalf of Fereydun. This period is considered mythological because it deals with the Iranian myths of creation, from that of humanity at large to elementary forms of civilization, as we know them now. The heroic age commences with Kaveh's uprising and ends with the murder of Rostam. This period is considered heroic because it deals with the trials and tribulations of Rostam and other heroes of the *Shahnameh*. The historical phase of the Persian epic commences with the reign of Bahman, the son of Esfandiar, and ends with the collapse of the Sassanids after the Arab invasion, which brings Iranian history to Ferdowsi's own time. To be sure there is certain validity to this division of the *Shahnameh*. But the exaggerated anxiety over the oral and written sources of inspiration for the *Shahnameh* has been at considerable cost to the integrity of the text as a singular act of creative consistency. Today we no longer worry much about the historical sources of Shakespeare's dramas, nor should we be any more attentive to the textual and oral sources of Ferdowsi's stories. The fact that Abu Mansur's *Shahnameh* was the written source at the disposal of Ferdowsi, or that Ferdowsi had access to a written text on Alexander, or that such oral historians like Makh or Azad Sarv were the source of his other stories should not and does not detract from the compositional originality of Ferdowsi's *Shahnameh* as an act of artistic ingenuity. It is now an established fact that Dante had access to the Mi'raj stories about the Prophet Muhammad, and that *The Divine Comedy* was most probably influenced by, if not modeled on, these stories. But that supposition says nothing about *The Divine Comedy* as a singular act of creative inspiration. Such false anxieties over the historical origins of the *Shahnameh*, and the fact that its stories appear in any number of other prose texts, are a direct result of the aggressive overnationalization of the Persian epic and the insistence to read it more as historical evidence of a postcolonial nation-state rather than the creative work of an artist who inevitably takes liberties in any number of directions and for any number of poetic and aesthetic purposes.

If we were to take the text of the *Shahnameh* as a singular work of art, odd as it seems to insist on this (because it is like saying, "If we were to take the text of *The Divine Comedy* as a singular work of art . . ."), and then control our anxiety over sources and influences, and rescue it from the exhausted project of state-sponsored literary nationalism, then the text itself would be a solitary sign of its creator's poetic ingenuity, from its *mythological*, to *heroic*, and then to its *historical* aspects, all of which are the integral components of a single work of art, issued from the creative corner of one astonishingly ingenious poet. Between the abuses perpetrated on the text by generations of its enforced canonization by literate Iranians into literary nationalism and now an insane assault on it by the proponents of the "oral formulaic" theory,[5] the text of the *Shahnameh* needs to be rescued for a whole new generation of close and attentive literary readings. If it is not exaggerated to the level of categorical breakdown in the making of the text, the division of the *Shahnameh* into mythological, heroic, and historical components can in fact facilitate a theoretical perspective on its narrative composition with lasting insights into its specific poetic disposition. The division is in fact remarkably akin to Giambattista Vico's theory of history, in which he divides the course of human life into divine, heroic, and human phases, presided over by gods, heroes, and humans.[6] But while Vico proposed these three phases as "the course that nations run" in realizing their nature and then articulating their corresponding customs, civil states, languages, characters, jurisprudence, authority, and then even reason and judgment, in the case of Ferdowsi's *Shahnameh* what we have is a particular mode of poetic disposition toward history that we can call *pararealism*—of being *at the supplementary side of* reality, alongside it and as a result a going beyond its tight grips, and thus resting in a shady location by the side of history, beside it, passing by it to one side, which results in being aside from its controlling demands. There is a sense of being *amiss* in *pararealism, beyond and subsidiary* to reality. It is that sense of being narratively parallel to and yet having a catalytic effect on how we read *reality* that I have in mind in the idea of a *pararealist* disposition of the *Shahnameh*'s poetics.

Taken together, the mythical, heroic, and historical components of Ferdowsi's *Shahnameh* constitute and sustain a poetic *pararealism* that suspends history from all its undelivered promises, where the *historical* still remembers the *heroic* and the *heroic* invokes the *mythical*. The *mythical* malleability of the *real* casts a long and lasting shadow over the *heroic* energy that animates the hidden promises of the *historical* world. The three phases are thus always simultaneous, informed by a *polychronic* conception of time and space. Through the poetic language, the immediately *political* becomes categorically *historical*, while the specifically *personal* becomes narratively *universal*. Outside the poetic act, the political and the historical are ordinarily the evident markers of the *real* in such metaphysical discourses of power that demarcate *reality*. Outside the political act, the poetic and the universal are ordinarily the markers of the *ideal* in such aesthetic moments that seek to subvert reality. But when in the disguise of delivering the *real* the poet sustains the *ideal*, pretending to relay *history* as he tells a *story*, then *the poetic word* is ipso facto posited against *the political world*. The *poetic word* in fact goes against the *political world*. In between *the poetic word* and *the political world*, the readers of the epic, its historical audience, we, are saved from narrative fears and delivered to sustained hopes, as the people that are thus formed are saved from their *history* and delivered to the *stories* that storytellers tell them—and thus is saved a whole culture for the promise it holds against the failures it has endured. Ferdowsi's inimitable poetry is in the language that it is because it is not, nor should it ever be, attainable. The *attained* is always already corrupt, but the *attainable* must always already be only one step ahead of the always-already *attained*. The *ideal* should always remain the twin tumble of the *real*, the other side of its coin; it must be looked at with the poet's forgiving eyes. How does Ferdowsi do it? With his eyes set on the details, the details that do not much matter to the actual story but that are the principal point of his poetry. It is as if the rest of the story is just an excuse, and that the real point is telling of these details. The teller of details, Ferdowsi can scarcely bring himself to tell a story without the *manner* of telling it taking over its *matter*. It is the detection, discovery, and theorization of that inner world that restores the *Shahnameh* to its worldly character, marks its claim to *world literature*, entirely independent of a theory of *world literature* outside its towering gates.

MIMESIS, VISUALITY, SEMIOSIS

The polychronic time zone of the *Shahnameh* brings its three temporal components together and gives the whole epic an entirely poetic rather than historical character. This dovetails with the three worlds of the *Shahnameh* I have outlined—the world in which it was created, the world in which we now read it, and the internal textual world of the Persian epic itself. The fact of this sculpted composure of the text is the pedestal upon which stands the poetic power of the text. Let me now add a semiotics to this poetics.

If poetry is the manner of this delivery paramount in the *Shahnameh*, visuality is its dramatic mechanism. What in effect I am proposing here is a theory of poetic visuality as definitive to our reading of the Persian epic. Let me explain. The poet sees things that are not part of the story that he is telling. He is seeing scenes while telling stories. Ferdowsi storyboards his stories. What the poet actually sees and shows is far more important than what he hears and says, for they constitute the emotive universe of the stories. This makes the application of extraneous ideas such as "oral-formulaic" theory to Ferdowsi's *Shahnameh* quite outlandish. What I am proposing here is a theory of Ferdowsi's visual "cinematography," decidedly to use an anachronistic and yet poignant term. There can very well be visual "cinematography" centuries before the mechanical invention of the cinematograph. Cinematography did not have to wait for the invention of the camera, the way I mean it here. Ferdowsi has a cinematographic mind. His mind works like a camera, his poetry reads like a script, his hemistichs and lines cut, frame by frame, edit, sequence by sequence, with the most impeccable precision and flow. The result is the primacy of *the visual* over *the verbal*. The verbal narrative yields to the poetic in the same manner that the poetic embraces the visual texture and contemplative disposition of Ferdowsi's poetry.[7]

Consider the scene where Seyavash is about to perform the test of fire to prove his innocence against his stepmother's false accusations and look closely at the manner in which Ferdowsi "cuts" his scenes, edits them one after the other—close-up, medium shot, long shot, interior and exterior shots—to generate a dramatic sense of the scene entirely independent of the narrative. In a particularly critical sequence first we have a long shot of the field where the fire is set for Seyavash's trial, next to which stands the Persian army and the general public, thus visually suggesting the political implications of the incident without ever uttering a word to that effect. Once this master shot is established, we have two consecutive fast close-up cuts of Seyavash's smiling face, kind and confident of his innocence, juxtaposed with his supporters' sad faces, an indication of the army's dissatisfaction with the king. Through an emotional register, rising to the political, the story starts to transcend itself. Then Ferdowsi cuts from this exterior shot to an interior dolly shot as Seyavash in full army regalia walks toward his royal father, which Ferdowsi's "camera" makes sure is detailed regarding the prince's clothing items, and he reminds us that Seyavash is still smiling for the sense of continuity from the exterior to the interior shot. Seyavash then dismounts, comes to his father, and expresses his obedience. We have a close-up of Key Kavous's face, ashamed and gentle. They have a short dialogue in which Seyavash assures his father all will be well, just before Ferdowsi shifts into an exterior long parallel cut between the army and the city, followed by another interior dolly shot of Sudabeh coming to her balcony when she hears the uproar from the city. By now all the principal actors are gathered in the sequence. From Sudabeh's POV Ferdowsi now shows us the fire through which Seyavash has to pass. Sudabeh looks worried. From this interior shot we again cut into an exterior shot of people in the street and soldiers angry and cursing the king. The political implication of these shots is not to be missed. From here Ferdowsi's camera now cuts to Seyavash via a crane shot as he gallops toward the fire and shows him and his horse disappear into the fire. A reverse shot now looks back at the field where the army is worried about Seyavash. We then see and notice that Seyavash has come out safely via the camera focusing on the expression in their faces. Here Ferdowsi pauses the scene for his own moment of "poetic implosion," wondering how—if Seyavash had gone through water he would have been wet—but nothing of the sort has happened. After this moment of pause, Ferdowsi goes back to crafting the sequence to show us how the army is delighted to see him alive and innocent. From here he cuts to Sudabeh, who is frightened by the fact that Seyavash is proved innocent, and she is scandalized.[8]

What we are witnessing here is the operation of an evident visuality lifting up that of poetic verbality, where the visual parallels and punctuates the verbal to the higher point of suspending its authority, a narrative dexterity that gives Ferdowsi's poetics a sense of pararealism, a mode of poetic realism that begins with the fact of *reality* but remains deliberately peripheral to it: it is real and unreal at one and the same time. At his best, Ferdowsi's uses of his eyes reflect perceptively the uses of his ears. The visual narrative then transfuses itself into a reality sui generis, irreducible to merely serving the verbal—and in fact transcending it in important ways. The dramaturgical operation of Ferdowsi's epic is as much contingent on his and our eyes as on his and our ears. The tight and seamless texture that holds the mythical, heroic, and historical layers of the *Shahnameh* together always suspends the signifying claims of *the real* on the suggestive signs of *other than the real*. This gives his sense of *reality* an *unreal* texture, his *realism* a *pRRreal* pliability to change, modify, and reconstitute itself. This in turn gives the Persian poetic mimesis evident in the *Shahnameh* an entirely different character from the Aristotelian mimesis. Ferdowsi's mimesis, predicated on his pararealism, contingent on his seamless sublation of history to heroism, and of heroism to mythology, is decidedly polylocal. It can modulate itself to a succession of sites and sights, poetic contingencies and narrative emergencies.

Ferdowsi's poetic narrative is verbally heteroglossic and polyvocal, which in turn translates and corresponds to a heterovisual and polyfocal pictorial imagination. What Bakhtin had detected in Dostoyevsky—namely, the heteroglossia of characters—is already evident in Ferdowsi's characterization, where his dramatis personae act, speak, and behave from the depth of their characters and convictions. The historical roots and textual sources of Ferdowsi's composition are what hold the *Shahnameh* together for Ferdowsi to have the necessary but limited poetic license yielding to unlimited dramatic leverage. To test this theory, we need both *performative* and *visual* support as corroborative evidence. The best *performative* evidence of this peculiar mode of mimesis is today evident in the Persian passion play, or *ta'ziyeh*, which though Shi'i in its immediate narrative disposition is in fact a heavily Persianized mode of epic poetry. It is crucial to keep in mind that what today we call *ta'ziyeh* might very well be considered an Islamic adaptation of the Persian epic narrative, with Imam Hossein and Hazrat-e Abbas as the moral equivalents of the *Shahnameh* heroes. With all its more recent gestations, *ta'ziyeh* itself is most probably rooted in the ritual practice of Seyavashan, where the sacrificial death of the hero is ritually remembered and mourned. What therefore we witness in the Shi'i passion play, or *ta'ziyeh*, could very well be the dramaturgical extensions of the *Shahnameh* stories into performative forms of public piety.

It is equally crucial to remember that soon after the active Islamization of Persian culture, the Persian epic narrative began to assimilate Muslim saints and characters into its repertoire. The earliest known epic poem, in the meter of the *Shahnameh*, and about the adventures of Imam Ali, is *Ali-nameh*, composed by a poet called Rabi' in 1089, which is only sixty or so years after Ferdowsi's death.[9] In *Khavaran-nameh* of Maulana Muhammad ibn Hisam al-Din, known as Ibn Hisam (d. 1470), we read the epic adventures of the first Shi'i Imam, Ali ibn abi Taleb, in the eastern lands of Khavaran, a narrative poem that incorporates the first Shi'i Imam into the ranks of Persian heroes. In *Sahebqiran-nameh* (composed in 1662), by an anonymous poet, we read of the heroic deed of Seyyed al-Shohada Hamzeh, the uncle of the Prophet Muhammad, who in this epic resuscitation appears in the court of the Sassanid king Anushirvan the Just, marries his daughter, and then goes to fight for the glory of the Persian king in Turan, India, and Asia Minor. *Hamleh-ye Haidari*, which was started by Mirza Muhammad Rafi' Khan Bazil's (d. 1712) and completed after his death by Mirza Abu Taleb Mir Fendereski, known as Abu Taleb Isfahani, is entirely devoted to the heroic adventures of the Prophet Muhammad and Hazrat-e Amir, Ali ibn abi Taleb. This genre continues with an astonishing rapidity in such other works as *Mokhtar-nameh* of Abd al-Razzaq Beik ibn Najafqoli Khan Donbali, known as Maftun, about the heroic deeds of Mukhtar ibn abi Ubaydah al-Saqafi's *Shahnameh-ye Heyrati*, composed by a poet known as Heyrati during the reign of Shah Tahmasp the First on the battles of the Prophet. Another poet, by the name of Asiri, again during the reign of Shah Tahmasp the First, composed yet another epic poem on the Prophet's battles. Another *Hamleh-ye Haidari* by a certain Mulla Beman Ali, known as Raji, a Kermani poet, is in the same genre. To all of these can also be added *Khudavand-nameh* of Malik al-Shu'ara Fath Ali Khan Saba Kashani, *Ordibehesht-nameh* of Sorush Isfahani (d. 1868), *Delgosha-nameh* of Mirza Qolam Ali Azad Belgrami (d. 1785), *Jang-nameh* of Atashi, and *Dastan Ali Akbar* of Muhammad Taher ibn Abu Taleb.[10] In this genre of epic narrative, the Persian poetic imagination actively incorporates Muslim saintly hagiography into literary and performing arts.

As for the visual register, Ferdowsi's polyfocality is coterminous with his verbal polyvocality, a multiplicity of sights corresponding to a multiplicity of sounds, coming together in a heteroglossia of sights and sounds. To test this idea of the polylocality of *Shahnameh* mimesis, and the multiplicity of the visually *seen* over the verbal narration of *the said* in Ferdowsi's poetics, we need to look at some of the illustrations that have historically accompanied the text of the *Shahnameh*, and where Ferdowsi's visual pluralism is best evident. Verbally polyvocal, visually polyfocal, the *Shahnameh* is read and seen like a movie, as it were. Ferdowsi's verbal polyvocalism sublates into his visual polyfocalism, which has in turn found its way into *Shahnameh* illustrations of both courtly and popular types. The defining feature of Persian painting is the categorical absence of one dominant unifocal perspective in them, as is evident in post-Renaissance European painting, for example. Let's begin by dismissing the possibility that we have an absence of a dominant unifocal perspective in Persian painting because those who were illustrating these manuscripts were congenitally cross-eyed, myopic, astigmatic, or suffered from any number of similar optical ailments and thus could not see properly. Bracketing that possibility, we can consider the sublation of Ferdowsi's heteroglossic poetic polyvocalism into heterovisual polyfocalism, which in turn in visual renditions of his epic result in the absence of a single, dominant, monofocal perspective. By way of a contrast, if we were to look at an Orientalist painting in the tradition of European paintings, for example, we would see how a European painter looks at precisely the same site that an Iranian painter looks at but comes with a dominant monofocal perspective that determines and dictates every minutia of his painting proportionate to the precision of that point.

The monofocality of the spatial perspective in turn translates into a monochronic conception of time, when and where everything in the painting points to not only a single dominant focal point but also a single dominant time, when everything in the painting points to one instance, one singular moment, 3:48 P.M., for example, when the sun was shining from that particular angle from that particular window. The *Shahnameh* illustrations, on the other hand, and by extension Persian paintings influenced by Ferdowsi's verbal polyvocalism and visual polyfocalism, entirely defy such a tyrannically monofocal perspective and opt for a polyfocal constellation of perspectives, as they in fact implicate a polychronic conception of time and narrative, when and where a multiplicity of instances is simultaneously depicted. The monofocal perspective in European painting implicates a monolocal spatial control that corresponds to a monochronic control of time and narrative. Ferdowsi's poetry is polyphonic and thus results in a polysonic narrative, which is in turn sublated into a polyfocal perspective in its visual illustrations—implicating a spatial freedom that corresponds to a polychronic freedom in its conception of time. This, I believe, is what Hossein Aqa Arab, an exceptionally gifted coffeehouse painter, meant when he said, "If we were to imitate the European painters and take the space of our work too seriously, half of our art and endeavor would be wasted. Because then we would have to sacrifice fifty live faces for four; and this, in my judgment, is wrong."[11]

The polyfocal space and polychronic time in the *Shahnameh* narrative, performance, and illustrations all point to a mode of pararealism that finds its astonishing way centuries later into Iranian cinema. What is happening today in Iranian cinema is in fact as much indebted to the wide spectrum of world cinema to which Iranian filmmakers have been exposed as it is subconsciously indebted to the classical modes of Persian storytelling, that of Ferdowsi in particular. Not only the works of Bahram Beiza'i, who is visually the most learned Iranian filmmaker, but also the entire cast of Iranian pararealism is rooted in the aesthetics and semiotics of the *Shahnameh*, in its verbal polyvocalism, visual polyfocalism, which is narratively polychronic, as historically sustained in *naqqali* and *ta'ziyeh* performances as well as in illustrated manuscripts and coffeehouse paintings.

My principal argument here dwells on those occasions when the poetics and semiotics of the *Shahnameh* override its ostensible historical roots and narrative derives. That poetics and that semiotics, intertwined, sustain but overcome the *Shahnameh* narratives. The Persian epic has been the subject of intense scholarship, beginning with the critical edition of the text and continuing with the minutest examination of its stories, but its poetics and aesthetics have been by and large overshadowed by its iconic confiscation for forced and manufactured ethnic nationalism as state ideology. This is what has most violated the text, and next to it has been its equally if not even more violent transmutation into an "oral formulaic" performance entirely at odds with its poetic and aesthetic foregrounding. Upon these predicates then arises this false pleading to "World Literature" to kindly consider Ferdowsi's masterpiece into the august gathering of its canons. The *Shahnameh* is integral to any definition and understanding of *world literature* not by any such pleading but by allowing the inner worldliness of the text itself to lay its claims to that standing.

TOWARD A THEORY OF NARRATIVE SUSPENSION

I have already argued how the three components of the *Shahnameh* (the mythical, heroic, and historical) are structurally interrelated, and once read together they point to a radically different narrative texture in tune with an aesthetic theory of the *Shahnameh* I have suggested as *polychronic*. I have also mapped out in some detail how the *polyphonic* and *polysonic* poetics and semiotics of the text override its historical narrative urges. Let me now map out that theory in more detail. The mythical beginning of the *Shahnameh*, the shortest of the three, begins with a praise of God and his creation, of the beauty of the spoken word, an account of the first human being, Kiyumars, who was also the first king, and his descendants. The heroic age makes up the bulk of the poem, which begins with Kaveh's uprising and the reign of Fereydun until the conquest of Alexander the Great, which links the heroic to the historical. Most of the towering *Shahnameh* heroes and their stories are in this second part of the epic. The historical age begins with a detailed account of Alexander the Great, followed by a brief allusion to the Arsacid dynasty, and concludes with a full account of the Sassanid Empire and its demise following the Arab invasion of Iran. The three phases are held seamlessly, narratively, structurally, thematically, and poetically together with an overarching dramatic potency, thus generating a unique polychronic time frame.

The mythological beginning of the *Shahnameh* casts a lasting shadow over the rest of the Persian epic. Human civilization as we know it begins to appear during this period, as do forces of good and evil, invention and destruction, creativity and corruption. Basic human instincts, like love and hatred, ambition and jealously, are also introduced in this stage. But first and foremost, we get to know how humanity first appeared on this earth. The charge of Kiyumars, the very first king ever, is in fact to bring humanity at large together to form a civilization. Under Kiyumars, humans learn the first two civilizing components of their communal life: how to dress themselves and how to make food. During the reign of Kiyumars, forces of evil enter human affairs. Siyamak, Kiyumars's son, becomes the target of Ahriman, the Supreme Demon, who dispatches his son to kill Siyamak and destroy Kiyumars's kingdom. Kiyumars is oblivious to this plot. Ahura Mazda, the Supreme Good, sends his emissary, Sorush, to warn Siyamak, who mobilizes an army against the son of Ahriman, but he is killed in hand-to-hand combat with him, leaving Kiyumars in mourning and his kingdom in ruins. The course of human civilization is thus interrupted by the demonic intervention of the forces of Ahriman, the Evil. These mythic battles define the course of human destiny, both internal to the *Shahnameh* and external to it, with ceremonial royalty, filial duties, successive wars, unsuspected treacheries, and wanton murder. The polychronicity of the *Shahnameh* narrative is here set on a solid mythic stage that embraces the rest of the text.

The first pattern of murder and revenge in the *Shahnameh* is established right here when in the mythological section Siyamak's son, Houshang, mobilizes an army of humans and beasts on behalf of his grandfather, Kiyumars, and avenges the death of his father, killing the son of Ahriman in a heroic battle. The pattern will be repeated multiple times in the *Shahnameh* and underscores its "Oedipal" foregrounding in multiple phases. Houshang rules for many years after the death of his grandfather and spreads peace and justice all over the world. His critical contribution toward making human civilization possible is to discover ore. He becomes the first blacksmith and invents the ax, the saw, and the hammer. He is also known for having invented agriculture. He devised a sophisticated system of irrigation. Under his reign people became self-sufficient in making food. He is also the one who discovered fire, by accidentally noticing a flash of light when trying to kill a serpent and prayed to the fire as a sign of Ahura Mazda, the Supreme Good.[12] This became the origin of the Iranian festival of Saddeh in winter. Rituals are thus initiated in human civility. Houshang also domesticated animals and used them for agricultural labor. The mythic foregrounding of history, as we read it here, thus expands apace for the rest of the Persian epic. History is anticipated with civilizational forestructures and warring factions. As we proceed to read the rest of the *Shahnameh* we remember how a polysonic poetics begins to resonate when this mythic state yields narratively to the heroic and the historical.

The battle between the forces of good and evil continue well through the reign of Tahmoures, Houshang's son, who succeeds his father. His title is Tahmoures the Binder of Demons. He consults with his vizier, Shidasb, and devises magic to capture the Leader of the Demons, Ahriman, then mounts him like a beast and rides on him to tour the world. The demons come back together and launch yet another battle against Tahmoures. He defeats them again, and this time around they plead for mercy and in return teach him the art of writing. They teach Tahmoures some thirty different languages and scripts. He also discovers the art of textile manufacturing and the use of barley and hay as food for domesticated animals. He then proceeds to identify game and cultivate the art of falconry. But the most significant event of his reign is the discovery of writing. Why should Ferdowsi acknowledge and attribute the most enduring feature of human civilization to forces of evil? What did the demons do to humans by teaching them how to write? What demonic device is the act of writing, jealously guarded by forces of evil, until they taught it to humans in a dubious compensation for their freedom? Or might we not reverse the question: did humanity not learn its most sacrosanct definition of civilization, the very alphabet of our cultured life, from our demonized enemies? Should we therefore not dare to overcome the fear of those thus othered for a gift hidden in their alterity? These and many other similar questions quietly begin to rise as we follow Ferdowsi telling us how the very alphabet of our civilized life came about. It is impossible to ignore or forget these earliest passages of the *Shahnameh* in its mythic part when we come to read its historical sections, where the narrative suspension he has created here comes to full fruition in the textual totality of his epic there.

Jamshid is Tahmoures's handsome and valiant son, the king under whose reign civilization as we now know it begins to take full shape. Jamshid becomes the first king, Mubad, combining political and religious authority that is at once royal and pastoral. He spends many years in the crafting and manufacturing of armaments. He perfected the art of making garments and distinguished between warring gear and dress for feasts. He also created the first social groups and divided his subjects into four castes: the Priests, the Warriors, the Peasants, and the Workers. He put the Demons in his possession to work and made them construct buildings and monuments. He invented the art of mining, excavating for precious metals while discovering perfumes and the art of bodily adornment. He was the first navigator. He invented the ship and traveled over the seas. He also invented the art of flying. He had himself a beautiful throne made and told the Demons to fly him over the lands. He was like a sun in the sky. All these achievements took hundreds of years, and Iranians celebrated him every year in their Noruz Festival, at the precise moment of the vernal equinox. He ruled for more than three hundred years, and during his reign he discovered the secret of immortality and taught it to his people. Jamshid's achievements, especially his victory over mortality, lead to hubris and a claim to Divinity. The nobles among his subjects do not dare to object. But Ahura Mazda takes back his charisma, and thus he begins to lose his gift of grace. During his reign time and history stand still, as earth, water, air, and fire fuse together. In each one of these early mythological phases we are rehearsing the momentous occasions when the very idea of "the human" is invented. Jamshid's reign is the epitome of a full mythic panorama of human existence—and as such his time becomes emblematic of the polychronic liminality of time and space in which the entirety of the Persian epic is cast.

Zahhak (the son of King Marda) is the evil king who comes to destroy Jamshid. Ahriman, the Supreme Evil, turns himself into a handsome and attractive man and appears to Zahhak. Ahriman seduces Zahhak to kill his father and ascend his throne. When Zahhak becomes the king, Ahriman changes his appearance and comes to Zahhak as a handsome cook. In gratitude to his new cook, Zahhak grants him any wish he has. Ahriman asks to kiss Zahhak's two shoulders. He does so and then instantly disappears. Two monstrous serpents grow precisely where Ahriman had kissed him. Zahhak's guards kill the serpents, but they immediately grow back. Ahriman now appears as a wise physician and tells Zahhak that his only cure is to feed the serpents the brains of two young men every day, so that they will not devour him. It is at this time that a group of Iranian nobility invites Zahhak to invade Iran and conquer Jamshid's kingdom. Jamshid escapes to the borders of China and lives yet another one hundred years in hiding. But Zahhak finally finds him and has him cut in half by a saw. We read these fantastic stories and we wonder, and we carry that wonder with us from the mythic to the heroic and from there to the historical phases of the *Shahnameh*. There is an organicity to these syncretic suspensions of times and narratives.

We read these stories as if in a different world, on a different plane. We never know where we are, who is telling us these stories, and how they are hanging in suspense our very conception of truth and reality.

Zahhak rules over Iran and attends to his two serpents by killing young men and feeding them on their brains. Jamshid had two beautiful daughters, Shahnaz and Arnavaz.[13] Zahhak captures and marries them and forces them to attend to his serpents. The two princesses secretly work with two pious men, Armayel and Garmayel, who were in charge of Zahhak's kitchen, to release the young men that have been captured to be killed fed to the serpents and instead feed the brains of two sheep to Zahhak's serpents. Despite such an act of heroism, Zahhak still rules for many years over the Iranians with tyranny and feeds his serpents on their brains. Finally, he has a dream one night that is interpreted for him by a daring interpreter as his reign coming to an end with a certain Fereydun coming and destroying him. Zahhak now desperately looks for this Fereydun. The reign of Zahhak is the epiphany of evil, pitting the force of his darkness against the Iranian realm. He is the negative force of history, setting it in motion. Before his demise, Zahhak's diabolic force is resisted by a defiant but leaderless nation, which becomes a nation by surviving Zahhak. Zahhak's reign is the mythic moment when Iran as a nation and Iranians as a people enter their history via a trauma. The trauma is ahistorical, anachronistic, narratively suspended on an immaterial moment when history was yet to begin, but the world was dreaming its dangerous dreams. It is a strange sensation to read these stories happening in a space whose location and logic are beyond our grasp. We are inside a world that has no material referent to it. The infinity of this moment lacks any beginning or end, totality or locality. Can there be a *world literature* without coming to terms with the factual immateriality of this inner world of the *Shahnameh*?

Fereydun is born to a certain Abtin and his wife, Faranak, in a remote part of the kingdom. Abtin traces his ancestry to Tahmoures the Binder of Demons. Abtin is captured and murdered by Zahhak's retinue. Faranak is desperate to save her son. She takes Fereydun to a certain prairie in which a famous cow named Bormayeh is pasturing. She entrusts Fereydun to the owner of Bormayeh and asks him to take care of her son, save her from Zahhak, and feed him on Bormayeh's milk. Fereydun grows up on Bormayeh's milk for three years, until Zahhak discovers his whereabouts, at which point Faranak comes back, rescues her son, and takes him to Alborz Mountain and entrusts his upbringing to a pious man. Zahhak captures Bormayeh and kills the good cow. Fereydun grows up with the pious man in Alborz Mountain. At the age of sixteen, he comes down to his mother and asks her who his father is. Faranak tells Fereydun who Abtin was and why he was killed by Zahhak. Fereydun swears to kill Zahhak and avenge his father. Faranak warns him that Zahhak is very powerful. But Zahhak is petrified by the prospect of Fereydun's coming and avenging his father and all other innocent men he has murdered to feed their brains to his serpents. Zahhak summons all the nobles of the realm and forces them to sign an affidavit that he has been a just and kind king. The rise of Fereydun in the company of his single mother and absence of any father fixes the enduring mother-son relationship as definitive to the familial trauma of the epic. In every turn of the narrative, the unfolding stories anticipate and reflect back on one another. The mythic world becomes a self-reflecting collage of mirror images generating, sustaining, reflecting back and forth the collective unconscious of the text.

Every episode of the *Shahnameh*, as we see, is contingent on the episode before and suspended by the next. Kaveh we soon learn is a blacksmith who storms into Zahhak's court exactly at the moment that he is collecting signatures on an affidavit testifying to his just rule. Kaveh admonishes the complacent nobles, denounces Zahhak for having killed his sons to feed his serpents, rescues his last remaining son, storms out of the tyrant's court, and leads a revolutionary uprising against Zahhak and on behalf of Fereydun. He makes a leather banner from his blacksmith apron and leads the popular uprising toward Fereydun's hideout. With the march of Kaveh soars the mythic and heroic components of the *Shahnameh* toward its historical ends, with every episode the myth of human origin advancing toward its heroic dimensions and historic consequences. By now we have completely exited the normative narrative of the world and find ourselves lost in the collective unconscious of the Persian epic.

Fereydun listens to people's complaints, adorns the leather banner of Kaveh with royal jewelry in his possession, puts on his crown and royal robe, goes to his mother, Faranak, to secure her blessing, and leads a war against Zahhak. First he summons his two brothers and commissions them to have the blacksmiths make him a special mace with the head of an ox, for which he draws the model on the ground. He then leads his army toward Zahhak's palace. At night during an encampment a handsome man appears to him and teaches him the secrets of Zahhak's fortresses and how to conquer them. Fereydun takes this as a sign of Divine intervention on his behalf. The following day he marches toward Zahhak's palace. He reaches Arvandrud, where the sailors refuse to let him use their boats. He marches into the river, and his army follows him toward the palace. Zahhak is not in his palace. Fereydun destroys his guards, rescues Shahrnaz and Arnavaz, ascends Zahhak's throne, and sits Jamshid's two daughters at his side. He throws a lavish party at Zahhak's palace. Kondro, Zahhak's chamberlain, secretly escapes the palace and reports to his king of the events. Zahhak initially refuses to believe that his nightmare is coming to pass, until he hears that Fereydun is intimate with his two wives, Shahrnaz and Arnavaz, Jamshid's daughters. Zahhak invades his capital, but his subjects attack his army. He secretly escapes the battlefield and goes to his palace, where he sees Fereydun intimate with his wives, Shahnavaz and Arnavaz. In a furious rage, Zahhak attacks the two princesses, but Fereydun strikes him with his ox-headed mace. About to kill Zahhak, Fereydun is stopped by the same Divine Emissary, who tells him to chain Zahhak on Damavand Mountain because it is not yet time to kill the tyrant. Fereydun does accordingly and straps Zahhak inside a cave in Mount Damavand, and rules over his realm with justice and fairness. At this point in the *Shahnameh* we have a solid sense of dramatic balance in historical narrative. Mythic figures appear and disappear, rise and fall, the un-time of a mythic world unfolds, history awaits itself.

WHEN HISTORY REMEMBERS ITSELF

From this point forward, we begin to see the unfolding drama of world history dreamed inside the memorial consciousness of the *Shahnameh*, in what we can now see is the collective unconscious of the Persia epic. Fereydun and his three sons become the focal points of the next story of the *Shahnameh*, by which event we now exit its mythological and enter its heroic phase. Fereydun ascends the royal throne in the month of Mehr (September–October) at the autumnal equinox—henceforth the Mehregan Festival becomes a Persian festive occasion. Fereydun's mother, Faranak, becomes instrumental in her son's spreading justice and fairness in the realm. Fereydun has three sons: Iraj, Salm, and Tur. Fereydun commissions his vizier, Jandal, to find three suitable sisters to marry his sons. Jandal goes around the world and decides that the daughters of the king of Yemen are best suited for Fereydun's sons. He asks the Yemenite monarch for the hands of his three daughters for the sons of Fereydun. The king is ambivalent because he is interested in the union but is reluctant to be separated from his daughters. He is also afraid of refusing Fereydun's request and inciting his anger, having the history of Zahhak freshly in mind. The Yemenite generals are offended by their monarch's weakness and ask him to be steadfast in his decision, either send off his daughters to marry Fereydun's sons with dignity or, if does not wish so, to simply ask Fereydun for certain impossible things in return that he will not be able to provide. The imperial power of the house of Fereydun has now reached its fullest potential. History, as provisioned by the mythic force of *The Book of Kings*, is now unfolding apace.

The imperial geography of the *Shahnameh* now begins to expand proportionately. The Yemenite monarch sends a message to Fereydun through Jandal in which he tells him that of course he would be honored if his daughters were to be married to his sons. However, he wishes to see his future sons-in-law in person, and would the Persian king mind sending them off to Yemen? Fereydun is wise and knows that his Yemenite counterpart is reluctant to send off his daughters. So he teaches his sons how to tell the three princesses from one another, because they look very much alike. Alerted to the Yemenite king's stratagem, Fereydun's sons go to Yemen and skillfully distinguish among the three princesses, marry them respectively, and head back to Iran. But the Yemenite king was relentless. He planted a number of other magical stratagems to trap the Persian princes. But having been bestowed with the Divine Gift of Grace, Royal Glory (Farrah-e Izadi), Iraj, Salm, and Tur undid all his magic and returned home in safety. Before they reach their father's palace, however, Fereydun himself decides to test his sons' wisdom and appears as a dragon to them, with which they again deal with caution and reason. Assured of his sons' capabilities, Fereydun welcomes his daughters-in-law and gives them Persian names: Arezu to the oldest, who marries his oldest son, Salm; Mah to the middle princess, who marries his second son, Tur; and Sahi to the youngest, who marries his youngest son, Iraj. By the end of this story Ferdowsi's gift of storytelling and expanded geography of the Persian Empire assume evident historical proportions. The heroic phase weds the mythic into the historical via a purgatorial phase that enables the world of the Persian epic to resonate with what we know and what we wish we knew about history. The heroic phase enables the mythic to connect with the historical seamlessly.

Human fragility and imperial rivalries now commence apace. Fereydun is concerned that after his death his eldest son will conspire against Iraj, his youngest. So while he is still alive he divides his realm among them: to Salm, his eldest, he gives the west; to Tur, his second son, he gives the east (China and Turkestan); and to his youngest, Iraj, he gives Iran and Arabia. Salm and Tur are jealous of Iraj and his more opulent realm and conspire against their brother. They lead their respective armies from east and west, encamp in the vicinity of Fereydun's palace, and send him a message to the effect that he has been unjust in dispatching them to the east and west of his realm and giving the best portion to Iraj. Iraj is reluctant to fight his brothers. He carries a friendly message from Fereydun to his brothers and pleads with them not to fight him. Salm and Tur are relentless, especially when they see that their respective armies are entirely drawn to Iraj and his Divine Gift of Grace. They take him to a tent and angrily behead him. The fratricide shakes the fabric of the epic narrative. We no longer think we are reading a work of fiction. We are in the bosom of murderous history.

When Iraj is killed by his two brothers, one of his courtier companions, Mahafarid, is found pregnant. Months after Iraj's death, Mahafarid gives birth to a girl. When this girl grows up, Fereydun marries her off to Pashang, his nephew, a valiant and chivalrous general in his army. From this marriage a son is born, Manuchehr, whom Fereydun holds as dear as if he were Iraj. Manuchehr grows up to become a valiant prince and is crowned by Fereydun as his successor. Salm and Tur again wage war, now against Manuchehr. But this time around Manuchehr kills them both. Fereydun dies soon after, and Manuchehr becomes the solitary and just king. Between Iraj and his grandson Manuchehr, generational successions in the *Shahnameh* have extended from the mythic to the heroic, giving a sense of historical continuity to the very idea of "Iran" as an imperial destiny. By now we have a sense of that imperial destiny as both worldly and otherworldly, material and moral, factual and imaginative. The imaginative geography is self-transcendental. It banks on stories it has already told us and it anticipates the stories we are yet to read.

It is during the reign of Manuchehr that Rostam, arguably the greatest hero of the *Shahnameh*, is born. The story of his birth begins with that of his grandfather Sam, the son of Nariman, who is the most valiant general in Manuchehr's army and rules in Zabol. After a long time of expectation, finally a beautiful woman bears Sam a son, who is perfect in every respect except his youthful hair is completely white. Sam is embarrassed to show his infant son to his court lest they laugh at him. He has the infant boy taken away from his mother and abandoned at the foot of the Alborz Mountain. The legendary bird Simorgh is flying down from Alborz in search of food for its children when it sees the infant and takes him to its children. He grows up with Simorgh and its children to become a beautiful and valiant hero. Meanwhile, Sam has nightmares over his abominable act of abandoning his own son to beasts and goes to find him on Alborz. Ahura Mazda forgives Sam his sin and Simorgh returns his son to him, telling the young lad that it has named him Dastan. Dastan is reluctant to leave Simorgh and his mountainous habitat.

Simorgh assures him that a better future awaits him with his natural father. To alleviate his anxieties, Simorgh gives Dastan one of its feathers and tells him that anytime he is in trouble all he has to do is to burn the feather and Simorgh will be there to help. Dastan follows his father to his court, where he receives his second name, Zal-e Zar, on account of being white haired. With the story of Zal, the son of Sam, the Oedipal (or what we might call Sohrabaneh) complex at the heart of the *Shahnameh* assumes its most potent form. Here we have to be careful neither to approximate such "Oedipal" moments to their Greek referents nor leave them theoretically mute. A father inadvertently killing his own son remains archetypal to the enduring significance of the Persian epic.

Zal becomes a valiant hero in his father's court. Soon Sam leaves his court to his son's care and leaves for Mazandaran to fight against Manuchehr's enemies, where demons had again revolted. Meanwhile Zal travels from Zabol to Kabul, a country that was under the authority of Mehrab. Mehrab, the king of Kabul, is a descendant of Zahhak's but a wise and good-natured man. Zal and Mehrab meet on a hunting expedition near Kabul. Zal hears of Mehrab's beautiful daughter Rudabeh and falls in love with her. Mehrab finds Zal a worthy hero and invites him to his palace. Zal refuses because he believes his father, Sam, and his king, Manuchehr, will object to his affiliating with a descendant of Zahhak's. Mehrab goes back to his palace and describes the valiant Sam to his wife, Sindokht, and his daughter Rudabeh. Rudabeh in turn falls in love with Zal and dispatches her five beautiful ladies-in-waiting to his hunting encampment. They meet Zal and invite him to come to Rudabeh's palace. Zal goes to Rudabeh and expresses his love to her, but, alas, he fears that his father, Sam, and his king, Manuchehr, will not allow him to marry a descendant of Zahhak's. Rudabeh bursts into tears and confesses her love for Zal. Zal in turn prays to God Almighty and promises to ask his father and his king to allow them to marry. Sam agrees to his son's request after he consults with astrologers and they assure him that from this union a hero of unsurpassed nobility and power will arise. But he stipulates that he needs to secure Manuchehr's permission. Zal and Rudabeh constitute one of the most beautiful love stories of the *Shahnameh*. Such stories border the Persian epic with intensely romantic episodes that enrich the sense of war and love, heroism and romance in a mutually enabling way. The text by now has become self-sustained, a world entirely independent of the uses to which it will be put throughout its long and tumultuous history.

Meanwhile, Sindokht, Rudabeh's mother, discovers her daughter's secret love for the Persian prince and is horrified by the prospect of exciting the Persian king's ancient animosity against Zahhak and his progeny. Mehrab is enraged at the news of his daughter's falling in love with Zal but controls his anger when he hears that Sam has in fact agreed to the union. He is baffled as to how Sam or Manuchehr could agree to a union with one of Zahhak's descendants. His fears are justified when Manuchehr hears of this story, is fearful of a son being born of this union and coming to take away his throne and return it to one of Zahhak's descendants, and he thus commands Sam, before he has a chance to plead with the monarch, to go to Kabul and destroy Mehrab. Sam leads his army to Kabul to perform his duty to Manuchehr, his king. Zal hears of this and intercepts his father's army and pleads with him not to attack Kabul, reminding him of the hardship he has endured since childhood. Sam is desperate and sends a letter to Manuchehr asking him please to spare Mehrab and allow Zal to marry Rudabeh. Mehrab is enraged by this whole episode and wants to kill his wife and daughter. But Sindokht asks her husband to allow her to take some gifts and go and talk to Sam. Sindokht meets with Sam and persuades him not to attack her kingdom and allow their children to marry. Meanwhile Zal himself carries his father's letter to Manuchehr and pleads with his king to allow him to marry Rudabeh. Manuchehr asks him to stay awhile until he consults with his advisers. His advisers and astrologers convene for three days and happily inform him that this indeed is an auspicious marriage and beneficial to his kingdom. Manuchehr keeps Zal at his court for another couple of days and tests his wisdom and courage. Finally, Manuchehr writes a letter to Sam and agrees to Zal's marriage to Rudabeh. The two lovers finally marry in happiness. Zal becomes the king of Zabol, and Sam returns to his services to Manuchehr in Mazandaran province. Ferdowsi is at his absolute storytelling height in telling the story of Zal and Rudabeh. He is intense, passionate, engaged, crafting the cliff-hangers with impeccable dramatic precision and psychological depth. We are no longer in the grand sweep of epic history. We are in the grips of the minutiae of palpable passions. The subconscious of the text now reverberates with the most potent human emotions. How did we get here, from those grand mythic beginnings to these detailed miniatures of worldly affairs? The *Shahnameh* is delivering itself from its own textual subconscious.

Soon after her marriage to Zal, Rudabeh becomes pregnant. After about nine months she is extremely heavy but cannot give natural birth. In desperation, Zal burns the feather received from Simorgh, who instantly appears and congratulates Zal that he is about to have a valiant son, but that he is too big to be born naturally. The mythical bird instructs that a very wise and skillful physician ought to be summoned and surgery performed on Rudabeh so that her infant can be born from her lower abdomen. So Rostam is born through a "Caesarian" (or what we might even venture to call Rostamaneh) operation. Rostam grows up to become the most valiant hero of the entire world, beginning with his childhood and his showing signs of an extraordinary physical power and moral rectitude. Among the early manifestations of his heroism is his avenging the death of his great-grandfather, Nariman, who was killed by a stone thrown from the Sepand Citadel. The Persian kings never conquered this citadel, and Nariman was dispatched by Fereydun to conquer it, but he lost his life in the process. Rostam follows his father's advice, disguises himself as a salt merchant, and infiltrates the citadel, disarming its guards and conquering it for his father and grandfather. The birth and emergence of Rostam as the imperial hero of the epic becomes a momentous occasion in the *Shahnameh* narrative. His triumphs and tragedies become definitive to the traumatic nexus of the text. Both his own tragic history and the stories in which he is involved define the Persian epic for what it is: the subconscious of a people, aware of their imperial past, cast into postcolonial destinies beyond their control.

The stories of Sam and Simorgh, Zal and Rudabeh, and ultimately the birth of Rostam are narratively the most important events during the reign of Manuchehr. But the most important political event of his reign is his battle with Turan. As Rostam grows to become a valiant hero, Manuchehr dies and entrusts his throne to his son Nozar, alerting him

that Turan is about to invade Iran and assuring him that his three generations of heroes, Sam, the son of Nariman, Zal his son, and, most
important, his grandson Rostam, will be his staunchest supporters. Soon
after the death of Manuchehr and as soon as his son Nozar ascends the
Iranian throne, Pashang, the king of Turan, seeks to avenge the humili-
ating defeat of Tur at the hand of Manuchehr and dispatches his son
Afrasiab to invade Iran. Nozar is defeated and killed by Afrasiab. Rostam and Zal mobilize the Iranians against the Turanians, while Zav Tahmasp and Garshasp, two inconsequential kings in an apocryphal part
of the *Shahnameh*, hold the monarchy together. This is the moment when
we have a premonition of the rise of Rostam as a central moral core of
the Persian imperial order. Rostam becomes definitive to the Persian
epic, his consistent heroism and tragic end emblematic of the moral predicament of the heroic age. On the moral map of the Persian epic, he is
the allegorical sign of the uneasy parental predicament of history: born
out of chaos, father to a tragic end, putting an end to his own posterity.

Finally, Zal and a group of Iranian nobles select Key Qobad as the
monarch. Key Qobad is a just and effective monarch who expels the
Turanians from Iran. Key Kavous, Key Qobad's son, succeeds his father.
His reign is inundated with one mishap and catastrophe after another.
He attacks the demons of Mazandaran and is captured by them. Rostam
has to go and save him. He attacks the kingdom of Hamavaran and is
captured by his future father-in-law, the beautiful Sudabeh's father. Rostam goes and rescues him. He fancies being able to fly and has himself
built a throne and carried by eagles but crashes in enemy territory. Rostam goes and saves him. Narratively, the most exciting event of Kavous's
reign is Rostam's Seven Trials, canonizing him as the greatest hero of the
entire *Shahnameh*. The most tragic episode of the entire *Shahnameh* also
occurs during the reign of Kavous, when Rostam inadvertently kills his
own son, Sohrab. (Matthew Arnold's "Sohrab and Rustum" is based on
this story.)

An equally tragic and politically far more consequential trauma during the reign of Kavous (as I have had occasions to refer to it before) is
the story of Seyavash, Kavous's valiant son. Rostam, as will be recalled,
raises Seyavash to become a gallant prince, worthy of the Persian throne.

Upon his return to his father's court, Sudabeh, Kavous's young wife, falls in love with her stepson. He, however, refuses to return her love, which enrages the stepmother, who in turn accuses Seyavash of trying to rape her. Seyavash submits to a public test of his innocence and gallops triumphantly through a bonfire. Disheartened, however, by the whole episode, Seyavash leaves his father's court and leads the Iranian army against the Turanian forces and defeats them at the border. He signs a treaty with the Turanians and sends a message to that effect to his father, Kavous. Kavous is enraged by the treaty and orders Seyavash to kill the Turanian entourage at his court. Seyavash refuses to betray the terms of his treaty with Afrasiab and seeks political asylum in Turan. He is initially welcomed but subsequently killed in a plot by Garsivaz, King Afrasiab's jealous brother, whom Seyavash had defeated in his battle against Turan. Seyavash marries two women while in Turan, initially Jarireh, daughter of Piran, Afrasiab's vizier, and subsequently Farigis, Afrasiab's daughter. Seyavash's son from Farigis, Khosrow, escapes from Turan, returns to Iran, succeeds his paternal grandfather Kavous, and wages a war against Turan to avenge his father. Among the casualties of the war, however, is Forud, Khosrow's half brother. The wars between Iran and Turan end with the killing of Afrasiab and the subsequent death of Kavous.

The tragic ends of Sohrab, Seyavash, and Esfandiar will collectively constitute the traumatic epicenter of the *Shahnameh*, where its mythic and heroic phases prepare the way for its historical consciousness. That historical consciousness is always already conscious of its mythic and heroic dispositions. In all these seminal cases, arrogant and self-centered fathers cause the death of their respective sons—changing the course of history with a tragedy that had predestined the fate of the *Shahnameh* heroes. Filicide of varied forms and dispositions connect the heroic phase of the Persian epic as the foregrounding of its historical drama. But around these three acts of deliberate or inadvertent filicide the three components of the *Shahnameh*—mythic, heroic, and historical—will ultimately lose their temporal distinctions and come together as a fusion of fact and fiction definitive to the entirety of Ferdowsi's masterpiece.

With the death of Key Kavous and Afrasiab the heroic age of the *Shahnameh* eventually comes to an end. The history of Iran as mapped out in the Persian epic is thus divided into three successive dynasties, each corresponding to a main narrative theme of the text: the Pishdadids in the mythic age and its early legendary kings, who established civilization against forces of chaos and mayhem; then come the Kiyanids in the heroic age, whose kings and heroes see their empire to its highest achievements as they fought against the external enemy, the Turanians; and finally comes the historic age of the Sassanids, the last dynasty to rule a unified Iran before the advent of Islam. Via a beautiful Alexander Romance, Ferdowsi links the end of the Kiyanids to the rise of the Sassanid period and ends with their defeat by the Arab army. Each era and dynasty is seamlessly linked to the next, producing a narrative suspension of stories and episodes in one panoramic view of transhistoric sweep, compared with which the limited span of Homer's epics pales, and yet the *Shahnameh* remains Shakespearian in its detailed dramatic episodes. The fact that we need to link two different European hallmarks, Homer and Shakespeare, to make the *Shahnameh* familiar to present-day readers is among other indications that its global reception will need to come closer to its own inner worldliness, held together by successive traumatic episodes.

THE IMPOSSIBLE MISSION

This detailed account of the *Shahnameh* through its varied narrative suspense has allowed me some comfortable space in which to draw you closer to its logic and narrative. Let me now take you back to some more specifics.

The impossible mission of Esfandiar on which his father sends him is to go and do nothing less than to capture, bind, and bring the world champion Rostam to his court, knowing too well this is an impossibility. It is a homicidal mission. Goshtasp wants his son Esfandiar to be murdered by Rostam, for his ambitious presence at his court he considers a threat to his throne. Rostam will never allow anyone to tie him and bring him to the royal court. He is a kingmaker, not the subject of any king.

Esfandiar travels to Rostam and commands him to accompany him as his father has demanded. Rostam loves Esfandiar and pleads with him to refrain from asking him an impossibility. He is willing to accompany Esfandiar on foot while he is riding on his horse as a sign of his humility. Esfandiar is blinded to reality and demands Rostam's total surrender and to be publicly humiliated and tied. Rostam refuses, and the two begin their tragic and doomed battle, despite their deepest love and admiration for each other. Rostam is almost defeated just as in his battle with his son Sohrab, but Simorgh instructs him that he can kill the otherwise immortal Esfandiar only by targeting his eyes, which he does and thus kills the ambitious prince. The battle of Rostam and Esfandiar is perhaps the most dramatic, the most "cinematic," of all battles in the *Shahnameh*.

At this point it is imperative to remember that the *Shahnameh* stories are *stories* not histories, left for us since time immemorial, however rooted in some distant historical fact they may be. Whatever roots they may have had in history, it is in the majestic hands of Ferdowsi the poet, the storyteller, that they are turned into works of art, very much as *King Lear* or *Hamlet* or any other work of Shakespeare may have had roots in some history. This means that the *Shahnameh* characters are narrative tropes not human beings, personae not persons. As literary tropes these characters transcend history to enter the realm of mythic realities. This means that these characters are not caught in actual *familial* but in a symbolic *societal* web of affiliations, integral to the world of the *Shahnameh* as an epic. From Deleuze and Guattari's collective work we have learned how *desires* are the products of social narratives not of familial relations. The production of *social desire* is therefore a plot narrative domestic to the world of the Persian epic. While for us this means a closing in of the social and the psychoanalytical, a literary-critical extension of it means that in the *Shahnameh* these stories are narratively performed, and as such the social context of the characters and the world in which they live becomes indicative of the human condition that has occasioned them. Theorizing that world therefore must begin from *the structure of desires* it invokes and move forward toward the manner in which such desires become conscious of their worldliness. At the dramatic heart of the major *Shahnameh* stories dwells this narrative constitution of desire.

In the tragedy of Rostam and Esfandiar, as a paramount example of such social formation of the structure of desire, we encounter the *Shahnameh* trope of how a son wants to succeed his royal father, but the father sends him on an impossible mission to get him killed, this time around though through his vulnerable eyes. The narrative proximity to *Oedipus Rex* is of course striking, but it should not distract from something perhaps entirely different. This is a case of parricide as well as filicide although by proxy. As it often happens in the *Shahnameh*, fathers deny, sons desire, while mothers conspire, as fathers either kill their sons directly (as Rostam does Sohrab) or send them to be killed (as Goshtasp does Esfandiar), or they plot to cast them out and get them killed (as Key Kavous does Seyavash). The exception is of course Zahhak, who in effect preempts this filicidal probability by conspiring with the devil and through him kills his father. Zahhak did what Seyavash, Sohrab, and Esfandiar wished but did not dare do. Similar to the Oedipal case of coveting the mother and killing the father, the plot of the *Shahnameh* approximates Esfandiar to the tragic indecisions of the frustrated Hamlet.

In my previous work on the fate of the tragic hero in Shi'ism I have found it useful to reverse the insights of Freud articulated in his Judeo-Christian reading of the archetypal psychoanalytic. Here in a similar move if we part ways with Freud and move toward Deleuze by opening the *familial* to the *societal*, we might see the tragic hero, the father, and the mother much more effectively into the epic cycle. The result opens the dynamic of the Persian epic onto an entirely different cast: neither conquest nor defeat but defiance, and in fact consistently a *deferred defiance*, now defines the Persian epic, so that Shi'ism (in which we have a paramount case of the murder of the son and thus of deferred defiance) can be read as a version of the paradigmatic pattern of the *Shahnameh* and as such a metaphysically sublimated epic.[14] I originally developed that idea of "deferred defiance" in juxtaposition to and reversal of the Freudian notion of "deferred obedience" that he considered contingent on the murder of the primordial father. The father, I proposed in my book on

Shi'ism, was not the figure who was killed but the son, the primordial son, Hossein in that case, and Sohrab or Seyavash or Esfandiar in this case. If we place Hossein, Sohrab, Seyavash, and Esfandiar next to one another, the whole historical case of Shi'ism becomes a textual commentary on this central trauma of the *Shahnameh*. That proposition opens the case of Shi'ism to the mythic panorama of the Persian epic, as it will lend the *Shahnameh* also an extended historical case beyond its textual referents. The move from Freud to Deleuze, with the particular twist I propose here, becomes even more important at this point.

In *Masochism: Coldness and Cruelty* (1967), Gilles Deleuze begins with the Freudian point, in "The Passing of the Oedipus Complex," either in an active-sadistic direction, where the child identifies with the father, or in a passive-masochistic direction, where the child identifies with the mother. In trying to separate these two directions, Deleuze then maps out a critical point where the son replaces his own body with the body of his father.

> So when we are told that the character who does the beating in masochism is the father, we are entitled to ask: Who in reality is being beaten? Where is the father hidden? Could it not be in the person who is being beaten? The masochist feels guilty, he asks to be beaten, he expiates, but why and for what crime? Is it not precisely the father-image in him that is thus miniaturized, beaten, ridiculed, and humiliated? What the subject atones for is his resemblance to the father and the father's likeness in him: the formula of masochism is the humiliated father. Hence the father is not so much the beater as the beaten.[15]

This insight has serious implications for all the critical *Shahnameh* stories, such as those of Rostam and Esfandiar or Seyavash and Sudabeh, and therefore for the entirety of the Persian epic. While for Freud the father's power makes him the primary figure of potential violence and domination for the child, for Deleuze it is the mother who is the critical figure in the child's world. Mother here is both the love object and the controlling agent, an ambivalent figure whose power of bodily proximity and comfort (which includes but is not limited to breastfeeding) both comforts and threatens the child. Recall the crucial moment when Esfandiar goes to his mother, Katayoun, drunk, asks for more wine, and then embraces her and starts complaining about his father. From here onward it is easy to see how the fusion of both the mother and the father are the perpetual source of anxiety for the son/prince in the Persian epic cycles. If the fear of the father is one of castration/denial of succession, the fear of the mother is one of denial of the womb/erotic proximity, most palpable in Seyavash's case but also evident in Esfandiar's drunkard encounter with his mother at the commencement of the story. The son/prince desires and fears losing the mother as much as he fears and covets the throne of the father. In effect he wants the throne to have the mother, for he identifies the throne with the power to possess and command the mother's love and affection. The fear of losing the mother is as compelling as desiring her, with the figure of the father sitting on his throne as an obstacle embedded in the persona of the son as the future king, the father. The play between seduction and rejection (Seyavash and Sudabeh or Esfandiar and Katayoun, or even Sohrab and Tahmineh) is the primary space where the son fears and desires the mother. To succeed the father as the king is to eliminate and replace him as the source of power and barrier between the son and the mother. Possession of the mother the prince identifies with absolute and permanent power over the throne and vice versa.

If we follow this Deleuzian psychoanalytic trope, then the moment of the physical death of Sohrab, Seyavash, and Esfandiar is in fact the moment of the symbolic death of their respective fathers Rostam, Key Kavous, and Goshtasp—namely, the moment when the son has substituted his body for the body of the father in revenge, and by directly or indirectly killing his son the king in effect commits regicidal homicide. This reading of the *Shahnameh* brings the central leitmotif of Shi'ism and the Persian epic together. The fact that Ferdowsi was a Shi'a might in fact be considered a deep subconscious condition of the plot narratives of his masterpiece having been plotted on the central trauma of Shi'ism. The analogy could work both ways, both the *Shahnameh* replotting Shi'ism or Shi'ism foregrounding the *Shahnameh*. Either way, what we have here is the central epic narrative of the Persianate empires replicating themselves at the heart of Islamic empires, which makes the Persian epic neither an epic of conquest nor an epic of defeat but an epic of perpetual, historical defiance. Neither Freud nor Deleuze could see the full historic proportions of their respective psychoanalytic conclusions, trapped as they both were in their blindingly European limitations. Nevertheless, their limitations are precisely what enable critical inroads into literary and societal domains beyond their Eurocentrism.

This dialectic of father-son relationship in the Persian epic sustains its traumatic course all the way to present-day history. We must first remember that Esfandiar is the epiphany of the tragic hero in the *Shahnameh*. He has to do the impossible, knowing full well his father, Goshtasp's, command to arrest Rostam and bring him to his court bound is an impossibility, a mission impossible, effectively a suicidal mission banking on the young prince's natural hubris and the old Rostam's pride. The encounter gives Ferdowsi the opportunity to show his love for both his heroes, without preference for one or the other. This is the battle between two good men caught in a bad encounter, conspired by a treacherous father reluctant to give up his throne. Goshtasp had repeatedly reneged on his promise to give up his throne for his son. First, he sends him off to fight Arjasp, the Turanian monarch, then he sends him off to spread Zoroastrianism around the world, just before he is asked to rescue his sisters from the Ru'in Fortress. Esfandiar does everything he is asked to do and overcomes his Seven Trials too. Goshtasp finally discovers through his court astrologers and prognosticators that Esfandiar is destined to be killed in Zabolestan by Rostam. So he dispatches his son to arrest Rostam, knowing only too well he shall not return from this task alive.

Rostam is initially defeated until his father, Zal, solicits the help of Simorgh, who teaches Rostam how to make an arrow from a special wood and target Esfandiar eyes, which are the only vulnerable parts of his otherwise invulnerable body. Ferdowsi's dramatic storytelling at this moment excels as it never has so powerfully before. His description of the heart-wrenching moment when Esfandiar's eyes are hit by Rostam's arrow is among the most astonishingly beautiful passages in the Persian epic. More than a thousand years after Ferdowsi's description of

Esfandiar's demise, the towering modern-day Iranian poet Ahmad Shamlou (1925–2000) picks up where the master Khorasani poet had left off and retrieves the painful memory of Esfandiar closing his eyes forever in one of his own most iconic poems, mourning the death of revolutionary heroes of his own time in his "Abraham in Fire," in which he brings together biblical, classical Greek, and *Shahnameh* tragic themes for a renewed rendezvous. Describing one such revolutionary hero, we read in Shamlou's poem,

> . . . and a lion-iron-mountain kind of a man
> Like this
> Traversed upon the bloody
> Battlefield of fate
> With his Achilles' heels.
>
> An immortal body,
> The secret of whose death
> Was the sorrow of love
> And the sadness of solitude—
>
> Oh you sad Esfandiar:
> You are better off
> With your eyes closed![16]

The trauma of Rostam thus killing Esfandiar remains archetypally definitive to an epic culture from the height of its imperial history to the depth of its postcolonial fate.

FOUR
EPICS AND EMPIRES

Shabi chon shabah ruy-shosteh beh ghir,
Nah Bahram Peyda nah Keyvan Nah Tir.

A night jet-black dark with its face covered in tar
Neither Saturn was visible, nor Mercury nor Mars—
The moon had so differently adorned its sight
Passing upon its forehead a streak of light.

The subjects of Key Khosrow, the royal king of Iran in the Erman region, report to their sovereign lord that their fields and crops are under attack by wild boars. Bizhan, the Persian warrior, is dispatched to force the wild animals out of these fields and restore peace. Happy with his victory, Bizhan ventures into the northern frontiers of the Iranian realm and crosses the border into Turan, the archenemy of Iran, where in an enchanted orchard the young Persian warrior meets Manizheh, the beautiful daughter of Afrasiab, the Turanian king. The handsome warrior and the beautiful princess fall madly in love. Manizheh smuggles Bizhan into her private quarters, where the two young lovers spend their days and nights singing and dancing their desires, far from the vindictive eyes and ears of Afrasiab. The fear of a forbidden love makes their union even more fervently passionate.

EPICS RISE, EMPIRES FALL

The story of Bizhan and Manizheh in the *Shahnameh* is an allegory for the triumph of passionate *eros* of epics over the political *ethos* of empires. Iran and Turan are mortal enemies—two warring empires at each other's throats throughout the course of the epic. Bizhan crosses the border between the two empires, as had Seyavash before him. Bizhan and Manizheh meet, and their happy, healthy, and passionate love for each other triumphs over their political divides. The *Shahnameh* is therefore the epic of two not one empire: Iran and Turan. Ferdowsi writes his epic sitting on the Iranian side, no doubt, but his story of Bizhan and Manizheh, among many other indications, is a clear sign that he is the simultaneous chronicler of a Self and an Other facing each other. He sees and shows Iran in the face of Turan, and he reflects Turan on the face of Iran. That innate dialectic constitutionally differentiates the *Shahnameh* from any assumption that epics are either one of triumph or one of defeat. The *Shahnameh* is the dialectical account of both. Before Bizhan, Seyavash, too, crosses the border of the two empires, falls in love, and marries Farigis, another daughter of Afrasiab, the emperor of Turan. From this marriage Key Khosrow is born, who will eventually become the next emperor of Iran, thus in effect uniting the two empires. Rostam, the principal hero of the *Shahnameh*, is also born of a mixed marriage between his father, Zal, who was a Persian warrior, and his mother, Rudabeh, who was the daughter of Mehrab Kaboli and the granddaughter of the Arab usurper king Zahhak. Most of the passionate love stories of the *Shahnameh* (Zal and Rudabeh, Seyavash and Farigis, Bizhan and Manizheh, and even Rostam and Tahmineh) are between an Iranian prince or warrior and a non-Iranian princess who has become a familiar foreigner in the course of Ferdowsi's narrative. Ferdowsi narrates the Iranian and Turanian victories and defeats in equal measure passionately and convincingly. The entire *Shahnameh*, one might thus say, works toward this passionate love affair between an Iranian warrior and a Turanian princess—their deep affections for each other the syncretic universe in which the emotive cosmogony of the *Shahnameh* works. The history of the *Shahnameh* throughout the ages will have to be read in the context of this paramount momentum at the heart of the Persian epic, where the prototypical heroic narrative in which one of the parents of the hero is either a supernatural being or a foreign woman assumes far more mortal, worldly, and human proportions.

Ferdowsi's *Shahnameh* has had a long and consistent history in the tumultuous course of the rise and fall of multiple empires, from its immediate context in the course of the Samanid (819–999) and Ghaznavid (977–1186), all the way to all the subsequent Muslim and Persianate empires up to and including the Mughals (1526–1857), the Safavids (1501–1736), and the Ottomans (1299–1923). Even before the rise of these later, almost simultaneous, Muslim empires, the *Shahnameh* was equally significant during the Seljuqid (1037–1194), the Mongol (1206–1368), and the Timurid (1370–1507) Empires, judged by the many illustrated manuscripts of the epic from these various periods. The text of the Persian epic has offered political legitimacy and narrative authority to these Persianate or proto-Persianate empires, enabled them to partake in the mythic, heroic, and historical pedigree of Persian monarchy. The key question for us is, what is the relationship between the ritual commissioning of the illustrated manuscripts in the royal atelier of these courts and the evident legitimacy that this gesture has historically offered them?

What does the central role of the Persian epic in the course of successive dynasties tell us about the link between epics and empires, when at the most triumphant point of their ascendency these royal families are drawn toward Ferdowsi's *Shahnameh*, commissioning its beautiful production, celebrating its content, claiming its blessings, naming their children after its heroes? What can the fascinating story of the torn-up and dismembered Shah Tahmasp (aka Houghton) *Shahnameh* tell us about the vagaries of Muslim empires, European colonialism, and art collection? This particularly luxurious *Shahnameh* was produced during the Safavid period and given as a gift to the Ottoman sultan Selim II (r. 1566–1574). It eventually reached the American collector Arthur Houghton Jr., who in turn tore this *Shahnameh* to pieces and sold each folio for an exorbitant amount of money. It was fortunately studied and published in two large-scale facsimiles in a limited and expensive edition by the distinguished Harvard curator Cary Welch and Martin B. Dickson of Princeton before its destruction. More recently Sheila Canby of the Metropolitan Museum has painstakingly traced all the pages of that *Shahnameh* and published a complete copy of it in a handsome edition.[1]

The fate of this particular text of the *Shahnameh* is emblematic of a larger context in which the symbolic significance of the Persian epic eventually loses its imperial habitat and in its dismembered fragments finds its way into European and U.S. museums and private collections.[2] This journey from Persianate royal courts to European bourgeois private and public spheres marks a key transitional stage of not just the text of the Persian epic but also in fact its poetic destiny. If as the prominent literary critic Franco Moretti proposes we are to read texts such as Goethe's *Faust* (1829), Herman Melville's *Moby-Dick* (1851), or James Joyce's *Ulysses* (1922) as examples of modern epic or "sacred texts" in what he proposes be called Western literary culture, then how are we to read the Persian epic in its colonial and postcolonial context?[3] In what way do classical texts like the *Shahnameh* carry the imperial memories of their past into the postcolonial history of their future? The *Shahnameh* is not a "modern" text. The very temporal or spatial or ideological designation "modernity" does not apply and is in fact entirely irrelevant to the Persian epic. But how does the fate of a literary masterpiece of a once imperial pedigree reflect on the aggressive theorization of "modern epic" as "the form that represents the European domination of the planet"? Suppose we were to disagree that there is a "solid consent around" that European domination. Suppose that European domination was and has been and continues to be boldly contested. Then what would be the receptive fate of classical epics like the *Shahnameh* in the postcolonial context of their continued significance?

AN EPIC OF DEFIANCE

Before we answer such questions we first need to know how we are to understand the place of Ferdowsi's *Shahnameh* as an epic and its relations to various Persianate empires it has historically sustained, informed, and legitimized, and do so in the context of other studies of epic and empires.

It is during the Samanids that the writing of the *Shahnameh* in both prose and poetry reaches its epochal height. This is not a coincidence. The Samanid monarchs see a decidedly political significance in the composition of these *Shahnameh*s. In those *Shahnameh*s the Iranian monarchs already detect (and rightly so) an alternative imperial consciousness to Islamic empires that were rooted in the Prophet's legacy, the Qur'an, as well as the active formation of an Islamic scholasticism and Arabic humanism that had culturally facilitated and instrumentalized Muslim empires. The genre of the *Shahnameh* posits a decidedly different political genealogy, and in their compositions these Iranian monarchs detect an alternative source of political consciousness for their reign, almost entirely independent of an Islamic lineage and pedigree. As the Umayyad and Abbasid caliphs were increasingly rooted in that Islamic consciousness, the Samanid shahs and amirs were aiming at an entirely autonomous source of legitimacy in the mythic and historic consciousness of *Shahnameh* narratives. Without a full grasp of this genealogical origin of Ferdowsi's *Shahnameh* no comparative assessment of it is possible.

A number of key factors come together to occasion the phenomenon of the *Shahnameh* and give it particular political significance—the first and foremost among them is linguistic, where the Persian language assumed increased dynastic and therefore cultural significance. The second is location. The eastern provinces of the Abbasid Empire were too far from Baghdad logistically to control them with the hegemony of the imperial Arabic in any serious way. To be sure, there were many learned men who left Khorasan and went to Baghdad to join in the intellectual effervesce of the Abbasid capital and caliphate. But at the same time there was enough political autonomy and intellectual gravitation in the east to keep people of Ferdowsi's poetic and political persuasion happy and content. The third factor is the factual evidence of the continuity of a cultural heritage in the region that demanded and secured the attention of gifted poets like Ferdowsi or, before him, Daqiqi. The fourth factor was the political need for a radically different and autonomous political and imperial consciousness, which the *Shahnameh* genre amply provided.

These and related factors came together and culminated in the Samanid period when Ferdowsi began the composition of his *Shahnameh*, which in turn became even more significant for the Ghaznavids, who were of Turkic origin and even more in need of a local and regional imperial consciousness independent of both their own Central Asian tribal origins and of the central caliphate in Baghdad whose nascent Islamic pedigree and Arab tribalism were at the root of both the Umayyad and the Abbasid Caliphates. From the Ghaznavid dynasty forward the writing of the *Shahnameh* becomes a key and critical factor for securing political legitimacy for both Persianate and Turkic dynasties, so much so that when the Mongol conquest happened in the thirteenth century, both the Persian language and the *Shahnameh* became definitive to their imperial imagination. Having originated in the Iranian, expanded to the Turkic, and now reached the Mongol Empire, the *Shahnameh* became positively archetypal in its reach and resonances, pushing against the whole spectrum of scholastic and humanist traditions that the Qur'anic revelation and the prophetic traditions (Hadith) had enabled in the eastern parts of Muslim empires. Eurocentric theorization of "comparative literature" to this day remains categorically ignorant of this or any other imperial context of production of epic narratives. These theorists take Homer and Virgil and their limited (however magnificent) localities and injudiciously universalize them into "epic and empire." There is something dialogical, contestatory, competitive about the very origin of the Persian epic that remains definitive to its genealogy. That dialectic must always be kept in mind when we place the text of the *Shahnameh* next to any European epic, classic or modern.

I use "eastern" and "western" provinces of Muslim lands only in an indexical way, for Islamic scholasticism and Arab humanism were very well represented in Khorasan in the east while the significance of the *Shahnameh* and Persian humanism extended well into Mesopotamia in the west and ultimately became integral to the Ottoman Empire in Anatolia. By the time we get to the fragmentation of the Mongol Empire (1206–1368) in the Ilkhanids and the Timurids the *Shahnameh* is categorically dominant in Persianate and Islamicate empires. By the time we reach the Mughals in India, the Safavids in Persia, and the Ottomans in Asia Minor and beyond the *Shahnameh* is definitive to the vast spectrum of the last three Muslim empires. This latest phase of Muslim imperial imagination gives three complementary registers to the *Shahnameh*, its stories and sentiments holding the widest reach of Muslim territorial expansion together. This consistent and expansive reach of the *Shahnameh* ipso facto gives it a global and comparative significance long before and beyond what European literary theorists have called comparative literature. In short, the significance, endurance, and multifaceted presence of the *Shahnameh* in global imperial formations from the Samanids and the Ghaznavids through the Seljuqid and Mongols, down to the Ottomans, Safavids, and Mughals, is simply too large to fit in the limited, provincial imagination of a comparative literary theory that begins with the Greek city-states and ends with the Roman Empire, before it reaches modern European imperialism and the rise of what Moretti calls modern epics.

The *Shahnameh* began neither as an epic of triumph nor as a eulogy of defeat. It is written neither by a triumphant Arab nor by a defeated Persian. It has victorious stories and it has plenty of tragedies. It is an epic, but it does not emerge from a militaristic logic of defeat and victory. It is neither exclusively triumphalist nor consistently tragic. It is both. It is therefore neither. It will refuse to succumb to any militarist logic of epics or empires. It casts old stories its author had collected as the modus operandi of political legitimacy, a book for Persian kings and princes, offering them a universal frame of reference and thus eternal and archetypal legitimacy. But it does so never abandoning its own internal poetic logic of a traumatic reading of history. Its internal narrative logic overrides the limited patience of royal courts and their scribes, calligraphers, and painters. It revives old stories and bygone empires and casts them as the blueprint of a new world order. By doing so it gives meaning, significance, and purpose to an otherwise chaotic and meaningless world. Contrary to the universe enabled by the Qur'anic revelation it does not reference itself on any metaphysical belief in Divinity, the Holy, the Unseen. It is its own poetics that posits its sense of transcendence. To be sure, the *Shahnameh* does not consciously posit itself as an alternative to the Qur'an. Ferdowsi was a Shi'i Muslim, and his book begins with praise for the Muslim God, his prophets, and other Shi'i saintly figures. But the fate of the *Shahnameh* as a royal text implicitly assigns it this significance. To understand the transhistorical significance of the *Shahnameh* we need to come to terms with the internal logic of its own temporality.

TIME AND NARRATIVE

The world is today fully conscious of successive empires that have come and gone ruling it: the Babylonians, the Achaemenids, the Romans, the Sassanids, the Abbasids, the Byzantines, the Ottomans, the Mughals, the Spanish, the British, the Americans. Each one of these empires have told their stories in epic or in other imperial forms. Are these epics and stories signs of a triumphalist assuredness or perhaps indexes of anxiety? What do the epics of empires past and present reveal about them? Quint tells the story of European empires and their genres of triumphalism or jeremiads of defeat. Moretti reads "modern epics" as indications of the triumphant "world system," of globalized capital, and thus he updates that triumphalism of "the West" in more specifically literary terms. When we look at the *Shahnameh*, however, we see how it presents itself as a self-consciously moral narrative, exposing empires it narrates or embraces as inherently anxiety-ridden, fragile, made sure of themselves only by epics that will do more to expose their anxieties than assure them of their triumphalism. Empires have been at the mercy of the Persian epic far more than the Persian epic has been in need of their endorsements. "There has never been a document of culture," Walter Benjamin observes in "On the Concept of History" (1940), "which is not simultaneously one of barbarism."[4] All empires are conscious of this fact and by virtue of it conscious of their original sins. They know and they see their signs of civilization as rooted in barbarity. This fact gives empires a consciousness of their fragility, mortality, temporality. The *Shahnameh* is a document celebrating its own triumphant moral rectitude marking the barbarity of empires that have failed to heed its wisdom. For this very reason, all empires have come close to the *Shahnameh* at their own peril. They have seen its name and nomenclature and did not bother with its poetic text and moral imagination. The *Shahnameh* is a like a Trojan Horse, to borrow a metaphor from a different epical context. It has entered the citadel of imperial legitimacy only to discredit it.

While teaching the *Shahnameh* to students at Columbia University in the first decades of the twenty-first century, many times they drew comparisons with the epics of their own time, epics pertinent to the American empire. The HBO series *Game of Thrones*, for example, or even comic heroes like Batman or Spiderman would come to their minds. My students and I would occasionally wonder what would Shakespearean histories reveal about their time. Discussions of Shakespeare inevitably drew us to their cinematic adaptations, particularly those of the Japanese master Akira Kurosawa. On one such occasions I took David Quint's reference to Sergey Eisenstein's *Alexander Nevsky* (1938) toward the end of his book *Epic and Empire* at its face value and complicated it by adding to it three other archetypal cinematic epics that he does not consider, for his reference to Eisenstein's epic points to other examples of this genre and thus charts a more expansive frame of comparative reference. In cinematic epic, I told my students, we can detect at least three dominant paradigms of (1) projecting an epic narrative into an imminent *future* in John Ford's Westerns, (2) an expostulation of *foregone* empires in David Lean's cinema, and (3) the *archetypal* positing of imperial power and violence in Akira Kurosawa's cinema.[5] The advantage of this cinematic typology of epic narratives over Quint's, though instigated by his reference to *Alexander Nevsky*, is that it is far more universal, for it embraces three modes of epic narratives: about a fallen empire by a British filmmaker, about a rising empire by an American filmmaker, and then about the archetypal articulation of empire by a Japanese filmmaker. Between the three, Ford (future), Lean (past), and Kurosawa (archetypal) pretty much exhaust the cinematic modes of epic filmmaking, and all other epic filmmakers—from Sergey Eisenstein to Richard Attenborough, are subsumed under these three exemplary epic filmmakers. If we place Quint's reference to *Alexander Nevsky* in this context, his ahistorical and atypical reference becomes both historical and typified. Once we do that, time and space, temporality and location, are brought back to our reading of epics, the two critical factors that Eurocentric theorists categorically camouflage under their false universalization of their nativist limitations.

However anachronistic these may appear, these cinematic samples were drawing my students ever deeper into seeing aspects of the Persian epic and its contemporary worldly significance we had not explored (or even suspected) before. It now occurred to me that my students did not have any issue with such apparent "anachronism," because the time of the Persian epic was atemporal, its frames archetypal, its world omnipresent. The fusion of the mythic, heroic, and historical time/narrative spectrums of the *Shahnameh* had crafted its own textual temporality. This recognition, dare I say this discovery, came about only by allowing the text of the Persian epic to speak to the lived experiences of my students, coming from the four corners of the globe, neither Western nor Eastern in any artificial bifurcation of their poetic sensibilities, without painting the text they were reading "Oriental" or "Western" but by allowing its foreignness to become familiar through a temporal encounter with their own lived experiences. Such moments were revelatory. I was more of a student in these classes than teaching them. The text I was supposed to know and to teach to my students was now speaking to me in a different, unsuspected, powerful new language.

If we were to carry Quint's typology forward to more modern epics it would have the advantage of expanding the typology from the literary to also include the operatic. Quint's reference to Milton's *Paradise Lost* (1667) and *Paradise Regained* (1671) and his treatment of Eisenstein's *Alexander Nevsky* point to the comparative assessment of more modern epics. With Moretti's *Modern Epic*, we finally come to a systematic classification of such masterpieces as Goethe's *Faust*, Melville's *Moby-Dick*, Wagner's *Der Ring des Nibelungen* (1848–1874), Joyce's *Ulysses*, Ezra Pound's *The Cantos* (1922–1962), T. S. Eliot's *The Waste Land* (1922), Robert Musil's *The Man Without Qualities* (1930–1942), and even Márquez's *One Hundred Years of Solitude* (1967) as "modern epics," which Moretti defines as literary, poetic, and operatic master narratives that reflect the European domination of the planet, in which political will to power and literary will to formal inventiveness go together and reflect each other.

Why is it, we were now ready to ask, that Moretti included Márquez's *One Hundred Years of Solitude* in his Western epic narrative of "world system," when in fact it comes from a Latin American colonial site of resistance to that economic and cultural domination, and this is precisely the issue that exposes the principal fault line of his theory? Cast in his proverbial magic realist register, Márquez's novel does not corroborate but in fact dismantles the "world system." The chief feature of Moretti's theorization is that it is decidedly synchronic. The "world system" is a status quo whose hegemony he takes for granted as global, and therefore all his "modern epics" are diachronically deterritorialized and dehistoricized, both those that dominate and those that resist. They are taken out of their temporal and spatial habitat to be fed into a globalized "world system" that knows and recognizes no boundaries. The key distinction that is effaced here is the particular kind of abuse of labor by capital we call colonialism. This is where his inclusion of Márquez becomes the key factor in forcing Latin America into Moretti's Eurocentric imagination.

The timing of a narrative, epic or otherwise, is crucial in its structural-functional or subversive presence in an imperial order. The temporal and spatial location of an epic determines at what point and where it has served and where and when it has dismantled the legitimacy of an empire. Taking "the West" for the world at large and turning its particularity whimsically universal and thereafter ahistorically mapping it against a defiant world is where comparative literature has started on the wrong foot and perpetrated its epistemic violence against the very texture of world history. This is where the multilayered temporality of the *Shahnameh* (its mythic, heroic, and the historical times) will have to teach *world literature* a new meaning of worldliness.

The comparisons with more modern epics—literary or cinematic—revealed a crucial fact. Having its own innate temporality, the Persian epic cannot be simply assimilated backward into the existing Eurocentric conception of "World Literature" for the simple reason that the dominant theorists of that worldliness have so far failed to come close to the unique temporality and the multilayered unfolding worldliness of the *Shahnameh*. We cannot simply "extend" the existing idea of "World Literature" as dreamed in Goethe's or Damrosch's generous imagination chronologically and geographically to include the *Shahnameh*. That will do irreparable epistemic violence to the Persian epic. The inner dynamics of the *Shahnameh*'s worldliness and the polychronic temporality upon which it thrives will have to be navigated and understood first before we know why the theorists of "World Literature" as we know it now must go back to the drawing board.

THE TRAUMATIC UNCONSCIOUS
OF THE *SHAHNAMEH*

Framed in these comparative contexts, is Ferdowsi's *Shahnameh* an epic of conquest or an epic of the vanquished, a linear or an episodic narrative? Is it a Virgilian triumphalist narrative or a Lucanian epic of defeat? In cinematic terms, does Ferdowsi in the *Shahnameh* project a future empire, a promised land, the way John Ford does in his cinema, or reflect on a bygone age, the way David Lean offers in his films, or does he pause for a paradigmatic moment on the nature and disposition of power in the making of any empire, as Kurosawa does in his cinema? And then when it comes to the question of *modernity*—which for the colonized word spells out as *colonial modernity*—how does the modern reception of the *Shahnameh* in the course of the nineteenth to twentieth-first centuries reflect the position of Iran and Iranians in "the world system"?

The reason we are led to ask these questions is not because of the potential insights that we might have into the inner working of the *Shahnameh* in a thematically, narratively, generically, and theoretically comparative context. We ask these questions because the very idea of "World Literature" is stacked against anything other than the self-designated hegemony of the Western canon. We need to ask these questions given to the world by "World Literature" in order to draft a different worldliness for the very idea of *world literature* beyond the epistemic limitations and aging blind spots of the discipline. But the even more compelling reason for asking these questions is the fact that we have invariably considered the *Shahnameh* as a *national epic*—and the key term "national" inevitably places the Persian epic on a political plateau of power and postcolonial nation building, of the imperial expansionism and narrative primacy of "the West," of colonial conquest and anticolonial resistance, of the formal courage to defy that hegemony and the literary and poetic imagination that has sustained that courage. In other words, by asking these questions we are not doing damage to the formal or poetic provenance of the *Shahnameh*—we are in fact, in a global and contemporary imperial context (the context of the inner narrative logic of the *Shahnameh*), paying homage to it.

Ferdowsi's *Shahnameh* does follow a linear and teleological narrative, which makes it a Virgilian epic of conquest in David Quint's dichotomy, and yet it also offers deeply emotional and episodic narratives, as in the case of Rostam and Sohrab, or Seyavash and Sudabeh, or Rostam and Esfandiar, which Quint would call an epic of the vanquished. Obviously, instead of cutting the *Shahnameh* to pieces to fit Quint's typology, we are better off overriding and expanding his dichotomy to accommodate the *Shahnameh*. The *Shahnameh* is linear, but that linearity is punctuated on a temporal spectrum ranging from the mythic to heroic to historical—namely, along three distinctly different temporal registers. The *Shahnameh* is episodic, too, but through poetic implosions of deeply dramatic stories that give renewed significance to that linearity. Ferdowsi does not follow Quint's dichotomy. The *Shahnameh* decidedly dismantles it.

The easiest and standard way of reading through this fusion of linearity and episodic epic is to consider Ferdowsi's composition of the *Shahnameh* as an expression of Iranian imperial consciousness at a time that these legacies were in fact threatened and compromised by the Arab conquest of Iran—part and parcel, in fact, of the Shu'ubiyyah movement, a literary movement associated mostly with non-Arab communities of the Arab empires. This reading, which dovetails with the coincidence of the composition of the *Shahnameh* with the Shu'ubiyyah movement, is not altogether false, although it does tend to overdetermine the text at the expense of its poetic and literary open-endedness. Even in its historical context one must think of the *Shahnameh* in the imperial occasion of the emerging eastern dynasties of the Samanids and the Ghaznavids rather than in the anachronistic "national" context of our current history—the way that it has been framed within the postcolonial nation-state formation, particularly during the Pahlavi dynasty. But more important, this reading subjects the poetic proclivity of the epic to its imperial context, while I wish to argue the exact opposite of that assumption.

Turning more toward the poetic presence of the text itself rather than its imperial context, my overriding argument is that Ferdowsi's sense of tragedy dwells in a staged drama that is embedded in an ultimately tragic sense of history—remembering the past in the heat of an urgent present. The tragic sense of the *Shahnameh*, I wish to argue, resides in the paradox of telling an epic of the world conquerors in the language of doomed heroism, at the time of imperial victory remembering the fate of doomed defeat, and as such its tragic trauma is founded on a fundamental Shi'i sense of history, perhaps by virtue of its Shi'i poet, and which in turn makes of Shi'ism a tragedy rooted in a *Shahnameh* leitmotif. *This fractured narrative fissure*, we might therefore suggest, betrays the *traumatic unconscious* of the text and is what ultimately holds the *Shahnameh* poetically together as a singularly creative work of art, the product of one creatively conscious poetic act. This *traumatic unconscious* and the fractured narrative fissure that betrays it I place somewhere near Freud's *psychoanalytic unconscious*, Jung's *collective unconscious*, and a fortiori and in particular Lacan's *linguistic unconscious*, by which he suggests that the unconscious is structured like a language. If I were to appropriate the inner working of this Lacanian linguistic unconscious—its fractured narrative fissure—I could see how it corresponds to the traumatic unconscious of the *Shahnameh*.

How could the *Shahnameh*, as a literary text, you may wonder, have any kind of *unconscious*—even linguistic? If, as Umberto Eco suggests, a text (like the *Shahnameh*) has an intention (Latin *intentio*)—just like its author (Ferdowsi) and its varied readers (us), then just like its author and readers, the intention of the text has an unconscious too, and that *traumatic unconscious*, conditioned by recollecting the moment of moral defeat at the time of political triumph, is definitive to the enduring significance of the Persian epic. The triumphant rise of Persianate empires with the Persian language as the lingua franca of these empires all the way from the Saffarids and the Samanids in Central Asia to the Mughals in India renders that *traumatic unconscious* entirely paradoxical and yet definitive to the decentered subject formation at the heart of Persian literary humanism.[6] Ferdowsi's *Shahnameh* partakes in and contributes to that defining force field of Persian literary humanism and thereby places the poetic disposition of the text itself over and above any empire that may use or abuse it. I therefore propose a categorical distinction between the symbolic significance of the *Shahnameh* as an epic lending empires the legitimacy they seek and its substantive content that effectively questions and dismantles that very legitimacy. The result is a superior poetic consciousness to the text that is upstream from any and all its political abuses, whether imperial or dynastic, classical or contemporary. The *Shahnameh* is a living organism. It lacks any and all dead certainties. It teaches uncertainty, fragility, vulnerability. Everything and anything that an empire projects and quintessentially lacks, the *Shahnameh* celebrates.

Reflecting this *traumatic unconscious*, Ferdowsi's *Shahnameh* works through the inner paradox of a self-referential epic, where every political triumph is ipso facto a moral defeat—the triumph of Rostam over Sohrab, the triumph of Rostam over Esfandiar, the triumph of Seyavash over the false accusations of Sudabeh. There is quite obviously something also Shi'i about this sense of tragic paradox, as indeed there is something of the inner sense of paradox of the *Shahnameh* evident in Shi'ism. There is thus something intimate connecting the Shi'i author to the epic texture of his *Shahnameh*. In reflecting this traumatic unconscious, the *Shahnameh* can ultimately be read as a Shi'i epic by virtue of its Shi'i author, or, conversely, Shi'ism in its entirety might be considered a story of the *Shahnameh* run historically wide into a world religion, by virtue of the antiquity of the origin of the *Shahnameh* over the more recent historicity of Shi'ism. These questions become even more compelling if we were to add such epics as *Ali-nameh* and *Khavaran-nameh* to the *Shahnameh* and wonder if these are all variations on the theme of Shi'i traumatic origin, or are these epic narratives of the first Shi'i Imam, and along with them Shi'ism itself, a narrative take on the *Shahnameh* that historically took flight and went its own way? Ultimately we will have to abandon these open-ended questions for the simple conclusion that the worldliness of the *Shahnameh* text has had more than just one narrative take. The point here is the coincidence, however we may opt to read that coincidence, between the *Shahnameh* and Shi'ism as two symmetrical modes of operation on the theme of a *traumatic unconscious* that triumphs at the moment of its defeat and is defeated at the moment of its triumph.

Ferdowsi's sense of epic—challenging the imperial triumphalism of any dynasty that seeks its endorsement by anticipating its poetic demise—is also evident in his cinematic techniques, if we were to use this anachronistic term and read the *Shahnameh* as if we were watching a film. While Eisenstein's *Alexander Nevsky* should be placed next to D. W. Griffith's *The Birth of a Nation* (1915) as a myth of national origin,

Ferdowsi's *Shahnameh* is more comparable to the triad of Ford, Lean, and Kurosawa as three modern epic filmmakers. What we witness in the *Shahnameh* is an ocularcentric intelligence and narrative technique that in cinematic terms mixes Ford's triumphant narrative with Lean's defeatist nostalgia in order to reach for the closest Iranian epic similitude to Kurosawa's archetypal epic narrative—because, one is now in a position to speculate, the centrality of the trauma of Hiroshima for Kurosawa is the sense of tragic futility at the heart of Ferdowsi's epic.

To demonstrate this point, we can compare two exemplary scenes from Ferdowsi's story of "Rostam and Sohrab" and Kurosawa's film *Ran* (1985). In this example we might compare the function of the (five-minutes, forty-second) *melodic implosion* in the central scene of *Ran* when the warlord Hidetora Ichimonji's children are murdering their father with the almost identical function of the (eight hemistich) *poetic implosion* in the central traumatic scene of "Rostam and Sohrab" when Rostam is about to kill his own son.

Jahana shegefti zeh kerdar tost . . .

Oh world your deeds are indeed strange,
Crooked and correct are both your ways.
In neither the father nor in the son did kindness rise,
Reason was absent, kindness concealed.
Even animals recognize their own children,
Whether the fish in the sea or onager in the field.
But from arrogance and ambition
Man cannot tell foe from a son.[7]

The central narrative trauma of the *Shahnameh* is its moral memory of a tragic end to any imperial act of triumphalism—just before the text itself is appropriated as the insignia of imperial triumphalism of a new dynasty. This act of remembrance, at once triumphant and defeatist, exuberant and tragic, eventually becomes the most cogent constitution of the very subtext of the *Shahnameh* as an epic. That destiny is made precisely at the moment when it is interrupted. That central sense of tragedy becomes definitive to the archetypal modus operandi of the *Shahnameh* as a self-conscious epic, precisely the same way that Kurosawa's cinema thrives on the traumatic birth of a nation at the moment of its near annihilation in Hiroshima and Nagasaki.

EPICS OVER EMPIRES

The *Shahnameh* as an epic has historically expanded in meaning and gained renewed significance as empires that had sought its power of persuasion have fallen and faded from historical memory. Who today other than erudite historians know or care to remember the Samanids, the Ghaznavids, the Mongols, or any other empire? But we keep reading the *Shahnameh* with newfound awe, inspiration, and delight. The entire logic and rhetoric of the *Shahnameh* are in fact predicated on the primacy of epic narrative overcoming the imperial power it once lent a helping hand locating in history. The *Shahnameh* tells the story of the mythic origin of humanity, of bygone heroic ages, and of the historical rise and fall of empires. It celebrates their rise, it mourns their fall, it reads and teaches their history—as it all the while enriches its own poetics of epic narrative. As the *Shahnameh* was used and abused to justify Persianate empires, Ferdowsi was building a dramatic bridge with his readers across time and space. I believe precisely the opposite view of David Quint in his *Epic and Empire* to be true: epics are not at the service of empires, celebrating or mourning them. Empires are at the service of epics, offering them dramatic events in myth and history to better tell their stories. The same I would propose about Franco Moretti: modern epics are not an expression of "the world system"; quite to the contrary they are the literary signs of resisting and dismantling it. The *Shahnameh* is the living testimony of both cases, an epic of multivalent perspectives contingent on the narrative angle it enables and overcomes. It is, as such, a living vindication of how epic narratives trump and triumph over the vacuous theorization of "the West" as imperially triumphant.

Love, desire, heteronormative passion, the effervescence of yearning
for another body to have, to hold, and to possess: in the story of Bizhan
and Manizheh and other similar *Shahnameh* romances we witness the
eruption of the repressed sexuality and subversive eroticism of Seyavash
and his stepmother, Sudabeh, or of Esfandiar and his mother, Katayoun,
as these episodes lend renewed significance to the love stories of Rostam and Tahmineh, Zal and Rudabeh, and thus poetically turns to
signal and unleash the imperial repression of desire into heroism. In
these stories we witness the rebellious urges of desire subverting the
imperial austerity of power. The more we move from the mythical to
the heroic phase and approach the moment when the turn to historical
is complete, history itself becomes the salvation of myth and eroticism
the defining moment of heroes. History is therefore a delivery, a deliver-
ance, a promised land, a destiny, and the *Shahnameh* an epic of defiance,
and not of triumph or defeat. Just like Shi'ism, it is an epic of protest and
defiance. It does not mourn defeat. It does not celebrate victory. It
absorbs and defies empires, turns them into stories, and keeps history
expectant of something else to come.

If we were to read the *Shahnameh*, as I suggest, as *an epic of defiance*
then its enduring significance within and beyond multiple empires
speaks of a confident truth that absorbs the political power of those
empires to posit a normative epic before and beyond empires. The epic
power of the *Shahnameh* therefore raises the political into the poetic,
sublates the personal into the mythic, transforms the historic into the
legendary. That narrative moment of defiance remains definitive to the
Persian epic beyond the political vagaries that have laid false claims on
it. As those empires, from the Ghaznavids forward, have abused the
Shahnameh for their own benefit, the *Shahnameh* has used them to
sustain its historic references to the worldly character of its aesthetic
sublimity. This very defiant trajectory of the Persian epic is also the
very reason for its enduring significance long after all those empires
have been laid to rest and postcolonial nations have emerged on their
premises to find renewed meaning in Ferdowsi's masterpiece.

As an epic, the *Shahnameh* breaks through an imperial *totality*
(a closed political system) and opens up into a poetic *infinity* (on an

unfolding symbolic register). It has survived through the thick and thin of successive empires and then weathered the postcolonial fates of nation-states not just by helping them to declare a momentary and passing claim to the anteriority of bygone ages but also in fact guiding them to find their ways into the interiority of an emergent morality always embedded in its own poetics. The *Shahnameh* stories are open-ended, internally related, textually self-referential. They are not closed in the circuitous claim of any literary masterpiece that is canonized for a dubious political purpose here or an imperial lineage there. How can peace be ascertained against the certainty of wars, the poetics of living against the politics of death? Empires and the nations they hold have endured more wars than enjoyed peace. But Levinas's warning is of a different vintage: "Such a certitude is not obtained by a simple play of antithesis. The peace of empires issued from war rests on war." It will not last and it therefore cannot sustain any enduring sense of unfolding being, of being poetically in the world. For that unfolding being to sustain itself, the humans that epics enable must rely on the emotive interiority of the poetic event itself. "It [the peace of empires] does not restore to the alienated beings their lost identity. For that a primordial and original relation with being is needed."[8] How is that "primordial and original relation with being" possible except through the meandering wonders of a poetic text rooted in time immemorial and unfolded in all bygone ages? The *Shahnameh* is the poetic delivery of itself. It is an *infinity* placed in history, through its playful and evocative distribution of time into the mythic, the heroic, and above all the historical.

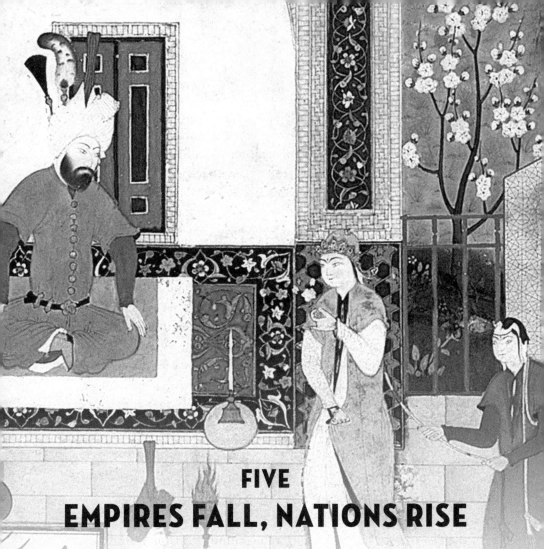

FIVE
EMPIRES FALL, NATIONS RISE

Zani bud bar san-e gordi savar . . .

There was a chivalrous woman brave and bold,
Habitually victorious in battlefields,
Her name was Gordafarid
Fate has never seen a valiant like her,

. . .

She put her battlefield armor on,
For there was no time left to waste,
She hid her long hair under her cuirass,
Putting it with a Roman knot under her helmet.

As Sohrab marches toward Iran to defeat Key Kavous, find his father, Rostam, and place him on the throne, the archenemy of Iran, Afrasiab, the emperor of Turan, hears of the young hero's approach and mobilizes an army and puts it at his disposal. Afrasiab warns his trusted generals, however, that Sohrab and Rostam must never recognize each other, otherwise his fate as the supreme Turanian monarch is doomed. As Sohrab proceeds at the head of this mighty army toward Iran he reaches the Sepid Dezh fortress. A local warlord named Gazhdaham was in charge of that fortress, and while his son Gostaham was too young to fight, his daughter Gordafarid was ready and willing. Initially a warrior named Hujir charges against Sohrab but is defeated and captured. Gordafarid, the valiant daughter of Gazhdaham, hears the news of this defeat and gets angry at Hujir, puts her armor on, and hides her hair under her helmet. Gordafarid and Sohrab engage in a fierce battle. Sohrab finally defeats Gordafarid, but she uses her charm and beauty, deceives Sohrab, and returns to the fortress. Gazhdaham writes to Key Kavous and asks for help, and the Persian monarch in turn dispatches Rostam to fight Sohrab.

REREADING THE PERSIAN EPIC

The *Shahnameh* has had a long and continuing history, from its very inception in an imperial age to its canonization well into our postcolonial history. In the aftermath of the collapse of the last three Muslim empires (the Mughals, the Safavids, and the Ottomans) and the rise of postcolonial nation-states it has been used and abused in the making of fragile state legitimacies. The trauma of nation building through the heat of European colonial domination could not have left the Persian epic intact. Perhaps the most blatant political use of the *Shahnameh* was staged when in 1934 the first Pahlavi monarch, Reza Shah (r. 1925–1941), hosted a major millennial celebration of Ferdowsi's *Shahnameh* soon after he ascended the throne. The Persian epic was thus put to use for the newly established dynasty seeking to overcome the revolutionary upheaval of the constitutional period (1906–1911), the collapse of the Qajar dynasty (1789–1924), and the chaos of the recently occupied Iran, seeking to link Reza Shah's reign to ancient Persian empires. The Persian epic thus began its prolonged history of aggressive transformation from an epic of successive empires to the classical text of a tug-of-war between the national sovereignty of a people and their historic battles with the abusive powers of the states that laid false claim on them. As the state commenced its militant appropriation of the Persian epic so did contemporary poets and literati begin appropriating the *Shahnameh* and its heroes for their own oppositional and militant purposes. Ferdowsi's text was pulled and pushed from one side to another.

Poets like Mehdi Akhavan-e Sales and Seyavash Kasra'i, novelists like Simin Daneshvar and Sadegh Chubak, and scholars like Mehrdad Bahar and Shahrokh Meskoub soon emerged as leading public intellectuals appropriating the figures of the *Shahnameh* for their own respective political causes. Heroes such as Kaveh the Blacksmith became proverbial to a new generation of the Iranian left appropriating his rebellion against an unjust king to their own political purposes. The accidental death of Sohrab at the hands of his father or the treacheries of Key Kavous against his son Seyavash were now read as signs of generational gaps and hostilities of the old and the new. This was all done under the pressing conditions of the fateful encounter of the Persianate world from India to Central Asia to Iran with European colonialism directly affecting the narrative cohesion of the *Shahnameh* from mythic to heroic to historical. It is upon that traumatic experience that we need to rethink the parameters of what it means today to place the *Shahnameh* in the domain of "World Literature," as it is understood by mostly European and U.S. literary scholars. The critical task today is to defamiliarize the *Shahnameh* in a manner that people (Persian speaking or otherwise) will want to go back to the original and read it again as a historical document organically linked to a tumultuous history. In any such attempt we are bound to raise more questions than answers. Here I would of course try to disentangle the Persian epic from its various ideological abuses, but even beyond that I am determined to retrieve a literary inroad back to the original epic.

THE WORLDINGS OF THE *SHAHNAMEH*

The *Shahnameh* has moved from being the singularly symbolic epic of successive Persianate empires to an epic claimed by postcolonial nation-states, chief among them Iran. The empires that have laid claim to the Persian epic, from the Samanids all the way down to the Safavids, have included territories that are now divided among multiple nation-states, each of which has a legitimate claim on the Persian text, with Iran, Afghanistan, and Tajikistan as the epicenter of the Samanid and Ghaznavid Empires that witnessed the initial composition of Ferdowsi's towering text. Be that as it is, from India to Turkey—namely, from the Mughal Empire, through the Safavids and its successors, down to the Ottoman Empire—all have a legitimate claim on the Persian epic. To reworld the *Shahnameh*, to place it in its existing world, we need to pay particular attention to the ways in which it has been deworlded, used and abused in the context of colonial modernity.

To look at the *Shahnameh* as a "modern epic," as an epic that has reached to inform postcolonial nations in their encounters with European colonial modernity, we need to consider three interrelated factors: (1) how the fate of the Shah Tahmasp *Shahnameh* became emblematic, (2) how the Pahlavi celebration of the Persian epic for its state-building project and after that dynasty even the Islamic Republic reflected the postimperial fate of the Persian epic, and (3) how poets like Mehdi Akhavan-e Sales and Seyavash Kasra'i, or scholars like Shahrokh Meskoub, or the preparation of critical editions by Djalal Khaleghi-Motlagh and others have come together to locate the text at the center of a national consciousness. We need to do so in order to see how the *Shahnameh* has moved from an imperial epic into a postcolonial allegory.

Before we consider these factors we must first remember how the *Shahnameh* was preserved, literally, in the course of its long imperial history. First and foremost, it was preserved through royal patronage, copying and illustrating, and calligraphy, and giving it as political gift. It was equally preserved via popular painting and reciting. The emulations of Ferdowsi's masterpiece by aspiring poets were equally instrumental in preserving it for posterity, as were various selections in subsequent generations, as well as citations in biographical dictionaries and books on poetry.

FRAGMENTS AS ALLEGORIES

The story of the *Shahnameh* as a "modern epic" is epitomized in the fate of the Shah Tahmasp *Shahnameh* and its dismemberment (literally) as an imperial text into colonial and postcolonial state-building projects.[1] As I indicated in some detail in the previous chapter, the destruction of this precious copy of the *Shahnameh* is a perfect allegory of what has been the postcolonial fate of the Persian epic. The text of this *Shahnameh* was given as a royal gift from a Safavid to an Ottoman emperor. Its destruction and dismemberment by forces of greed and disrespect for anything inherently and in its totality priceless is the story of the epic itself and its manhandling by political forces of one persuasion or its opposite.

The Pahlavi dynasty subjected the Persian epic to monarchical state building by overinterpreting its content to its own advantage, while the Islamic Republic that succeeded it did the same abuse to the text by the over-Shi'ification of its author. Meanwhile, leading oppositional poets like Mehdi Akhavan-e Sales and Seyavash Kasra'i put the Persian text to exactly the opposite use of turning it against tyranny. Either way, the *Shahnameh* was turned into an allegory, bereft of its own power and prudence. Meanwhile, learned *Shahnameh* scholars began preparing erudite critical editions of it, which inevitably resulted in its systemic fetishization beyond its imperial poetic habitat. The Iranian diasporic communities soon joined forces and appropriated the text for their desperate identity politics—the best example of which are the expensive and luxurious editions of the text as published by Mage Publications in Washington, D.C., which had originally commissioned a new translation by the learned British poet Dick Davis. Another contemporary artist based in the United States, Hamid Rahmanian, updated that appropriation for a younger generation by preparing a new translation by Ahmad Sadri and adding to its state-of-the-art internet-facilitated collages. Financed by rich expatriate benefactors, Cambridge University established a whole center for the study of the *Shahnameh*.

Against this background, the prominent *Shahnameh* scholar Mahmoud Omidsalar published deeply informed polemical monographs on the book,[2] while "oral formulaic" theorists abused the Persian epic for their own whimsical reasons. Art historians began to pay exclusive attention to the various aesthetic qualities of the paintings that accompanied old manuscripts, almost entirely independent of the substance of the epic. Art dealers were of course not to be disregarded, for they too began to partake in the lucrative market of selling torn-out folios from old manuscripts. Private collectors prided themselves on possessing such copies, while museums competed to have more copies than any private collector. Encyclopedia entries about the author and the text of the *Shahnameh* soon began to appear, as well as learned essays in academic journals examining the minutiae of the epic. The fragmented fate of the Shah Tahmasp *Shahnameh* becomes emblematic of its postcolonial allegorization in ever more fragmented context, and thus paradoxically the *Shahnameh* went back to the state that it was in before Ferdowsi had started collecting and putting it into a singular poetic narrative, though this time in fact worse for now the Persian epic was both there and not there, ever evident in fetishized form, emptied of its ennobling aura and myth.

ABUSING AN EPIC FOR AND AGAINST THE RULING STATE

Memories of old empires have animated the postcolonial state formations that have laid a false and falsifying claim on the *Shahnameh*, dragging it deeply into their limited political imagination. In this transition the tumultuous seas of bygone empires are being poured into the tight torrents of postcolonial nation-states—and no postcolonial state has represented this abuse better than the Pahlavi dynasty (1926–1979) and its systemic epistemic violence against the *Shahnameh*. The Pahlavis were of course not the only perpetrators of this violence. While during the Pahlavi dynasty it was heavily abused to lend legitimacy to a discredited monarchy, during the Islamic Republic that succeeded it, it has been officially ignored, or overtly Shi'ified by virtue of its Shi'i author, or sought to be compromised by the recently discovered manuscript of *Ali-nameh*, an epic composed almost at the same time as the *Shahnameh* about the first Shi'i Imam. At the center of all these ideological abuses has remained the text of the *Shahnameh* itself. As Iran and its neighboring countries have entered the colonial and postcolonial stages of their encounter with European modernity, so has the *Shahnameh* been dragged left and right to sing and dance to melodies not its own.

Not just the violent forces of state building over the past two centuries but also even forces hostile and opposed to it—all the way from the Qajars to the Islamic Republic—have resorted to the *Shahnameh*, abusing the Persian epic for their own anti-Qajar, anti-Pahlavi, or anti–Islamic Republic rhetoric. The *Shahnameh* has thus been pulled and pushed by multiple political forces all categorically oblivious or indifferent to the inner logic and rhetoric of a primarily poetic text. In all these cases what is ignored, disregarded, and distorted is the text itself, its poetic logic and rhetoric, its aesthetic power and literary audacity. In this environment, the perfectly competent and lucid English translation by recent scholar-poets like Dick Davis and Ahmad Sadri are assimilated backward into a fetishized antiquarian interest in "Persian heritage" integral to an iconography of exilic identity politics. The epic poem is here overfetishized, hypernationalized into lucrative, oversized coffee-table publications useful mostly as a centerpiece of the expatriate Iranian diaspora for gatherings—burying deeply the gems that are thus decorating someone's living room. There are of course exceptionally learned pieces of scholarship in both Persian and English dealing with various minutiae of the Persian epic. But the general contour of such scholarship is framed within a nostalgic remembrance of bygone empires, now falsely finagled to be assimilated forward to a "national heritage." Over the past two centuries, the *Shahnameh* has been the epicenter of such systematic abuses. Gaudy internet-based vanity shows based mostly in Los Angeles—invariably featuring a verbose, vulgar dilettante staring into a bewildered camera—are the depth of this depravity.

The origin of all such political abuses might be traced back to the earliest generations of Orientalist-colonialist encounters with the *Shahnameh*. By the late nineteenth century, the *Shahnameh* had become the focus of the attention of leading European Orientalists in Germany, Italy, the United Kingdom, France, and elsewhere in Europe. The publication of Matthew Arnold's "Sohrab and Rustum" (1853) might be considered the epicenter of this age of European attraction to the Persian epic.[3] It is important here to keep in mind that the European reception of the *Shahnameh* extended well into its colonial dimensions, as, for example, when the Persian epic was published in India, with the same anti-Arab sentiments rooted in European racialized modernity, or during World War II, it was abused by the Allied forces in a series of propaganda postcards.[4] The title of the *Shahnameh* in one of its earliest editions published in Calcutta (1811) reads as follows: "The SHAH NAMU, being a series of HEROIC POEMS on the ancient HISTORY OF PERSIA from the earliest times down to the subjugation of the Persian Empire by its MOHUMMADAN CONQUERERS under the reign of KING YUZ-DIRD."[5] The origin of such a racialized reception of the Persian epic was of course Europe, where literary critics like Charles Augustin Sainte-Beuve (1804–1869) were totally enamored of Ferdowsi's masterpiece: "If we could realize that great works such as the *Shahnameh* exist in the world, we would not become so much proud of our own works in such a silly manner."[6] From this colonial context of racialized identities, and at the threshold of the constitutional revolution of 1906–1911, a strong ethnonationalism emerged rooted in a deeply flawed reading of Ferdowsi's masterpiece.

In the course of the twentieth century, following this colonial pretext, both Pahlavi monarchs (1926–1979) had sought to appropriate the *Shahnameh* as the epic narrative of Persian monarchy to which they had now laid a dynastic claim, hoping that it would provide the ideological foregrounding of their short-lived house. For the Pahlavis and their project of monarchic nationalism, Ferdowsi's *Shahnameh* became a key poetic text in their ideological project of state building, with monarchy as the definitive institution and defining moment of that nationalist modernity. Reza Shah had decidedly modeled his persona and monarchy on pre-Islamic Persianate legacies. By 1934 he was constructing a mausoleum over the grave site of Ferdowsi in Tus. He made a recognition of Ferdowsi's epic a bedrock for his "modernization" ambitions. Leading Iranian scholars of his time were encouraging Reza Shah to honor Ferdowsi and publicly celebrate him. The monthlong millenary celebrations he decreed were launched in 1934. "The main thrust of the millenary celebration . . . was the gathering of some 100 distinguished scholars and dignitaries in Tehran and Mashhad for a conference that would be responsible for the flourishing of Iranian studies in general and for research on Ferdowsi and the *Shahnameh* in particular."[7]

At the height of the reign of the second Pahlavi monarch, Mohammad Reza Pahlavi (1941–1979), and soon after the 1971 celebration of the two thousand five hundredth anniversary of Persian monarchy, an annual lecture series was established on Ferdowsi at Mashhad University. These and similar celebrations of Ferdowsi's *Shahnameh* by the Pahlavi monarchy marked the widespread institutional project of a political apparatus to assimilate the Persian epic into its anxiety-ridden legitimacy consciousness. Much of the nationalistic scholarship of the Pahlavi period has its origin in this inaugural moment. As Ali Ahmadi Motlagh rightly argues, the most important result of such celebrations was the "re-entry of Iran into the global community as a tenable, sovereign nation-state that by virtue of having a national epic could be considered a culturally legitimate civilization. This latter motif can also be detected in the 1990 celebrations of Ferdowsi as Iran attempted to rebuild its image and pick up the pieces after a brutal 8-year war with Iraq." But long before that war, and still at the time of the Pahlavis, in the words of the program leaflet handed out during the millennium celebrations of Ferdowsi at the School of Oriental and African Studies in London in October 1934, "Ferdowsi . . . gave to Persia what Homer gave to Greece and Virgil to Rome, an epic that not only perpetuates the tradition of her ancient greatness, but makes a universal appeal to the spirits of man . . . Firdausi's *Shahnameh* consecrated their heroic past and voiced their national pride. A thousand years later, Persia, resuming her place in the family of nations, salutes his memory as the earliest precursor of her renaissance."[8] Ferdowsi's epic was by now a cornerstone of nation building for the Pahlavi monarchy.

The oppositional forces to the Pahlavi regime were of course not to be left out of this battle for the soul of Ferdowsi. The leftist intellectuals soon realized the symbolic significance of the Persian epic and sought to appropriate it to their advantage. Late in the nineteenth century, and in the wake of the constitutional revolution of 1906–1911, Mirza Aqa Kermani (1854–1897) wrote his *Nameh-ye Bastan* (The book of antiquity) as a conscious imitation of the *Shahnameh*. This tradition remained constant with other critical thinkers throughout the Qajar and Pahlavi monarchies. Opposing the Pahlavi monarchy, leftist literati, poets, and scholars like Abolqasem Lahuti, Abd al-Hossein Nushin, Bozorg Alavi, and F. M. Javanshir (pseudonym of Farajollah Mizani) had their own take on the Persian epic, seeking, for example, to appropriate the story of Kaveh the Blacksmith for their own (however legitimate) political purposes. "Leftist readings of the *Shahnameh*," as Ali Ahmadi Motlagh rightly puts it, "gravitated towards depictions of the plight of the proletariat, most significantly manifested in the story of Kaveh and Zahhak, whose resolution involves an uprising by the people under the banner of a blacksmith."[9] There were of course plenty of royal injustices in the *Shahnameh* to lend support to such abusive readings. The Persian epic was being manhandled decidedly to meet the political ends of the time—in one way or another.

Later the ruling regime of the Islamic Republic sought to appropriate this leftist proclivity and carve Ferdowsi's poetry to its own size and measures. Soon after the end of the Iran-Iraq War (1980–1988), in 1990, the state organized a major conference to commemorate the millenary of the composition of the *Shahnameh*. The Islamic theocracy sought to up the ante against the background of the 1934 conference of the Reza Shah period. As Ali Ahmadi Motlagh sums up the event, "Going simply by the numbers, it blew away the 1934 millenary conference. No less than 104 papers, out of 270 candidates, papers were delivered by more than 120 people from 23 countries alongside who [*sic*] joined 170 scholars from Iran." Tehran University was the host of the international gathering. In welcoming remarks, the *Shahnameh* was suggested to have been inspired by the Qur'an, its author a devout Shi'a.[10] the Islamic Republic was now actively competing with the monarchy it had toppled in claiming Ferdowsi and his *Shahnameh*.

For millions of Iranians leaving their homeland for a life abroad the *Shahnameh* was not to be entirely irrelevant either. They soon began to abuse the Persian epic for their own political purposes in opposition to the Islamic Republic. They began featuring it as part of their wedding ceremonies, substituting it for the Qur'an. "What is most significant about the reception of Ferdowsi among the Iranian community in exile," Ali Ahmadi Motlagh suggests, "is an overriding anxiety that has naturally resulted from the limbo of being an outsider in both one's original and one's adopted society."[11] Soon a second and third generation of Iranian-Americans emerged who now sought to have a reappraisal of what their parents had told them was a significant text. Some of these younger Iranians ended up at Columbia University taking my course on the *Shahnameh*. In the first few sessions of our course, I had to compete with the extended shadow of their fathers and grandfathers as to what the *Shahnameh* was and what it signified.

THE *SHAHNAMEH* AS METAPHOR

Appropriation of the text of the *Shahnameh* or the figure of Ferdowsi as an insignia of cultural modernity (on a European prototype) or, alternatively, literary nationalism was not limited to the political domain, but political purposes certainly conditioned and facilitated them. The writing of learned essays, encyclopedic entries, literary historiographies, and above all the preparation of a critical edition of the *Shahnameh* based on all the extant manuscripts became the defining moment of scholarly "modernity" and literary nationalism, a practice that European Orientalism proper extended to the realm of Persian studies from the domain of European classics, but which the Iranian scholarly literati picked up in the twentieth century and pushed forward with an abiding sense of national pride and even prejudice. Iranian scholars of the *Shahnameh* outperformed their Orientalist predecessors in collecting even more scattered manuscripts, collated and compared them even more diligently, and sought to prepare a critical edition that surpassed anything that had been done by Europeans before. Preparing the most accurate text of the *Shahnameh* thus emerged as the modus operandi of a scholarly pride that in and of itself laid the claims of "modernity" on the *Shahnameh*. The Persian epic was "modern," or more accurately became "modern," because modern textual criticism was so diligently applied to it.[12] Preparing a critical edition of the *Shahnameh*, previously done by Russian or French scholars, was now integral to Iranian literary nationalism, with or without a formal state sponsorship.

From the political to the literary, from the scholarly to the hermeneutic, the *Shahnameh* emerged more than any other text as the locus classicus and the master signifier of Iranian claims to state-sponsored, Eurocentric, "modernity," or, alternatively, to militant Islamism. The *Shahnameh* was the subject of learned conferences and symposia, printed and illustrated, narrated and recited, staged and filmed, glossed and annotated, critically edited and taught at all levels of school, high school, and college curricula. The *Shahnameh* became the primary poetic disposition of a nationalist modernity, integral to the machinery of making modern subjects suitable for a modern nation-state, with a prolonged monarchical history and character. If the Pahlavis emphasized the monarchic traits of the text, the Islamic Republic celebrated the Shi'i identity of its author. Reading the *Shahnameh* was thus trapped inside two diametrically juxtaposed hermeneutic circles, pulled and pushed to serve the ideological agenda of two opposing states. Predicated on both these abuses, and when it comes to the treatment of the *Shahnameh* over the past century, we witness a fundamental failure of a monarchic adaptation of the *Shahnameh* under the Pahlavis as the modus operandi of their legitimacy, as indeed their refusal to be co-opted by the triumphant Shi'ism of an Islamic Republic that is at odds with their own epistemic paradox.

That paradox has a wider frame of reference, far beyond any national space or political territoriality. Allow me to share a more specific example that may clarify this point further. My habitual joy at teaching my own children the *Shahnameh* stories has taught me a much different location for when the Persian epic comes alive with unpredictable zest and energy. Once I took a children's version of the *Shahnameh* written in simple English prose to Jamaica while vacationing with my younger children Chelgis and Golchin. They were still in elementary school and reading these stories of the *Shahnameh* and summarizing them in an "illustrated manuscript," as it were, we made as part of their summer activities. They soon began reading the stories of the *Shahnameh*, discussing them between themselves, acting them out, writing summaries of the stories in their own handwriting in their notebooks, and illustrating each story with their crayons. As I watched them learn and illustrate the *Shahnameh*, it occurred to me that today as we read the Persian epic the book is no longer even related to the domain of original intentions and destinations and certainly beyond being either triumphalist or defeatist. It operates in an entirely different register and therefore resonates in uncharted territories. It is, at this point, an epic of ennobling loss. I was conscious of teaching my children something on a Caribbean island that no longer was, had nothing to do with their material surroundings as American children born to immigrant parents, and yet did so without any sense of regret. I did so with a sense of achieving something for them ennobling in having been forever lost, letting them partake in the dramatic relics of something fleeting, something allegorically historical but effectively poetic beyond their adopted homeland where they were born and being raised. That contemporary "reception" of the *Shahnameh* among ordinary Iranians in and out of their homeland, teaching the Persian epic to future generations, is as relevant as when it is used and abused for or against any ruling state ideology. The *Shahnameh* has entered a transnational public sphere far beyond the control or even intentions of state building.

The three atemporal components of the *Shahnameh*, I remember thinking to myself as my children took a break from drawing Rostam and his Rakhsh and went swimming in the pool, have by now become almost entirely allegorical. The mythic, heroic, and the historical are now all fused together. We no longer care to remember where or when one ends and others begin. It seems to me that it is that sense of ennobling loss and nostalgia, embedded in the tragic totality of the epic, that is now definitive to the very idea of "homeland" even (or particularly) when you are in it. We have all become deeply textual, literary, in our sense of the tragic loss that has been coterminous with our notion of "nationhood," so far as the *Shahnameh* has had anything to do with that sense of a homeland. Iran is therefore a floating signifier, a mere allegory for what we think once was but in effect could never have been, for the poetics of its allusions rooted in the Persian epic undercuts its historicity. No state, no ideology, no political movement could ever have control over that interface between the *Shahnameh* and its readers. What was the *Shahnameh* to my children on that Caribbean island, or to any other children born to parents who have known, loved, and cherished the *Shahnameh*, children being born and raised in New York, going to public schools with other children mostly from Latin-American or African-American heritage? What were Rostam and Tahmineh to them or they to those bygone heroes? How could they have related even to their own, *Shahnameh*-inspired, names, beyond the allegorical relics of a homeland, rooted in textual evidence, reminiscent of a distant epic of a bygone age neither they nor their parents could ever completely fathom? Here, the *Shahnameh* had become a metaphor, far beyond its own subconscious.

At home or abroad, in Persian or any other language, the *Shahnameh* today offers its readers a sense of literary wholeness otherwise lacking in lived reality. The more the world around the *Shahnameh* becomes increasingly fragmented, the more wholesome appears the open-ended horizons of the Persian epic. The sense of nostalgic loss, of wishing for a totemic totality, is what holds the tragic tenacity of the *Shahnameh* together today. The *Shahnameh* is the full constellation of Iranian meta-historical memory, wrapped inside a volume in a nutshell. You enter the text and you need not exit it ever to learn that full and unfolding, but ultimately unattainable, history. It is not that people don't realize that much of the *Shahnameh* is just stories and not histories. But the poetic fusion of the two adjacent realms leaves no room for anything else. The

Shahnameh makes the poetic act inaugural. It has its own temporality, spatiality, locality. It is not European modern. It is Persian presence. To our historical consciousness, to our worldly presence, to the fact that we exist it asserts itself. As a poetic act, the sense of transience, of fate, of tragedy and triumph, becomes coterminous with the moment when we enter, embrace, and dwell in the *Shahnameh*. The Persian epic can never be fully owned, for it owns its reader at the moment of any and all encounters. The epic has long and tiresome passages, especially in the historical section. But the dramatic power of its poetic openings, its mythical sections and heroic deeds never lose sight of the rest that it chooses to narrate. It narrates an eternity in the here and now.

Once in the course of a class presentation on the *Shahnameh* illustrations through the ages a student became visibly shaken by the sudden realization that in every frame of a painting the whole epic dwelled. A simple sense of wonder and awe I witnessed in another student when I shared with my class the contemporary poet Mehdi Akhavan-e Sales's poem "Akhar-e Shahnameh" (The end of the *Shahnameh*). The fact that more than a thousand years after its composition the Persian epic could still elicit such powerful emotional resonances seemed unreal, uncanny to him. I have had similar senses of tragic totality when listening to the recitations of Mahmoud Darwish of his own poetry, declaring the triumphant tragedy of his own people. For all I know Darwish had no knowledge of Ferdowsi, never perhaps even read the *Shahnameh*, even in its Arabic translation. But the sense of the fragility of fate evident in Darwish's poetry is decidedly epic. That I know for a fact for I know from our own example in Iran when reading poets like Mahmoud Darwish, Faiz Ahmad Faiz, Nazem Hekmat, Pablo Neruda, or Vladimir Mayakovsky we read them with a sense of revolutionary epic. We read them with a sense of enabling fragility of time and space, both ours and not ours. Our own towering national poet, Ahmad Shamlou, once said some nonsensical gibberish about the *Shahnameh* to provoke people. Little did he know or cared to know how our active memories of the *Shahnameh* were the foregrounding of our reading of his own poetry, or that in time his own sense of the tragic sense of our futurity, his nostalgia for our future, as it were, was instrumental in helping us read the *Shahnameh* more purposefully in our own time. Now put all those poets I named together—Darwish from Palestine, Faiz from Pakistan, Hekmat from Turkey, Neruda from Chile, and Mayakovsky from Russia—and all of them provoked by our reading of the Persian epic and ask yourself if "World Literature" has any inkling of this *world literature*.

All of this is to say that the text of the *Shahnameh* has historically and narratively defied any and all kinds of political abuse—the intention of the text (as Umberto Eco would say) defying the intention of an imperial or anti-imperial, monarchical or antimonarchical, reading. Because of its inherently tragic disposition, which is always predicated on a moral paradox, and the fact that it is the epic of the conquerors in the language of the vanquished, the *Shahnameh* has a built-in narrative resistance to political or even literary abuse that ultimately disabuses itself for posterity. The intention of the text itself was resistant to the intention of all such abusive readings, and the *Shahnameh* remained defiant, conspiring with the intention of its author to agitate alternative readerships. Three epic narratives in twentieth-century Persian poetry, cinema, and literature borrowed from the central trauma of Ferdowsi's *Shahnameh* and worked against its abusive adaptation by the Pahlavi monarchy for imperial nationalism: first was Mehdi Akhavan-e Sales's epic poem "Chavoshi," where the central tragic trauma and narrative paradox of the *Shahnameh* informed its modern dispensations in another epic poem "Khan-e Hashtom va Adamak" (1968); second was Amir Naderi's film *Tangsir* (1973); and third of course was the magisterial epic of Mahmoud Dolatabadi *Kelidar* (1977–1984)—all three of them entirely predicated on the *Shahnameh* and its tragic disposition (although Naderi's cinematic proclivity toward John Ford overrides his Kurosawa disposition). The masculinist disposition of all three narratives is then effectively countered by Simin Daneshvar's *Savushun* (1969), which radically compromises the phallocentric disposition of the epic altogether.

What we have here is a will to resist power and not a will to power—all evident in such recent adaptations of the Persian epic as Loris Tjeknavorian's opera *Rostam and Sohrab* (2003), the Iranian rapper Taham's video clip "Rostam & Sohrab,"[13] Behrouz Gharibpour's puppet opera *Rostam Sohrab*, (2004),[14] and Hamid Motebassem's operetta

Simurgh (2009).[15] As a poetic constellation of enduring master signifiers, the *Shahnameh* is the locus classicus of assigning meaning to the
world. If Moretti's *Modern Epic* is offered as a European will to power,
we can see in these adaptations of the *Shahnameh* a defiant will to resist
power. To the degree that the *Shahnameh* was abused against the subconscious of the text, it has effectively dodged, as it were, and surfaced
in its oppositional renditions in Mehdi Akhavan-e Sales and others.

Among the most potent oppositional readings of the *Shahnameh* is
Bahram Beiza'i's *Sohrab-Koshi* (Sohrabicide, 2007), a play that marks a
critical turn to Ferdowsi's epic by arguably the most eminent playwright
in contemporary Iran.[16] Bahram Beiza'i (b. 1938) is a towering figure in
Iranian performing arts, both as a playwright and as a filmmaker.[17] He
updates the tragic encounter between Rostam and Sohrab, turning the
classic story into a timely commentary on the nature of violence, power,
and retrograde traditions. Some in Iran interpreted Beiza'i's reading of
the story as a criticism of the encounter between Tradition (Rostam) and
Modernity (Sohrab). Others read it as an allusion to Sohrab A'rabi, a
young man who was murdered in the course of the Green Movement in
Iran.[18] Beiza'i composed his play in decidedly archaic prose to give it an
archetypal air of authenticity. The play is a dramatic adaptation of Ferdowsi's text with a potently political twist to its timely resonances. The
result is a performing diagnosis of the classical text that everyone thought
they knew, but Beiza'i gave it a different urgency. He stages it as a flashback but in effect it flashes forward to bring the old story to life. In inter-
views, Beiza'i began speculating about the character of Sohrab and
interpreted his name or the mythic origin of his maternal origins creatively. The result is a timely twist to the classical story that it brought
the Persian epic to meet the most urgent questions of the time.

Could Iranians, as a people, or the Afghans, the Tajiks, the Indians,
or any other people who have been narratively touched by the *Shahnameh*, have had any other history than the one they have lived, with the
Shahnameh as the defining moment of their historic consciousness? Isn't
Bahram Beiza'i's *Sohrabicide* or Mehdi Akhavan-e Sales's "Khan-e Hashtom" the exegetic bookend of the *Shahnameh* in enclosing and encoding a quintessentially tragic sense of history? Are we not as a people, and

isn't our entire history, a mere commentary on the text of the *Shahnameh*? Can we ever escape its ennobling sense of tragedy, which graces and sacrifices us at one and the same time, doomed always to be defeated by a hidden fate narrated into an epic of triumph at the time of defeat, triumphant only at the time of defeat—a quintessentially Shi'i disposition written into a historical consciousness of epic proportions, or, put differently, a *Shahnameh* leitmotif coagulated as our inevitable choice of a public religion? Isn't the story of Imam Hossein, as the defining trauma of Shi'ism, just another apocryphal *Shahnameh* story that has not made it into any critical edition for it has made it into our collective consciousness as our public religion? Look at the streets of Iran today and see the names of young men and women murdered by order of a Zahhak or a Yazid (take your pick) but ultimately at the hand of their own father: Sohrab A'rabi, Ashkan Sohrabi, Neda Aqa Soltan, Kianush Asa, Taraneh Mousavi, Mostafa Ghanian, Hossein Akhtar Zand, Ramin Ghahremani, Mas'ud Hashemzadeh, Behzad Mohajer, Amir Javadi Langerudi, Mohsen Ruholamini, Farzad Kamangar . . .

ANOTHER WORLD TEXT

The *Shahnameh* becomes a "modern epic" not because it was composed during the course of European colonial modernity, which it was not, but because it was literally and figuratively dismembered in the selfsame tumultuous history, aggressively fragmented into folio pages and into the scattered registers of the original. What made European colonial modernity possible made the textual totality of the *Shahnameh* impossible. That fragmentation of the Persian epic in and of itself turned it into an allegory of itself, a metaphor for the collective consciousness and the agential defiance it had harbored during its entire history. In other words, the *Shahnameh* became a "modern epic" and a "world text" by virtue of and at the moment that it was dismembered, disjointed, and catapulted from its imperial territories onto fragmented nations. That very fragmentation, however, has also allegorized the *Shahnameh,* made it into a powerful parable of postcolonial nations, from which traumatic experience it has emerged to reclaim the world in which it now finds itself. Nativist nationalism has been chiefly responsible for destroying the imperial provenance of the *Shahnameh*. This linguistic nationalism has categorically deworlded the worldly text, nativized, nationalized, denatured it, from which weak perspective *Shahnameh* scholars are now pleading to be accepted into the hall of fame of "World Literature." That is the worst kind of "World Literature" from its very inception. It was and it is a sham. It has robbed the world and its creative forces to claim and call itself "World Literature." The whole Eurocentric idea of "World Literature" needs to be categorically dismantled and texts like the *Shahnameh* restored to this and not their lost worlds, by making them speak to the fragmented realities of a colonially ravaged world.

Franco Moretti's identification of a number of modern epics as the literary, poetic, and operatic master narratives that reflect the European will to power posits a very tempting question to the *Shahnameh* as the epic drama of a people entirely outside the purview of his considerations and today located entirely in the postcolonial shadow of his imperial imagining. How can the contemporary reception of the *Shahnameh* be read in light of the Iranian encounter with colonial modernity—namely, at the receiving end of what Moretti considers the European will to dominate the world and its corresponding literary will to formal inventiveness? The opposing site of that European will to dominate has of course been the universal and variegated will to resist that domination by any means necessary, including literary and artistic. How has the postcolonial reception of the *Shahnameh* in the course of this European colonial modernity fared in the course of that global encounter?

To the texts Moretti has selected as modern epics, he attributes "the cognitive metaphor of the world text," which he is perfectly entitled to do. However, his world, the world he theorizes, is not *our* world, meaning the world at large from Asia and Africa to Latin America and Oceania. His world is Europe and his world is Eurocentric. Our world is neither European nor Eurocentric. But more important, we, the rest, no longer wish to be called non-European. We are not "non-European." Non-Europeans authenticated Europe, nativized themselves and the worldliness of their own arts, literature, and culture. We are altogether liberated from Europe and look at literary theorists like Moretti quite fondly as colleagues and friends, though we see them as incurably provincial in their Eurocentrism.

Moretti's notion of "modern epics" or "world texts" has, however, a crucial insight into how they work when he says these texts "reveal a kind of antagonism between the noun and the adjective: a discrepancy between the totalizing will of the epic and the subdivided reality of the modern world." How beautiful is that insight, and how sad it makes me to see its author so utterly indifferent to the world he inhabits but does not know by reducing it to his Eurocentric imagination. "The totalizing will of the epic" is precisely what was violently destroyed in the *Shahnameh* when one of its most precious copies was torn into pieces precisely by the "subdivided reality of the modern world" between the colonizers and the colonized. Texts like the *Shahnameh* have multiple lives, and their fragmentation in the course of colonial modernity is precisely what Moretti so accurately calls "the totalizing will of the epic and the subdivided reality of the modern world." That subdivision is actually fragmentary and allegorical, as indeed that "totalizing will of the epic" is uniquely Virgilian and as such entirely inapplicable to epics like the *Shahnameh*, whose internal logic and polyvocal rhetoric prevent them from any such totalizing will. In the *Shahnameh* the heroic and the historical are intertwined and predicated on the mythical—a fact that is absent in the Virgilian epic and as a result does not enter into Hegel's conception of epic, which is at the root of Moretti's reading of the "modern epic" or "world text." It is not that Moretti does not know an epic like the *Shahnameh*. It is the fact that his "world system" is so completely closed ever to get to know it that is the issue.

A central dilemma of Moretti's, how can there be any epic in the age of the nation-state, is a moot nonstarter on the colonial site. In the age of European empires of course we have anticolonial reconfigurations of epics. All you have to do is to count the number of progressive revolutionaries in Iran and other Persian-speaking countries who have named their children and grandchildren Kaveh after Kaveh the Blacksmith in the

Shahnameh. This is not even to go near epic novels like Mahmoud Dolatabadi's *Kelidar,* which would certainly qualify for the category of "modern epic" if we were to extend the category to "colonial modernity" to make it more globally accurate. What Moretti calls a world text, like Wagner's *Der Ring des Nibelungen* (1848–1874) or T. S. Eliot's *The Waste Land* (1922), are actually European or Eurocentric texts, and their transfusion into the vacuous abstraction of "Western canon" is the clearest indication that such imperial hubris has no claim on the real world whatsoever. *One Hundred Years of Solitude* (1968) is not a reversal of Goethe's *Faust,* as Moretti surmises, thus perpetrating irreparable epistemic violence on Márquez's masterpiece. To do so he has to posit a "core" for "the world-system" he imagines and perforce a "periphery" to it. But magic realism is not a response to polyphony, nor is it there to tickle the "Western" fancy and offer it reenchantment. Consistently Moretti reduces Márquez's novel to a figment of the "Western" imagination, robbing the literary landmark form Latin America of its own worldly demand for theorization without being a commentary on *Faust.* He categorically collapses and flattens out the condition of colonialism and treats Márquez's magic realism as something of a panacea, a noble savage cliché, response to the cul-de-sac of "European modernity."[19]

Why is it that a monumental novel like Mahmoud Dolatabadi's *Kelidar,* a modern epic and a world text, entirely foregrounded on the tragic heroism of the *Shahnameh,* at one and the same time, does not even enter Moretti's horizon? Is Iran not on this planet and part of this world? Doesn't an epic written in Persian merit the term "epic"? Why, if not? Whatever the answer to such critical questions might be, the result of them is the serious compromising of the moment when Moretti and Eurocentric theorists like him come near the term "world." What is the point of even informing these theorists what Mahmoud Dolatabadi's *Kelidar* is all about, give a synopsis of it, describe its plots and characters, literary prowess and dramatic power? They have, by virtue of writing in Italian or English or French, claimed and coined the term "World Literature"—entirely oblivious of the presence of the Italian colonialism in Libya or British and French colonialism in the rest of Asia and Africa.

They have an imperial claim over "their mother tongue," which has come to us not through their kind and gentle mothers but the settler colonialism of their brutish and violent fathers. So they have their myopic world and we have the expanse of the entirety of the planet to our name to read and theorize.

Why is it that a massively popular film epic like Amir Naderi's *Tangsir* is scarcely known outside Iranian film critics circles? Why, as David Quint references Sergey Eisenstein's *Alexander Nevsky* (1938) toward the end of his book on European epics, can we not reference Amir Naderi's masterpiece epic? Why is it that Moretti cannot see any "modern epic" beyond the limited imagination of a European literary theorist? What would happen if we did consider Naderi's *Tangsir* as a "modern epic" and a world text? It will ipso facto dismantle both Quint's and Moretti's projects as having any serious implications for the real world beyond their fetishized conception of "Europe." But that is not the point or even necessary. The point rather is the fact that current gestations of the Persian epic in films and fiction and opera radically reconceptualize how we imagine a "modern epic" or even a classical epic, for that matter. It will in fact confuse the Christian calendar ordination of classic, medieval, modernity altogether and posit an entirely different chronological order—no, not an Islamic calendar but a worldly calendar. Naderi in *Tangsir* turns defiant struggles of a simple working-class man who had worked as a servant to British colonialists to amass a small fortune to provide for his family into a national folk hero. The local merchants and authorities conspire to rob Zar Mammad of his life savings, and he unearths his long-buried gun to kill them all one by one publicly and in revenge for the terror they had perpetrated on him and takes his wife and son and runs away and disappears into the widening sea. It is nothing but the astonishing nativism of European theorists that they think their little hometown is the center of the universe and never as much as bother to get to know another world outside their captured imagination— and then monumental civilizations like China, India, Iran, or Egypt should bring their literary masterpieces to the door of these literary critics and plead for consideration to be admitted into "World Literature."

DEWORLDING A WORLDLY TEXT

The *Shahnameh* became worldly in the context of worldly empires. With the collapse of those empires, it has lost that worldliness and yet has not gained its presence in the world in which we read it today. Against the dignity and mighty heritage of its origin, it has been relegated to the ghetto of "Third World Literature," and thus its historic and innate worldliness has been taken away from it. Repositioning it in the context of its current world habitat requires a constant attention to its fragmentation, nationalist fetishization, its overpoliticization, and therefore the epistemic violence launched against its poetic power and epochal endurance.

Lost to all manners of paying merely iconic attention to the *Shahnameh* is the urgent necessity of placing it at the center of a new critical reading in the totality of its narrative logic (the way its episodes are related and connected to one another) accentuated by its poetic rhetoric, lending it overdue legitimacy via conversation with current literary critical issues, to restore life and liberty to its poetic character, honor and dignify it with a serious comparative literary attention. The text has been terribly domesticated into nativist (nationalist), Orientalist (Eurocentric), iconic (identity politics) back alleys of insular and closed-circuited regurgitations. A decade and a half into the twenty-first century the dominant modes of encounter with the *Shahnameh* (with very few notable exceptions) are still very much on the model of nativist nationalism, old-fashioned Orientalism, or fetishized talismanic identity politics.

As a worldly text, the *Shahnameh* has been systematically deworlded in the service of ethnic nationalism against nations, of politics against poetics, of empires against epics. So the key question concerns how the *Shahnameh* has fared in helping nations imagine themselves from bygone empires to postcolonial entities. The origin of linguistic and literary nationalism, as the political and ideological source of state-building projects, is deeply rooted in European colonialism. The very idea of Goethe's *Weltliteratur* is predicated on a forced nationalization of literatures hitherto integral to varied imperial worlds. The same is true of the idea of "modern epic" that either exclusively considers masterpieces of European literature or casts an exotic look at Márquez's masterpieces to appropriate them for a Eurocentric reading. The same holds true for the notion of "comparative literature in the age of multiculturalism," ipso facto taking literary masterpieces out of their natural habitat. The West–non-West bifurcation has systematically nativized and deworlded texts such as the *Shahnameh* and compromised their imperial pedigree. The mythic, heroic, and historical time and narrative of the *Shahnameh* has suspended the timing of European chronology. Yes, the text of the *Shahnameh* was written a thousand years ago, but that does not make it medieval, or ancient, or modern, for it is written, composed, and read on an entirely different temporal scale.

The only way to retrieve and restore to worldly texts their worldliness is to replant them in their current history. That worldliness will not be restored unless and until we de-Europeanize their reception and reconstruct them to their own worldly conditions, from where we can then start embedding them in the world. We need to de-Europeanize their reception and reconnect them to their own worldly conditions. The *Shahnameh* lost its own worldliness sometime in the eighteenth and nineteenth centuries when Europeans discovered it embedded in their bourgeois public sphere. That sphere became transnational and spread with the force of global capitalism (referring to its Europhilia chapter). One might argue that Shah Tahmasp's *Shahnameh* was the last time it had its worldliness. What happened to it, torn into pieces and sold into slavery to various private collections and museums, is what happened to its worldliness. Iranians and other Persian-speaking worlds rediscovered their own *Shahnameh* dwelling in the veritable and European bourgeois public sphere. Thus the book was alienated from itself as it was from its original readers. Therefore, the fragmentation of empires into nations was itself another simulacrum of the worldliness of the *Shahnameh* being lost to itself.

Whether they critically edited, translated, or abbreviated it, they appropriated it into their own nationalized public sphere, from where it went back to Iran and other Persianate regions as postcolonial nation-states. These postcolonial nation-states are fragments of those empires, as fragmented pages of the Shah Tahmasp *Shahnameh* were the enduring relics of the last time it was produced as a worldly text and exchanged between two empires. This coincided with the postcolonial nation-states, which now dominated it for state building and forced and manhandled it into the making of a nationalized literature. This forced the *Shahnameh* into a "Third World Literature" category that was deadly to its own worldliness. "All Third World Literature" was then declared allegories of the nation, which was all fine and dandy for the First World theorists. They got to theorize "their "World Literature" and cannibalize the literature of others. Third-Worlding a literature is to deworld it, rob it of its own worldliness. But what is its own worldliness? In my *World of Persian Literary Humanism*, I have outlined and theorized it, arguing that it is the world to which it belongs, and it is upon that world that it needs to be placed, definitive to a transnational public sphere and allow it to resume resorting agency in its readers. That leads us into colliding worlds, the world in which the *Shahnameh* is alienated from itself ("the West") and the world in which it is alienated from its readers ("the Rest").

The task at hand is to take the *Shahnameh* back from "the West" and give it back to "the Rest," the rest of the world, which is *the world*—this is the only way it will become integral to a renewed understanding of *world literature*. The task is to make the *Shahnameh* meaningful and significant to "the Rest." Unless and until the *Shahnameh* is made meaningful and significant to people in Asia, Africa, and Latin America it will never be restored to its worldliness in a new world. We must once and for all divest this ill-founded power in "the West" to decide where "the world" is. Almost the entirety of *Shahnameh* scholarship of the past two centuries has been geared to convince Europeans, and by extension North Americans, that the Persian epic belongs to their "World Literature," that it is a masterpiece. But why? By what authority is that particular audience to be privileged? This world to which the *Shahnameh* now belongs is no longer an empire, but a world that is at the receiving end of an amorphous American empire. Here we must reverse the persistent folkloric attempt to pit Ferdowsi against Sultan Mahmoud. That folkloric history marks the consistent push to claim Ferdowsi for nations (peoples) that read him and wrest it away from empires that have historically abused it. In the same vein, Ferdowsi's *Shahnameh* has now returned to the people who read it. If Ferdowsi were alive today, he would have composed his epic in English—not because it is an imperial language but because it is the language of the colonized. Every single word of the original Persian so meticulously preserved has to be kept as the national treasure of multiple nations that hold that language precious to their collective heritage. But the Persian epic must be made to sing and seduce in all colonial languages we have inherited and made our own, by confiscating them from our former colonial masters. That is the meaning of the *Shahnameh* being part of a *world literature* that is currently beyond the horizons of their "World Literature."

EPICS OF ANOTHER WORLD SYSTEM

The *Shahnameh* has historically created its own world, moving, as it has, from empires to nation-states, and it is precisely on that passage that it has announced itself as a piece of *world literature*, or as a "worldly text." It is imperative to keep in mind here that the *Shahnameh* (as a text, a poetic event, a moral force) is neither Islamic nor Zoroastrian nor indeed exclusively of any other specific denomination—although Zoroastrianism and Islam inform its moral universe, and Shi'ism might in fact be considered a historically unfolded "story" in the prototype of the *Shahnameh*, or the sense of the tragic in Shi'ism might be considered coterminous with the Persian epic. Above all, the *Shahnameh* is a literary work of art, and it is as such that its moral imagination thrives on itself and works. The moral universe of the *Shahnameh* is the narrative outgrowth of its poetic idiomaticity. That idiomaticity has been rich and multisignificatory, ready to be interpreted in varied historical circumstances, from what European historiography calls medieval to modern.

To think of the *Shahnameh* in a comparative framework of epic narratives we need to dwell on its defining traumatic moments. The central traumas of the *Shahnameh* dwell in the three stories of Rostam and Sohrab, Rostam and Esfandiar, and Seyavash and Sudabeh. These three stories bring out the most potent, visceral, and emblematic power of the Persian epic. The entire narrative disposition of the *Shahnameh*, I believe, is informed by these three tragedies. To think about the *Shahnameh* as a "modern epic," instead of going through Moretti's Eurocentric "world system," I suggest we bring three master epic filmmakers—Akira Kurosawa, John Ford, and David Lean—to meet Ferdowsi in their respective imperial idioms. Cinematic epic, I believe, is far more universal and is staged on far more democratic grounds than the deeply distorted field of "comparative literature" and therefore entails a far more enabling take on comparative epic. Comparatively, the central liberating trope of John Ford is the love and admiration of the young first-generation Irish-American of the New Promised Land—as perhaps best anchored between *How Green Was My Valley* (1941) and *The Long Gray Line* (1955), among many others. The central trauma of David Lean is the pathology of the British Empire—as massively canvassed in *Lawrence of Arabia* (1962), *Ryan's Daughter* (1970), and *A Passage to India* (1984). The central trauma of Akira Kurosawa is the horror of Hiroshima he witnessed as a child and that subsequently defined the entirety of his cinema—as perhaps best demonstrated in the two masterpieces *Throne of Blood* (1957)—based on Shakespeare's *Macbeth*—and *Ran* (1985), based on Shakespeare's *King Lear*. Ferdowsi in his Rostam and Sohrab, Rostam and Esfandiar, and Seyavash and Sudabeh can transhistorically be placed in this epic quartet, where he echoes Kurosawa and corroborates Lean and Ford.

My contention is that the combined effects of the central traumas of the author and the text in each of these cases constitute the subconscious of the text and inform their kinesthetic. This means that the details of every sequence in the film or text—from every single shot to camera movement to mise-en-scène to editing, costume design, set design, and so forth—is also informed by that central trauma. This means that there is something celebratory and jovial about John Ford's cinema, something nostalgic and pathological about David Lean's, and something tragic about Kurosawa's. Kurosawa is the closest epic filmmaker to Ferdowsi in the defining moment of both their kinesthetics. The centrality of

Japanese medieval theater—in both Noh and Kabuki traditions—and the attraction to Shakespeare's dramas are the clearest signs of Kurosawa's inclinations toward archetypal epic—which might add additional dramatic reasons for the similarity of his cinematic aesthetics to Ferdowsi's epic.

Both Iranian and former Soviet filmmakers have paid some attention to the *Shahnameh* in their film oeuvres. Abdolhossein Sepanta made *Ferdowsi* (1934) for Reza Shah's celebration. The Pahlavi monarch did not like his portrait of Mahmoud and Ferdowsi and forced him to go back to India, where the film was made, and change those scenes and ordered his ambassador to India to act as Mahmoud! Two other negligible films were made based on the *Shahnameh*. M. Ra'is Firuz's *Rostam and Sohrab* (1957) and Siyamak Yasami's *Bizhan and Manizheh*, both melodramatic flops. Fereydun Rahnema made two noteworthy films, *Seyavash dar Takht-e Jamashid* (Seyavash in Persepolis, 1967) and *Pesar-e Iran az Madarash bi-Khabar ast* (Iran's son has no news from his mother, 1973). The most prolific filmmaker of the *Shahnameh* was Boris Kimyagarov (1920–1979), from Tajikistan, who made a few films based on *Shahnameh* stories, including *Legend of Rostam* (1971), *Rostam and Sohrab* (1972), and *Legend of Seyavash* (1977).[20] There are also Indian and Azeri film adaptations of the story of Rostam and Sohrab, as well as an opera by Loris Tjeknavorian.

There is an active moral imagination at work in Ferdowsi's *Shahnameh* that holds the epic emotively expansive and narratively together. The same is of course true of John Ford, David Lean, and Akira Kurosawa's respective modes of epic cinema. This, however, is not true of the American empire, which lacks any claim to any legitimacy or hegemony, and it is an empire almost despite itself. It does have a claim on Christianity, but it is more because it posits itself against Islam. John Ford's cinematic oeuvre is the closest this empire has come to giving itself an epic narrative. But Ford's cinema was the product of a first-generation young Irish imagination, which did its service and was in turn crushed under the myth of white settler colonialism. That myth does not allow for any other mythic form, folkloric or artistic, to give American imperialism even a semblance of hegemonic legitimacy.

The Persian epic once gave a lending hand to rising Persianate empires before it narratively dismantled them. Today there are no such empires, and no postcolonial nation-state has any exclusive claim on the *Shahnameh*. The Persian epic has escaped them all. Today the *Shahnameh* belongs to a global readership that reads it in its original Persian or English translation fully conscious of its fragmented allegorical power and poetry. Today the *Shahnameh* is a "modern epic" to the degree that modernity is colonially mitigated. Today that epic is a "world text" to the degree that its worldliness helps to overcome the postmodernity of an empire that no longer has any claim to hegemony and rules the world with brutish vulgarity. Today the *Shahnameh* can rely only on its *infinity* overcoming its *totality*. Today chances are millions of more people can read the *Shahnameh* in its English translation than in its original Persian. Chances are more millions of people read it in English outside Ferdowsi's birthplace of Khorasan than either in Khorasan or in multiple postcolonial nation-states around his birthplace. Yes, Iranians, Afghans, and Tajiks have an equally legitimate claim on him. But chances are these very Iranians, Afghans, and Tajiks are reading him in Persian or English outside the postcolonial boundaries of their recently manufactured political divides. How does the *Shahnameh* speak to them beyond these manufactured colonial borders depends entirely on how the stories of the *Shahnameh* are liberated from their fetishized commodification as identity totem and into the liberating domains of poetic emancipation from the power and prosody of political power.

TRANSGENDERING DESIRE

Afrasiab's treachery in trying to use Sohrab to kill Rostam and defeat Iran is indicative of the subplot of the ensuing trauma of a father inadvertently killing his son. Afrasiab thought he would either kill Sohrab if the son triumphed over his father, Rostam, or else exact a terrible revenge upon Rostam if he ended up killing his own son, which is what he did. In the advancing army of Sohrab therefore the political order of the two empires of Iran and Turan is being mitigated by the remissive space of Samangan, where Sohrab was in fact conceived, born, and raised. That remissive space is where we have a premonition of Gordafarid as the simulacrum of a "transgender" warrior. It is important to remember that Ferdowsi makes the point that the reason Gordafarid went fighting was that her younger brother Gostaham was too young and therefore her father, Gazhdaham, conceded that his daughter should fight Sohrab. Ferdowsi also makes the point that Gordafarid hid her long hair under her helmet. That Gordafarid is a beautiful young woman disguising herself as a man is therefore a major theme in her battle with Sohrab.

In the battlefield of the erotic encounter between Sohrab and Gordafarid the transgender desire in the *Shahnameh* finds its fullest display. This transgender desire as the productive unconscious of the text overwhelms and subverts the reproductive organism of desire and stages the pure desire as the poetic will of the epic against the patriarchal order of the empire. Here is where the *bazm* (feasting) component of epic overtakes its *razm* (fighting). The battle scene between Sohrab and Gordafarid is the simulacrum of a lovemaking scene in disguise. From the armament they use to Ferdowsi's deliberate phrasing, Sohrab and Gordafarid are making love in this scene in a disguised scene of fighting. The final delightful recognition that Gordafarid is a woman and not a man has a decidedly orgasmic tone to it. Gordafarid's running back to her fortress and teasing Sohrab invites him to penetrate the fortress for more. The erotic ruse is the suspension of patriarchy, replacing of pure desire for reproductive coupling as a precondition of patriarchal tension that will soon result in Rostam's killing his own son. The battle between Sohrab and Gordafarid is therefore a dramatic staging of the trauma of filicide, where the *Shahnameh* the epic poem dismantles the *Shahnameh* the imperial narrative.

CONCLUSION

Chonin ast kerdar charkh-e boland . . .

In one a crown and in the other a rope
When a man sits happy with his crown
With a tie of a rope someone brings him down
from his throne
Why would one fall in love with this world
Since we all have to pass by those who went
before us?

The story of Alexander the Great occurs at the end of the heroic period in Ferdowsi's *Shahnameh* just before the beginning of the historical. It is a transitional story in which the *mythic* and the *heroic* feed and fuse into the *historical*, a crucial fusion of multiple narratives to generate a whole new register on the time and place of the Persian epic. In this story, the historical account of Alexander is brought to bear on the heroic age of Dara, who stands for Darius III, the last Achaemenid king, who was defeated by the Macedonian general in 330 B.C.E. The key character trait of Alexander in the *Shahnameh* is his keen inclination toward justice, wisdom, and fairness. This segment of the epic, along with the sections on Ardeshir and Anushirvan, reads like a mirror for princes, a manual of leadership and governance with equanimity and justice. Upon ascending the Persian throne, and following a well-established tradition, Alexander delivers a royal sermon in which his first prayer is to wish upon all kings to have their soul blessed with *kherad* (reason).[1] He reminds himself that the only victorious might is truly that of Almighty God, and good kings fear Him most. He considers Time the only true judge and promises his subjects to have his court always open and welcoming to those who seek justice. This he says is in gratitude for his victorious fate. He forgives taxes for five years. From the poor he says he expects nothing, nor will he put any pressure on the rich. Alexander then proceeds to marry Roshank, the daughter of Dara, ascend the Persian throne, and rule and unify Iran, Turan, and China before he moves to conquer India.

There is an active transformation of the historical Alexander (356–323 B.C.E.), who had destroyed the Achaemenid Empire, into a wise and worthy Persian king. In both the *Shahnameh* and other Persian sources, based on Arabic, Persian, and Pahlavi materials, Alexander has a resoundingly positive character. Ferdowsi places the Macedonian conqueror straight in the line of Iranian monarchs, incorporating the world conqueror into the pantheon of wise and worthy kings. A brief mention of the Arsacid dynasty follows the story of Alexander and precedes that of Ardashir I, founder of the Sassanid Empire, after which Ferdowsi brings his epic to a close with the Arab invasion. The *Shahnameh* is, as a result, the epic of multiple empires, and even Alexander coming from Asia Minor is actively and comfortably incorporated into the imperial pedigree of the Persianate world.[2] There is no trauma of defeat here, as there is never an ecstasy of triumph in any part of the *Shahnameh*. For Ferdowsi these are just stories gathered from tumultuous histories of multiple empires, collected only to teach the world enduring lessons of the way life works.

WHENCE AND WHEREFORE "WORLD LITERATURE"?

Why bother with Alexander or any other magnificent stories in the *Shahnameh*? Why be so cautious, careful, and judicious in separating and then seeing together the *mythic, heroic,* and *historical* components of the Persian epic? Here in the conclusion I must place my reading of the Persian epic in the larger context of my most recent work. Over the past few years, in four consecutive books I have mapped out in some detail and from multiple perspectives the formation of a postcolonial subject on an emerging transnational public sphere. I have done so, using the example of Iran but for far larger frames of comparative and theoretical references, in order to document the manner in which we can think of a global history of our presence outside the dominating Eurocentric historiography and its nativist and colonialist consequences. In these four books I have had a decidedly historical reading of the postcolonial subject predicated on a non-Eurocentric reading of the world pronouncedly outside the European perspective and in fact epistemically violated by it. In *Shi'ism: A Religion of Protest* (2011), I focused on the central significance of Islamic scholasticism in the historical formation of that public sphere initially in Isfahan under the Safavids in the sixteenth century and the eventual rise of the postcolonial subject on its premise in the aftermath of Iranian encounter with European colonial modernity. In *The World of Persian Literary Humanism* (2012) I shifted gears from Islamic scholasticism and moved toward Persian literary humanism as the other crucial component of that selfsame public and parapublic spheres and the multifaceted aspects of the formation of the postcolonial subject. These two studies complemented each other and pointed ways toward a more transnational assessment of the issues I had raised systemically decentering "Europe" from our global history. In *Persophilia: Persian Culture on the Global Scene* (2015) I sought to demonstrate how this composition of the transnational public sphere worked through systemic acts of border crossings from the European bourgeois public sphere to its peripheralized colonial edges and back to it, where the postcolonial subject becomes in effect transnational through precisely such border crossings. Here I neither privileged Europe nor ignored it but placed it on a map of the globe that recognized both European imperialism and modes of postcolonial residences to it. By navigating the place of "Persia" in varied layers of European bourgeois imagination I showed how Iranians, too, began to conceive of their own national homeland on an entirely transnational public sphere. In *Iran Without Borders: Towards a Critique of the Postcolonial Nation* (2016), I brought all these works to a focal point and mapped out a view of Iran as a postcolonial nation formed on that transnational public sphere. The postcolonial subject of my sustained investigation was now historicized, liberated from any parasitical existence on the falsely manufactured binaries of "Islam and the West," "Tradition and Modernity." By historicizing this postcolonial subject, I had also decolonized it, liberated it from a Eurocentric false consciousness.

Now in this book on the *Shahnameh*, I have sought to extend that project and opted for a detailed reading of the link between the Persian epic and the multiple empires it has served up to the postcolonial age in order to make the question of "modern epic" more complicated as a case study of the public sphere and postcolonial subject formation through the rise and unfolding of multiple *worlds*—not just the one colonially dominant, and imperially manufactured, the *world* that European and U.S. literary theorists of "World Literature" consistently theorize. Their liberal conscience now invariably bothers them and they wish to incorporate the world they do not know into the world they do know—and thus the more they do so the more they appear like the Christopher Columbus or the Indiana Jones of literary theory. A key reason for my critical perspective on what is today called "World Literature" is this overall project of rethinking the transnational public sphere and the postcolonial subject from a decidedly anticolonial and non-Eurocentric site—in order, in effect, to reveal at least one world these theorizations consistently cover and epistemically violate. This is perhaps the most important angle from which I have come to read the Persian epic against the grain of "World Literature" as it has been imperially narrated with a sustained epistemic violence against all its repressed alterities. Those concealed, denied, repressed, denigrated, and blindsided worlds are the most significant blind spot of "World Literature" theorists today, no matter how cleverly the old card of transnational tokenism is played out to sugarcoat the epistemic violence definitive to their project.

My attention to both the *locality* and *temporality* of the Persian epic, interpolated in terms structural to its poetic worlding of the world it has inhabited and informed, is rooted in this project I have followed over this past decade. Let us remember how at the moment of entering the *historical* phase of his narrative, directly from the *mythic* and the *heroic*, Ferdowsi opts for a completely legendary account of Alexander, made allegorical through his poetic rendition of a fictional account of the Macedonian warlord and world conqueror. This choice pushes the *mythic*, *heroic*, and *historical* moments of the Persian epic toward the *poetically fictional*, which in effect inaugurates a whole genre of Persian Alexander Romance after Ferdowsi, though the source of Ferdowsi's own account predates him by centuries. The temporal space thus created between fact and fantasy becomes poetically fictive and as such it categorically overcomes the political narrative of any empire that wishes to lay a temporary historic claim on the Persian epic. Those empires are at the service of this epic, to offer it stories to tell, and not the other way around. The story of the historical Alexander was actively fictionalized based on a Pseudo-Callisthenes account, on which Ferdowsi's version, too, is based. This account is rooted in an apocryphal narrative attributed to Callisthenes of Olynthus (ca. 360–328 B.C.E.), a Greek historian (a great-nephew of Aristotle's) who had accompanied Alexander during his Asiatic expeditions. This account had already turned Alexander (very much on the model that Xenophon had turned Cyrus the Great into a model of imperial leadership in his *Cyropaedia*) into an exemplary world leader. Though accounts of incorporating Alexander into Persian imperial pedigree predates him, Ferdowsi furthered that account by actively valorizing him into the pantheon of Persian epic poetry. That plus the strategic location of the Alexander story at a narrative moment when the *mythic* and *heroic* become *historical* generate and sustain a whole different conception of "world" and "worldliness" in the *Shahnameh*, which in turn demands and exacts a vastly different conception of "World Literature" if we were to seriously consider it in that frame of reference. "The world" in "World Literature" cannot be simply a decidedly Eurocentric world. It must not just come to terms with other worlds (in the plural) but above all recognize the world internal to the worldliness of a work of literary art like the Persian epic. This is where much of "World Literature" theorization by European and American theorists is entirely blindsided.

The *Shahnameh* has been the epic of many and multiple empires. Many empires have arisen, fallen, and laid tenuous claims on the Persian epic, and yet they have all come and gone, and the *Shahnameh* has survived them all. With each and every fallen empire, nothing has happened to the living, worldly character of the *Shahnameh* except lending increasing legitimacy to its literary wisdom and poetic poignancy. Today the *Shahnameh* has finally reached one of its most ironic destinations— and it is here, and in its worldly character, that it poses a serious challenge to the very notion of "World Literature" as it has been imperially theorized. Through its widespread availability in its English translations it now lives through the farthest colonial reaches of an empire that cannot even read let alone lay a claim on its original. It has, also, providentially, as it were, remained outside the reach of those imperial literary theorists who write about "World Literature" entirely ignorant of it, or limited to an Orientalist nod to its existence. With that paradoxical ending, the *Shahnameh* is finally liberated from the false claim on it of any empire. Not just any single postcolonial nation-state but in fact the active theorization of "World Literature" as the ideological force of Euro-American imperialism cannot lay a claim on its world and worldliness. It now lives through its stories shedding light on histories, basking in its poetic defiance of all political and ideological claims on it. Liberating the Persian epic from the shackles of tiresome politics, of the pestiferous ethnic nationalism in particular, and marking its artistic powers will restore *The Book of Kings* to its neglected place as a piece of *world literature* in its own right, now made accessible, especially through its English translations, to a global readership made of postcolonial nations. It is in that manner that as a text that has overtly served but effectively subverted multiple empires, before it was plunged into its postcolonial history, we may ask how the *Shahnameh* has fared in the context and configuration of what today is called "World Literature" as the ideological force field of Euro-American imperialism the world over.

My argument regarding the Persian epic as *world literature* is rooted in how I have read the *Shahnameh*. This seminal worldly text forces the theorists of "World Literature" to look at themselves in its mirror and see their unabashedly imperial theory humbled to its limited locality. I know of no other way than seriously engaging with the Persian epic that these theorists could face the provincial limitations of their own colonially accented theories. I believe the project of "World Literature" as it is received and speculated on today is epistemically flawed and imperially rooted, and therefore no amount of liberal meandering can save it. The project is in dire need of not just some serious reconceptualization but also indeed coming to terms with its imperial provenance. The opportunity of engaging with the *Shahnameh* for a decidedly global audience has given me a unique opportunity to sketch out the general contours of this renewed understanding of what it means to think of *world literature* outside any compromising and sarcastic quotation marks.

If you were to take a look at the excellent volume edited by David Damrosch, *World Literature in Theory* (2014), you would see both the momentum of its extraordinary attempts at articulating itself in ever expansive and liberal terms and yet its irreparable limitations in opening up to literary worlds beyond its incurable Eurocentricity.[3] Marking the Eurocentricity of such volumes is not an accusation but a truism—a seeing through their imperial origins. We must understand and appreciate and benefit from such volumes for what they have to offer and move on with the task at hand, which is neither to accuse nor to excuse but to overcome the very idea of "World Literature" as we have received it from these senior custodians of the overexposed and outdated idea. Damrosch's volume aptly begins with Goethe in 1827 and duly jumps to John Pizer's 2006 piece "The Emergence of *Weltliteratur*: Goethe and the Romantic School." There is a flashback to the Hungarian theorist Hugo Meltzl's speculations about "Present Tasks of Comparative Literature" from 1877 and a citation of Hutcheson Macaulay Posnett's "What Is World Literature" from 1886. We have then tokens of the Oriental in the form of a piece by Rabindranath Tagore, "World Literature" (1907), and Zheng Zhenduo's 1922 piece, "A View on the Unification of Literature"— bringing them into a "conversation" that never actually took place. These are considered "the foundational texts" of the origin of "World Literature." Then follows specific reflections on Yiddish or French or Francophone (three pieces here) as "World Literature," with Edward Said's "Traveling Theory" or Franco Moretti's "Conjectures on World Literature" duly thrown into the ring. The volume is then brought to a conclusion with Zhang Longxi's telling the readers of the volume that yes, the idea of "World Literature" began with Goethe and Marx, but it has been consistently changing until we get to Moretti's telling us that we need to do "distant reading," concluding with an honest but nevertheless embarrassing confession that the business of "World Literature" is today theoretically insolvent: "The history of world literature is unabashedly Eurocentric and modernist, closely mapping on the European expansion in the colonialist era and the subsequent decolonization in the mid-twentieth century, but completely oblivious of the Hellenistic and Roman world and ignorant of the formation of literary constellations outside Europe, such as the Persian and Ottoman Empires, or the East Asian region with the Chinese written language and culture playing a pivotal role in pre-modern times."[4]

"Closely mapping on the European expansion in the colonialist era" is a thinly camouflaged euphemism for imperialism. "World Literature" is imperialism in literary theoretical terms. Zhang Longxi further admits, "From Goethe and Marx to Casanova, Moretti, and Damrosch, the concept of world literature has been theorized mostly in the context of Western literary studies."[5] Indeed—in fields theoretically contingent and coterminous with European and now American imperialism. Very little can or need be added to these concluding remarks in a volume summarizing the history of "World Literature" theories. That whole spectrum of "World Literature" as has been thus theorized now appropriately belongs to a literary theory museum with a fine and shiny glass cover for posterity to spend a fine Sunday morning beholding and marveling at the momentous history of an ideological movement at the service of a Euro-American imperial imaginary that considered itself "World Literature."

As is evident in Emily Apter's excellent volume *Against World Literature*,[6] even when these eminent literary theorists write critically about their discipline and field the idea, practice, and theorization of "World Literature" are nonetheless very much a closed-circuited speculation among a handful of quite erudite North American and Western European theorists very limited and in fact myopic in their preoccupations with what they know and yet entirely oblivious to the even more they do not know—but genuinely care to know and appropriate and assimilate backward to what they know. But what they do know and call "World Literature" has nothing to do with the real world, with the multifaceted, multilingual, multicultural worlds rising and rooted around them. What they do know quite well is *their* world, their North American and Western European world, which they imperially cast upon the real world from their respective offices in a department of English and comparative literature. As David Damrosch says aptly about Emily Apter's book *Against World Literature*: "Herself a leading figure in the opening up of comparative literature toward global perspectives, notably as author of *The Translation Zone: A New Comparative Literature* (2006), as contributor to several collections on world literature, and as a founding board member of Harvard's Institute for World Literature, Apter is well situated to assess the field from within."[7] And one might as well stay there, "within," and never venture out into the real world, the world outside departments of English and Comparative Literature.

In *Against World Literature*, Apter makes a very simple and even obvious point, that there is a power and politics, a blatant epistemic violence, perpetrated in any and all acts of translation from any language into English or French or any other European language. But she remains rather oblivious to the fact that all these European languages are in fact colonial languages for the world at large. What am I doing writing these lines in English, or Fanon in French, or Spivak and Said in English? None of us are European or of European descent. We are all colonials turned into postcolonial theorists. When they translate a Chinese or Arabic or Persian literary text into English or French they have not translated it into a European language but into a colonial language, a language read and understood far more by Asians, Africans, and Latin Americans than by Europeans—or those of European descent. The world did not learn these languages at a Berlitz school, or on an Ivy League campus. The world learned these languages at colonial gunpoint, in the trenches of anticolonial battlefields—the way Native Americans learned English from their European colonial tormentors, long before—just like my own university, Columbia—European colonialists built Ivy League universities on stolen Lenape lands. The dubious project of an English translation of a French speculative self-indulgence on "untranslatability" of philosophical terms, as in Barbara Cassin's *Vocabulaire européen des philosophies: Dictionnaire des intraduisibles* (2006), with which Emily Apter has been affiliated, is the limit of these European and North American theorists' imagination to come to terms with the fact that they are indeed globally irrelevant and provincially trapped in one or another colonial language they falsely think is theirs. This whole project, again as Damrosch rightly calls it, is "speciously unified via a Euro-universalism projected onto the globe at large." That "Euro-universalism" remains at the heart of this imperial theory they call "World Literature." Within that "World Literature" no non-European poet or theorist can ever stand up and say "I" with a confident voice of her own subject positions and pride of place. To paraphrase James Baldwin on a similar occasion, the minute a non-European person stands up and says she too has a right to exist the entire edifice of "Western civilization," or, in this case, "World Literature" will crumble. My consistent search for the particularities of a postcolonial subject comes to this edifice of "World Literature" and must either prostrate to it in obedience or crush it in defiance. I do not believe the world has ever been in the mood for prostrating to any imperial ideology in obedience.

Nodding toward a "planetary geography," as Apter does,[8] is a nice political gesture but has no literary significance so far as the very practice of "World Literature" as this limited number of Euro-universalist theorists perform it—a mode of theorization that by their very professional practices suppresses any alternative worldliness of literatures about which they know very little or nothing at all. Taking the Palestinian conceptual artist Emily Jacir out of her Palestinian context of dispossession or the Moroccan literary theorist Abdelfattah Kilito out of his multilingual milieu and assimilating them backward to familiar tropes represent literary and artistic cannibalism not "World Literature." To be sure, North American and Western European practitioners of "World Literature" are perfectly liberal minded and openhearted literary critics whose company you will much prefer to Euro-universalist literary critics who have scarcely heard of or care to hear about any Chinese or Arab or Iranian writer. But it is precisely in their openmindedness that the cul-de-sac of their "World Literature" as a defunct theoretical practice has become most evident—for it is precisely in their collegial liberalism that you discover the impossibility of any other alterity they fathom to become a self to their own worldliness. My bone of contention therefore with the whole enterprise of "World Literature" from Goethe to Damrosch and Apter is neither ad hominem nor Europhobic. Their theoretical practices ipso facto posit a negative dialectic toward the very existence of worlds beyond their literary horizons.

Replacing the term "world" with "planetarity"—or pointing out that Chinese or Japanese literary scholars are joining the "World Literature" club—will not solve but in fact exacerbate the fundamental flaw in the very assumption of "World Literature. The practice keeps assimilating backward into the limited but self-indulgent quagmire of the very idea of "World Literature" and its flawed worldliness. Noting the tokenism of Apter toward the Moroccan literary theorist Abdelfattah Kilito, Damrosch rightly notes,

It is refreshing finally to find some discussion of a theorist based out-side Paris or the United States, and yet like many Moroccan intellectu-als, Kilito does much of his critical writing in French, appearing in such journals as *Poétique*; he recently published in Paris a kind of sequel to his 2002 volume, *Je parle toutes les langues, mais en arabe* (Actes Sud, 2013). In discussing the work of a Moroccan theorist who holds a PhD from the Sorbonne, recipient in 1996 of the Prix du rayonnement de la langue française of the Académie Française, Apter has not moved so far from the Rive Gauche after all.[9]

Damrosch then concludes with an apt observation and yet a facile hope for sustaining the idea and practice of "World Literature" he still champions:

> The world is a large and various place. Those wishing to chart new plan-etary cartographies are finding many languages to study beyond the French–German–English triad that long dominated Western compar-ative studies, and they are developing new methods appropriate to the expanded scope of our field. The tough linguistic and political analy-ses that Emily Apter rightly wishes comparatists to pursue will best be carried forward by widening our cultural and linguistic horizons, and by employing the full variety of critical and theoretical approaches that can be included in our cartographic toolboxes today.[10]

This last plea is alas futile and regurgitates the selfsame Euro-universalism about which Damrosch rightly complains and to which he has in his own long and illustrious career contributed significantly by arguing that "World Literature" dwells in "an elliptical space created between the source and receiving cultures," thus reducing other *worldly* literature to national literatures and sustaining his and his colleagues' theoretical speculations as pertinent to the continued legitimacy of the "World Lit-erate" project.[11] But the way these distinguished theorists have under-stood "World Literature" is an impossibility. The very idea of it emerges in and remains confined to an incurable Euro-universalism, whether via Goethe's literary ecumenicalism or Moretti's world-system model; it is there for the theoretical entertainment of European and U.S. literary theorists, and as such as an ideological camouflage for Euro-American imperialism, and by and large they have a good time feeling superior to their even more belligerently Eurocentric colleagues. But the epistemic violence they ipso facto perpetrate upon the worldliness of non-European literary traditions, beginning by casting them into the ghetto of non-European, is irreparable. But that is not a merely literary theoretical flaw. That is the ideological domain where the moral agency of non-Europeans is stigmatized and made impossible.

My purpose here is not to rehearse the deepest flaws in the theory and practice of "World Literature" as these leading scholars understand it, and as I have had other occasions to discuss in some details.[12] Books and innumerable learned essays have been devoted to that task. As a founding member of the Institute for Comparative Literature and Society at Columbia University I have had the institutional duty of getting to know and teach this literature in detail. I am, as you might say, an outsider-insider to the project. There is a foreignness to my familiarity with this field. In the United States, this field is still very much an appendix to English departments. That fact at once enables and disables the field beyond reproach or repair. There are serious advances and insurmountable dead ends in the discipline as we know it now. I am neither the first nor the only one to think so. The field is in a creative crisis and keeps chasing after its own tail. In Pascale Casanova's *The World Republic of Letters* (2007), for example, she opts to read "the world" metaphorically, as "stylistic refinements" of political and economic realities, and sees the hegemony of any such culture over others as merely linguistic and aesthetic. This to me is pure Paris-centered literary romanticism disguising the innate violence of Eurocentric theorization. Her model of "literary capital" is preternaturally Paris and could not be possible be Cairo or Delhi. Paris is the Mecca and the Ka'ba of literary art for her—all the power of course to her and her beloved city. To me, however, as much at home as I am in Paris as in Istanbul, Delhi, Tehran, Cairo, or Mexico City, this is delusional chauvinism.

Yes, as Fernand Braudel and Immanuel Wallerstein, among others, have argued the capitalist economy is global—but by the same token it is polyfocal. Mumbai is as important on its map as Cairo, Istanbul, Paris, or Buenos Aires. This French self-universalism is medieval in its nativism of the village cartographer. Inevitably Casanova's three totem poles of "World Literature" are "Latin, French, and German." All the power to her—there is nothing wrong with these three magnificent languages and their literatures. But no French or American theorist has the right (except for the imperial might they exude) to cut Arabic, Bengali, Chinese, Japanese, or Persian languages and literatures to limited horizons of their provincial imagination. Casanova sees Kafka, Joyce, and Faulkner as key figures in her reading of this "World Literature" and in her systemic disregard for any other world she indeed offers some brilliant insights into the literary worlds she examines. We read these insights and learn and wonder. What is Hecuba to her or she to Hecuba? The *Shahnameh, Mahabharata,* or any other literary work from "oversees" has no place in her literary dreams. They are all "Greek" to her. Even when such vertiginous Eurocentrism is challenged it is challenged from the selfsame unconscious imperial imaginary. In their edited volume *Shades of the Planet: American Literature as World Literature* (2007), Wai Chee Dimock and Lawrence Buell offer a model of how an imperial literature can be recast as "national literature" and reflected upon from its peripheries. The result is geared toward detecting "alternate geographies, alternate histories"—though only in theoretical speculations rather than factual basis in those literary alterities.[13] My concern is not just to map out other worlds that have existed and that continue to exist outside the limited imagination of their "World Literature" but also to stress that within those worlds there is a cosmogonic universe in which real human beings have stood up and said "I," and yet that agency is now systemically violated by the imperial imprimatur of this "World Literature." The task at hand is not to force-feed those literary worlds into this "World Literature" and apply for a legal residency permit for them as "aliens" (get them a literary "Green Card" as it is called in the United States). The task is to see, recognize, acknowledge, celebrate, and critique at the same time, those alienated worlds.

Beyond that imperial imaginary that has historically enabled both the theorization of "World Literature" and certain liberal reforms within it there is a vastly different, and epistemically enabling, world—the world critical thinkers like the Argentinian-Mexican philosopher Enrique Dussel have explored and theorized in such groundbreaking works as *Philosophy of Liberation* (1980). Dussel links the philosophical hubris of this Eurocentric theorization (from which the very notion of "World Literature" has emerged) directly to the imperial arrogance of military conquest and colonial exploitation. "Spatially central, the *ego cogito* constituted the periphery and asked itself . . . 'Are the Amerindians human beings?' that is, Are they Europeans, and therefore rational animals? The theoretical response was of little importance. We are still suffering from the practical response. The Amerindians were suited to forced labor; if not irrational, then at least they were brutish, wild, underdeveloped, uncultured because they did not have the culture of the center."[14]

That "culture of the center" is not just in the normative and material foundations of the imperial cosmogony that has called itself the West and centered itself globally but even more decidedly in its epistemic hubris. That "ontology," Dussel adds, "did not come from nowhere. It arose from a previous experience of domination over other persons, of cultural oppression over other worlds. Before the *ego cogito* there is an *ego conquiro*; 'I conquer' is the practical foundation of 'I think.' "[15] Opposing this epistemology of conquest is the ontological predicate of categorically dismantling "World Literature" via a head-on collision. Any and all debates with "World Literature" are geared toward epistemically dismantling it—for good. All other liberal kinds of "provincializing Europe" or "alternate geographies, alternate histories" simply cross-authenticate that imperial hubris and all its epistemic formations. "The center has imposed itself on the periphery," Dussel rightly says, "for more than five centuries. But for how much longer? Will the geopolitical preponderance of the center come to an end? Can we glimpse a process of liberation growing from the peoples of the periphery."[16] Yes we can. We indeed must—for the idea and practices of a construct like "World Literature" as one particularly poignant ideological arm of Euro-American imperial imaginary have no room for any of its epistemic alterities. The instant it recognizes their presence and veracity it must denounce itself and join the ethics of their liberation.

Serious scholars of the *Shahnameh*, without whose monumental work the very idea of this discussion would have been impossible, object to the very proposition of bringing the Persian epic into this debate. They could not care less, they tell me, if the theorists and practitioners of what today passes for "World Literature" consider or do not consider the *Shahnameh* part of their incurable parochialism. My purpose here, as is quite evident, shares that sentiment and completely dismisses that plea to bring the *Shahnameh* into the pantheon of this "World Literature" as it is theorized today. My first and foremost purpose is once and for all to dismantle the very idea of this "World Literature" as we have received it, from Goethe to Damrosch and beyond, and put the masterpieces of world and worldly literatures, outside any scare quotes, after we have ascertained why is it that they are masterpieces, on an equal footing for a renewed global reading on the fertile ground of what Spivak rightly calls "the death of a discipline."

Gayatri Spivak's *Death of a Discipline* (2003) remains the most powerful, the most cogent, and the most earnest attempt to save "World Literature" from its innate pitfalls by forcing it into a direction it simply cannot travel, not by virtue of any will or wherewithal it lacks but simply because of its incurably imperial origin in the European liberal imagination that it can never shed for good. Spivak wisely places the discipline of Comparative Literature and with it "World Literature" next to "Area Studies," though of this latter mode of knowledge production she has a limited idea available to someone rooted in English and Comparative Literature department and a devout and professed "Europeanist." Spivak rightly points out the origin of Area Studies in the Cold War but does not see the root of this mode of knowledge production in Orientalism of the classical colonial vintage, which was the subject of Edward Said's groundbreaking scholarship.[17] Spivak then moves to argue for a strategic solidarity between Area Studies as she understands it and "Comparative Literature" as she wishes it to be. "Area Studies," she points out, "exhibit quality and rigor . . . combined with openly conservative . . . politics."[18] She is right on the first point and wrong on the second. She is right that Area Studies still thrive on philological and hermeneutic moves rooted in their Orientalist heritage, but scholars now ghettoized in that field by English department scholars have long since turned the table of power upside down and staged a will to resist power (rather than being subservient to it). She wants the discipline of "Comparative Literature" from which "World Literature" has emerged to "supplement" Area Studies and proposes, "We must take the languages of the Southern Hemisphere as active cultural media rather than as objects of cultural study by the sanctioned ignorance of the metropolitan migrant. We cannot dictate a model for this from the offices of the American Comparative Literature Association."[19] As always this is vintage Spivak brilliance—but the issue of literary confidence and aesthetic sensibility is far beyond linguistic competence of the highest degree imaginable to Spivak. Linguistic competence of the sort she envisions, and as in fact she fully recognizes, will never remedy the fundamental flaws of the disciple from its very inception by migrant European literary scholars finding a haven in the United States.

One of the main culprits in domesticating, nativizing, exoticizing, and thereby categorically alienating and deworlding the *Shahnameh* from itself and its readers is in fact this bizarre phrase of making it accessible to "the Western reader" when translating it into English. Who exactly is this "Western reader" facing a translated *Shahnameh*? What sort of a creature might that be? The person who is born to the English language or English is her or his primary language of literary, poetic, or scholarly expression? Is an Indian, a first-, second-, or tenth-generation immigrant to Canada, or the United States, an Australian, "a Western reader"? Is the thing called the Western reader a so-called white person alone? Let me speak from experience: Suppose an African-American, a Native-American, a Latino, Asian, Arab, Japanese student at Columbia University starts reading the *Shahnameh* in English for she or he knows no Persian. Is that student a "Western reader" too? The trouble with this phrase is the potent sign of the racialized encoding of the term "Western reader." You cannot go around the globe conquering the world, enslaving its inhabitants, stealing its resources, and imposing your language and culture on people and when they speak English back to you (so you understand them), then suddenly this language becomes a "Western language." English and French and such are not "Western languages" and those who speak them are not the "Western" public. People around the globe have confiscated these languages, very much as a Native American confiscated a Winchester gun from his colonizers and tormentors. That gun is now his—as English, French, or German now belongs to people in Asia, Africa, and Latin America. These are imperial languages, just as Persian, Arabic, or Ottoman Turkish were also once imperial languages. When we translate the *Shahnameh* form Persian into English we are translating it from one bygone imperial language into another dominant imperial language. For all we know Chinese might very well be the next dominant global language of our future. Until then we need to remember that the global reach of English has had to do with the British and now the American empire. As such all the subjects or citizens of that or this empire speak, read, write, obey, or defy in it. The translation of an epic from the language of one empire to another kept afar by a long historical distance must keep us aware of two or more worlds that these two languages and empires have historically informed and accompanied.

Some eight centuries before Goethe dreamed of the idea of "World Literature," and long before the idea became an ideological arm of Euro-American imperial hegemony over the world at large, in a world far away from his imagination, a Persian poet had crafted a world (as all poets often do) that had brought forth the poetic heritage of his bygone ages forward and let them shine on worlds yet to come. The richness and complexity of Ferdowsi's world predates and overrides the theoretical imaginary of Goethe as the progenitor of all those who have subsequently theorized the idea of "World Literature." The point of comparison is neither chronological nor spatial, nor indeed exclusive to Persian, Chinese, Indian, or Egyptian literary heritages. It is to mark the competing worlds that enable critical and creative thinking. The world Goethe and his European and American descendants have enabled and theorized is theirs and theirs only—and there solidly to cover up and abort the rise of alternative worlds. That world has nothing to do with other worlds, of which they know very little, and yet they do their best to assimilate backward to theirs. My attempt here is not to superimpose or place one (Persian) world against theirs (Eurocentric). Quite to the contrary. We must dismantle not just Eurocentrism but the very imperial foregrounding of any such One-Worldly arrogance. I wish therefore to make an example of this one world I know well, to point to all the other worlds (Chinese, Indian, Asian, African, Latin American) this outdated Eurocentrism embedded in "World Literature" has consistently and with imperial hubris systematically marginalized, darkened, and overshadowed.

Can the postcolonial world have an epic of its own—not an epic of triumph or defeat, of which two exclusive choices the triumphalist imperialism of "World Literature" is particularly fond—but an epic of resistance and resilience, an epic in which we can read the trials and tribulations of the very condition of our coloniality? Can this epic be a relic of the past recast in the hopes of our future? I have read and proposed reading the Persian epic as a postcolonial epic, a "world text" not of the First, Second, or Third World but of worldliness of an entirely different sort, of the postcolonial world liberated from its First World theorizations, the sort that habitually consolidates and confirms the global configuration of power, of an unjust and cruel "world system." Can we read the *Shahnameh* as a world text that has survived empires to come here to speak of bygone and defeated imperial hubris to the empire that thinks itself triumphant, exceptional, everlasting? Could White theorists of the First World (thus self-designated) perhaps stop expecting Brown theorists to bring their "national literatures" to their attention so they can grace and bless them with their "distant reading" for they are too busy theorizing "World Literature" to bother with their own close readings?

The *Shahnameh* stories are today liberated from their courtly contexts and their abusive manhandling in the course of colonial nation building. The monarchy and the Islamic Republic that came near it over the past century had little to no impact on or use for its subversive poetics. That monarchy collapsed and this Islamic Republic is categorically alien to it—caught up in the paradox of its own abusive power with a fallacious claim on Shi'ism. The text is now freed from the golden chains of all those exquisite courtly illustrations and gaudy conferences alike and thematically renewed in the tradition of its "coffeehouse paintings," the sustained aesthetics that saw it dwell in the emerging public spheres of its immediate habitat, where real people gathered and told themselves

Shahnameh stories. From those coffeehouse paintings, a renewed public pact is now evident between those ancient stories and our thinking
postcolonial truth against power. The Persian epic has been the trusted
companion of millions of human beings through the thick and thin of
their colonial encounters with European modernity. It is now rich and
reflective of the hopes and aspirations, sufferings and dreams of those
very people.

Could we perhaps consider the Persian epic as a world text by virtue
of having endured multiple empires before it was literally dismembered
into scattered pages of its former glories—and in the scars of that dismemberment it carries the marks of its postcolonial worldliness? If
so, could we then think of the *Shahnameh* as textual evidence of the
multiple nations that have known and lived it to come to terms with
their postcolonial truth and realities? Read in this light, suddenly the
Shahnameh has things to teach a world that shares its sustained history
of imperil domination and colonial abuse. The world on which "World
Literature" is theorized is the same world that has conquered, colonized,
and ravaged this planet. That world, that brutalized, denied, denigrated,
and vilified world, cannot, could not possibly, be part of this "World Literature," by definition. Any claim to the contrary is a sad practical joke.

When Fanon, in *The Wretched of the Earth*, said, "At whatever level we
study it . . . decolonization is quite simply the replacing of a certain 'species' of men by another 'species' of men. Without any period of transition, there is a total, complete, and absolute substitution,"[20] this is also
what he meant: that the very conception of "the world" in which we live
will have to change. For it is impossible to imagine that other "species"
of humanity without decoupling it from the colonial commentary on
capitalist modernity that conceived of this "World Literature" to begin
with. What made "World Literature" possible, the normative imaginary
that considered the world its property, made it impossible for any non-
European text to be part of it without denying its own worldly habitat.
Europe mapped itself against the world—from its mineral and material
resources to its cheap slave labor to its cultures and civilizations it termed,
defined, museumized, and cannibalized. The postcolonial world must
claim its own epics and narratives, the truths of its own historical

whereabouts. Unless and until the entirety of the "World Literature" project is categorically dismantled, from *A* to *Z*, from top to bottom, and its textual evidence disassembled and put on an equal footing with all other worldly texts, there is no hope for a *world literature* with a global claim to emerge. The *Shahnameh* as an allegory of itself, as an indexical reference to itself, is an allusion to that possibility.

REWORLDING THE *SHAHNAMEH*

Let me now be more specific and ask in what particular sense can we then argue the *Shahnameh* is integral to the idea of not "world" but in fact a "worldly literature," not to plead to be admitted into the pantheon of what Western European or North American literary theorists falsely claim and call "World Literature" but to mark the worldliness of literatures they so subjected to an epistemic violence when they enshrined them into *their* idea of "World Literature"? First and foremost, I have argued that the historical and textual experiences of the Persian epic must today be placed in its contemporary worldly context. The *Shahnameh* is the poetic embodiment of successive *worlds* it has encountered and now actively remembers. This remembrance must be defetishized and placed in conversation with the real world in which it now lives. The abuse of the Persian epic by postcolonial states to fake legitimacy cannot be the deadpan destiny of the *Shahnameh*. The fate of the *Shahnameh* cannot be talismanic, reduced to its symbolic significance, thus bereft of its organic encounter with the world in which it now lives. The creative adaptation of its stories or the critical edition of its finest prints are all necessary but not sufficient. Of all its varied expressions in our time I will point to one particularly powerful poetic encounter with it in an epic poetic narrative by Mehdi Akhavan-e Sales (1929–1990) as singularly significant evidence of how it has emerged to mark its postcolonial fate as a piece of modern epic, world text, or worldly text, or through a decidedly and self-consciously positing on the colonial site. This among many other similar encounters have made the

Shahnameh worldly to its current and immediate content. It is in a poem like "Khan-e Hashtom" (The eighth trial, 1967) that the *Shahnameh* has extended its presence into a critical transnational public sphere fully aware of its postcolonial fate.

The most politically potent poem of Mehdi Akhavan-e Sales's on a *Shahnameh* theme is his masterpiece "Khan-e Hashtom."[21] In this landmark poem, Akhavan summons his legendary command over Persian epic poetry to bring Ferdowsi's *Shahnameh* forward to visit his contemporary issues.

> *Yadam amad han . . .*
> Oh I just remembered:
> I was telling you this that night too—
> It was so bitterly cold.

The narrator proceeds to tell the story of how during one bitterly cold evening he had found refuge in a warm and cozy coffeehouse where a master *naqqal* was the center of everyone's attention. The *naqqal* looks, acts, speaks, and carries himself like a Khorasan nobleman, dressed and presented in a manner that invokes the image of Ferdowsi. Akhavan sets the stage so we have a sense of the cold winter outside, a warm gathering inside, with the *naqqal* in total command of his audience. Then he tells his audience how Ferdowsi has already narrated the "Seven Tasks of Rostam," and now,

> I recite the Eighth Trial,
> I whose name is Mas!

"Mas" here stands for Mehdi Akhavan-e Sales, placing himself directly in the line of Ferdowsi, and it is in that line that he begins to tell his story as the continuation of the Persian epic poet's:

> This is the story, yes, it is the story of pain,
> This is not just any old poem,
> This is the measure of love and hate,
> The measure of manhood and cowardice,

This is no abstract nonsensical verse—
This is a rugged rug of misfortune,
Soaking with the blood of Sohrabs and many Seyavashes—and
It's like a blanket over the coffin of Takhti[22] . . .
Yes, I am the narrator, the narrator am I:
Let me repeat as I have repeated only too many times:
I am the narrator of forgotten stories,
An owl sitting on the ruins of the cursed land of history—
An owl on the roof of this Ruinousville,
The turtledove cooing on top of these destroyed palaces.

The mirror of history, the narrator tells us, is broken, but by some sort of strange magic the image in the broken mirror appears unbroken. The master *naqqal*, Mehdi Akhavan-e Sales's own self-projection, now stands in the middle of the crowd, pointing with his fist and mace toward "the West" with hatred, and toward "the East" with contempt. What follows is an agony, a pain, a deeply rooted cry for freedom from the depth of the ditch into which Rostam was cast by his own brother and murdered. Here Akhavan turns the sense of tragedy in many *Shahnameh* stories into a contemporary lamentation against treachery and treason, tyrannical backwardness from inside and colonial domination from abroad. Rostam, now poetically resurrected into a contemporary defeated hero, is deep inside the ditch, full of poisonous daggers and arrows, with his brother looking over him with treacherous satisfaction.

Now that pole of confidence and hope for Iranshahr,
That champion of fearsome battles,
The towering hero,
The son of the Ancient Zal, world champion,
That Master and Rider of the matchless Rakhsh,[23]
The hero whose name when calling for a rival to fight
Would make the pillars of the world tremble in fear,
The hero who had no rival in combat,
That superior warrior, that old champion triumphing over lions,
He who upon his Rakhsh looked like a mountain upon a
    mountain,

A thicket of lions in armor,

He from whose lips—

Just like a key to the lock of a treasure house full of pearls—

The Smile would never fade away,

Be it a day of peace and he committed to love,

Or a day of war determined to fight . . .

Yes, now Tahamtan and his valiant Rakhsh

Were lost in the depth of this poisonous ditch full of daggers,

The Hero of the Seven Trials was now trapped in the maw of
the Eighth.

The telling of this Eighth Trial brings to a timely height the epic narrative of the *Shahnameh*, makes it real, palpable, contemporary. Akhavan's epic language echoes Ferdowsi's, mirrors his sentiments, updates his heroic diction. Akhavan's "Eighth Trial" is the epitome of the postcolonial moment when the fate of the nation with a solid command over Ferdowsi's legacy remembers its epic heroes and summons them to address its contemporary predicaments.

The sequel to "The Eighth Trial" is "Adamak" (The little man, 1968) that follows soon after its prequel poem and depicts the selfsame coffeehouse on a winter night crowded with an equally enthusiastic crowd, although this time gathering around not a master *naqqal* but a television set. Akhavan's denunciation of the television set here becomes emblematic of his condemnation of modernity and machine, made powerful and poignant by his prominent contemporary public intellectual Jalal Al-Ahmad in his classical text *Gharbzadeghi* (Westoxication, 1962). This sequel poem is the epitome of the moment when Ferdowsi's *Shahnameh* is brought to bear on an epochal condemnation of colonial modernity, albeit with a deep sense of nostalgia.

He who now tells stories—from inside the magic box—

The souvenir of the West:

Is a wolf-fox thieving trickster of a novelty—

Its seed is European its mother American,

The most pernicious enchanting thief—

Though the crowd knows this,
They still gather with commotion around that magic box,
The thief of their world and thief of their faith,
As if this cunning stranger were that precious master *naqqal* of
    yore.

Akhavan then turns his camera to a corner of the coffeehouse where we see the old master *naqqal* sitting in solitude, his heart full of anger and watching from a distance the European magic box. Times have changed, and Akhavan has a painful sarcastic message for the children of his time:

Sweet dear children, very good children,
Let's celebrate the living heroes,
Listen to us, the past is dead,
Long live the present and the future,
As for you who love the dead heroes,
Now it is our turn to live, we the living,
You see and you know us,
We whom they talk about and you know well,
As for you the lovers of dead heroes,
We are now Sam of Nariman, the Ancient Zal,
We are the legendary Rostam and the brave Sohrab,
We are Faramarz, we are Borzu.[24]

Delivering this bitter sarcastic farewell, declaring the death of old heroism in the face of the changing machinery of modernity, the master *naqqal* gets up and leaves the coffeehouse, and before he exists he goes to the window and upon its steamed glass plate with his thumb draws the shape of a little man, which as soon as it is shaped starts melting into a little apparition . . . of Rostam.

Mehdi Akhavan-e Sales's "The Eighth Trial" and "The Little Man" are the extended logic and rhetoric of the *Shahnameh* into the postcolonial modernity of Iran as the site of a now politically poignant reading of the Persian epic. These poems are by no means the only ones. They are two among many others, though Akhavan Sales had a particular penchant for such politically charged renewed epic narratives in his poetic redisposition. In these and similar poems the heroes and epic narrative they occasion are foreign, but the scenes they provoke are decidedly familiar and contemporary. Akhavan Sales assumes the heroic voice of Ferdowsi, an incarnation of the Persian poet, underlined by the fact that he too comes from Khorasan. He turns the Persian *Book of Kings* decidedly against the atrocities of his time, marks his nostalgic yearning for bygone ages, rehistoricizes the Persian epic, and places it on the map of a postcolonial nation. Poems like these by Mehdi Akhavan-e Sales mark the living organicity of an epic like the *Shahnameh*, pushing forward its stories, heroes, and dramatic forces into uncharted contemporary territories. Ferdowsi in effect lives in Akhavan as his *Shahnameh* does in much of his nostalgic poetry. The Persian epic becomes a living, breathing text in the poetry of Akhavan, its unresolved dramatic tensions retrieved for contemporary history. There is no "translating" this organicity of the text and its "supplements" into any other language or any conception of "World Literature" as we understand it. The task at hand is categorically to abandon the failed but still poignant project of "World Literature" and to try to understand the living worldliness of texts such as the *Shahnameh* beyond any straitjacket admission into the vacuous pantheon of a Euro-universalist "World Literature." The discursive formation of "World Literature," its "dispositive" (apparatus), is self-referential and any and all its encounters with "other literatures" by definition cannibalistic and anthropological.

Such poetic supplements to the *Shahnameh* as Mehdi Akhavan-e Sales's are not fortuitous but in fact integral to its narrative and temporal logic. What has textually sustained the enduring significance of the *Shahnameh* for generations past, present, and yet to come is its poetic fusion of three interrelated narrative modes: mythic, heroic, and historical, working together in the inner dynamics of an imperial world in and of itself. That is the reason there has never been any Persianate empire without first and foremost appealing to the archetypal power of the *Shahnameh*, the commissioning of its glorious production in the royal ateliers. The result is a triangulated poetic narrative that underlies all those segments and sustains a sculpted tragic subject at the heart of the epic narrative. It is right here that we need to posit and postulate the position of the *Shahnameh* as worldly literature. From Goethe to Damrosch, Moretti, Said, Spivak, Apter, and others, all think and operate within a known or contested world, all, without a single exception, Euro-universalist even (or particularly) when they contest it. Oblivious therefore they all remain to the forgotten worlds, invisible worlds, the hidden worlds, and the possible and impossible worlds, and all their innate worldliness.

Fully conscious of the rise and fall of empires, the *Shahnameh* is the product of an imperial world and as such it becomes integral to all the subsequent imperial worlds it narratively inhabits and politically informs. It becomes poetically iconic to those worlds and definitive to the spirit of those ages and eventually stays afoot until the twists and turns of history lead to the collapse of all those empires and witness the rise of postcolonial nation-states. What has sustained the *Shahnameh* as a prototype of worldly literature is not just the multiple and successive world empires that have given rise and then arisen by it to the point of informing postimperial nation-states that have a claim on the Persian text. But the fact that the text itself is made of a triangulated narrative of mythic, heroic, and historical moments, which the poet places within a singular poetic event, allowing for each to animate the others. This in turn sustains a triangulated, sculpted, and ultimately tragic subject best evident in its central *heroic* figure Rostam (excluding the *mythic* and the *historical* parts), who is born to an unwanted and outcast child, fathers a son whom he inadvertently kills, and his own final demise is in the hands of his treacherous brother. Though engulfed by tragedy, Rostam is not a tragic hero. Quite to the contrary: he is a worldly hero, embedded in a world of triumphant battles, erotic encounters, and festive celebrations of life.

Because of such fresh and unexamined domains of an enduring epic, I offer the *Shahnameh* as a prototype of a worldly literature precisely because contrary to Homer's *Odyssey* or Virgil's *Aeneid* it has not yet been *worlded* into the overriding fiction of "the West" and thus remains a fertile ground to the unfolding worlds way beyond the charted territories of the "world" we know as the ideological forestructure of Eurocentric imperium. The *Shahnameh* is a worldly epic because it does not belong exclusively to any given postcolonial state but remains entirely animated within multiple nations that could justly claim it. Its fusion of mythic, heroic, and historical moments gives it a miasmic and amorphous temporal character true to that transnational public sphere upon which it continues to thrive.

WORLD AS THE SITE AND THE SUBJECT OF HISTORY

Ferdowsi's *Shahnameh* speaks of both thriving nations and of bygone empires, of expansive and enabling myths and of tragic and debilitating history, and it speaks of noble heroes and corrupt kings. Its narrative was and has remained dialogical; no monarchy or empire could ever claim one triumphant side without embracing the other judgment, appropriate its politics without subjecting itself to its ethics. The psychological disposition of the epic subject is always contingent on the narrative site of the unfolding drama in combined forces of mythic, heroic, and historical fusion of the narrative. This epic subject becomes fatherless (with Sohrab as the epitome of *Shahnameh* heroes) and suspends the "mommy-baby-daddy" triumvirate, while history is absorbed into the heroic and the mythic in order to alter the matrix of time and narrative upon which the patriarchal father is posited and empowered. This subject and site of history posit a different world we need to discover in which the *Shahnameh* becomes a piece of "worldly" literature.

To come to terms with the worldly disposition of the *Shahnameh* as an epic, we need to understand *the epic subject* it posits through its *mythic, heroic,* and *historical* phases as, respectively, solitary, tragic, and omniscient. The epic subject is the creature of a time and timeliness decidedly different from those in which it has been successively received through its subsequent political histories. The epic subject of the *Shahnameh* is inaugural. That epic subject was an allegorical microcosm of the empires it had informed and that had informed its knowing possibilities the instant Ferdowsi puts pen to paper and starts writing the *Shahnameh*. Today, how can a postcolonial subject relate to or be rooted in an epic subject thus framed? This question must be answered thematically in terms domestic to the poetic idiomaticity of the *Shahnameh*. The mythic subject (Jamshid, for example) is all knowing, cosmic, present at the moment when the world was conceived, articulated, and delivered. The epic subject is primary like Kiumars, all powerful like Jamshid, omnipresent like the poetic voice of Ferdowsi himself. Ferdowsi as omniscient narrator of the drama of existence is the prototype of the epic subject in its opening mythic moment. Ferdowsi's voice is the paramount parameter of assurance in constituting the epic subject as coconscious of the authorship of the text. We recite with Ferdowsi when he says solemnly, "In the Name of the God of Soul and Reason." We effectively cocompose that inaugural benediction of the epic. The very utterance of the phrase "In the Name of the God . . ." is a declaration of intention and purpose, a beginning anticipating a delivery and moving toward a conclusion and an end. A totality is therefore announced at the very beginning of the text as a text—and the epic subject at the moment of its mythic initiation casts a long and lasting shadow over the world the Persian epic posits and inhabits.

As we move from the *mythic* toward the *heroic* the epic subject becomes self-conscious, deliberate, self-referential, now fully aware of the longevity of its own subjectivity. Rostam here is the combative consciousness of the epic, totally aware of himself, and in every heroic move he and his friends and foes make he is as much conscious of his mortality as he is of the immortality of the time that frames him. The sense of the tragic here makes the epic subject fragile, fragmentary, and therefore allegorical. The *heroic* brings the world closer to the *historical* while still seamlessly rooted in the *mythic*. By the time we move from the *heroic* to the *historical*, say from Alexander to Anushirvan, history is already pregnant with its own alterity and as such can never be allowed a metaphysics of its own certainties. Such certainties are offered vertically via the rootedness of the *historical* consciousness in the *heroic* and the *mystic*, and not teleologically by virtue of a self-unfolding Hegelian *Geist*. The time of the Persian epic is therefore decidedly, consciously, and purpose-fully un-Hegelian. This non-Hegelian world cannot be subjected to a "World Literature" rooted in Goethe's Hegelian consciousness.

In the term "World Literature" we must dwell first and foremost on "World" and then on "Literature"—for as we see them today both these terms are loaded with their Euro-universalist history. European impe-rialism divided the world to rule it better with little to no regard for the worlds that existed before or that could emerge within or adjacent to or could come after it. "Literature," too, has a generic European ring to it. For my purpose here I take the word *adab* (which I have translated as "literary humanism")[25] more seriously. The world of the *Shahnameh* occurs in the world of *adab*, as Persian literary humanism, and in that world it expands from the mythic through the heroic down to the his-torical, and the tragic hero who dwells upon the ever-widening spectrum of this time immemorial dies to be born a fatherless child. Ferdowsi is the first and foremost hero of his own epic, born to a drama out of a poetic wedlock an outsider to his own profession. The apocryphal anec-dote about Ferdowsi barging in on three court poets (Farrokhi, Onsori, and Asjadi) is the symbolic indication that he is an entirely alien figure in his own literary homeland. He does not belong. The three court poets, according to this hagiographic account, were having a picnic, and Fer-dowsi asks to join them. They look at his ruffian appearance and do not wish him to join their august gathering, so they tell him they are three prominent court poets and he can join them only if he can complete a quatrain of which they will compose three hemistichs. They then delib-erately chose a rhyming word of which they are certain there are only three words in the Persian language. Ferdowsi surprises and outshines them and comes up with the name of a *Shahnameh* hero that rhymes with those three words and of whom the court poets were ignorant. The folkloric stories about him and Sultan Mahmoud are all an indication of a defiant poet son contentious with his patron father. Mahmoud here is a fictive character, so is Ferdowsi. Mahmoud has always been a poetic trope—as in the stories of Mahmoud and Ayaz, his favorite slave with whom he had a homoerotic relationship that eventually crossed the boundaries of history and entered mystic dimensions. Stories of a thank-less Mahmoud and a dutiful Ferdowsi all point to the inaugural mythic moment of the Persian epic being predicated on a moment of paternal betrayal. That inaugural moment suspends the entirety of *The Book of Kings* on a moral predicament in which no ruling monarch can ever be completely morally victorious (there is always "a dram of evil" in the very best of them), no world can be eternal, no power legitimate, and nothing but the poetic *sokhan* (*logos*) be the ethical logic and rhetoric of history. That world is worldly and can never yield to the authority of an imperially postulated "World" in "World Literature."

In any reading of the Persian epic, we must keep in mind how Ferdowsi keeps the mythic, the heroic, and historical moments together and, just like Ibn Khaldun or Giambattista Vico, sustains a theory of history predicated on his fusion of these three instances seamlessly interwoven to posit an alternative temporal space. We also need to recall how the Persian poet himself, Abolqasem Ferdowsi, has lived his mortal life through the three components of the mythic, heroic, and historical, having come together in his own lifetime, his epic poetry and the structure of his narrative fusion of the three into one, and lived that world in person. Ferdowsi narrates these three phases into one another, weaves them into each other, whereby the stories that are not his are recalled through a formal structure that is indeed his, whereby the *Shahnameh* becomes the narrative testament of this fusion of the three temporal moments. Time, narrative, subjectivity, and worldliness are therefore held tightly together in the course of a single epic text that crafts its own world and worldliness. Subsequent empires and their history are therefore instantly assimilated into a transhistorical frame of reference beyond their political control. Theorizing that worldliness, predicated on that particular fusion of times and narratives, demands its own logic and rhetoric.

The *Shahnameh* has been used and abused, exoticized or neglected, and like all other classics it has been more cited than read. In a successive conflation of epic and empires, multiple empires have lived mythic, heroic, and historical lives and are thereby verified or dismantled by the fusion of those three. The Persian epic is therefore tragically triumphalist, as Quint would say, and triumphantly tragic, at one and the same time. Empires have fallen, upon their ruins nations arisen, as colonialism has severed the mythic and the heroic from the historical and therefore dismantled the possibility of meaning to history within the Persian epic narrative, but instead the art (mythic) and politics (heroic) of anti-colonial struggle have replaced them to give meaning to a hapless history. The postcolonial person is therefore bereft of the three temporal moments held together and under the false consciousness of any colonized mind the integral agency of the postcolonial person must be restored. The imperial, colonial, and the national come together to form a defiant subject through false consciousness and the tragic loss at the heart of all triumphalist vainglories. The *Shahnameh* will give you an entirely different perspective on Iranian (or any other postcolonial) cultural identity and history. It is decidedly non-Islamic (not anti-Islamic) evidence of Iran that cannot be reduced to its Islamic identity. The Pahlavis abused it for their own dynastic reasons, while the Islamic Republic by and large ignores it, for it can see no legitimizing reason in it. But both that abuse and this neglect are the political indexes of the literary significance of the *Shahnameh* that has survived and will survive both the Pahlavi dynasty and the Islamic Republic in order to reach a much wider postcolonial world and worldliness.

THE WORLDLY INTERIORITY OF THE PERSIAN EPIC

How is that worldliness to be assayed? The *Shahnameh* is the textual epiphany of the Persian epic and its winding encounters with multiple world empires, from the Samanids and the Ghaznavids in the tenth and eleventh centuries to the Safavids in the sixteenth century and finally the Qajars in the nineteenth century. In the age of its postcolonial predicament with the Pahlavis and the Islamic Republic, the Persian epic finally, and for good, parted ways with its historical abuses. It has now finally lost its political usefulness and is poised to safeguard its poetic power. The Persian epic can no longer support or sustain any imperial or dynastic designs on it. It can only historicize, humble, and dismantle any state that comes near it. Over the past two centuries it has in effect become a deeply subversive text because of its extraordinary adventurers having served and subverted multiple empires in its long and illustrious history. With all its imperial pretensions now historically overcome, the *Shahnameh* is here to stand on its own narrative devices, poetic prowess, political innuendos, textual unpredictabilities. Here the *Shahnameh* stands, like all other world masterpieces, in and out of itself provincializing any and all theories of "World Literature" that have failed to come to terms with its varied and multiple worlds, the world in which it was created, the world it poetically posits, and the multiple worlds in which it has been received and read.

Much of the artistry of the *Shahnameh* was lost to the empires that sought to abuse it—for they had no use for it. What has, for example, the story of Zal have to do with any empire? Not just the story of Zal, every other story of the Persian epic is the whole of the *Shahnameh* in a miniature painting. Zal is born to a beautiful mother and a noble father. Zal is albino, born with white hair and a white complexion. The father is ashamed of his son's appearance. The newborn boy is left out in the wilderness to fend for himself—an infant, defenseless, vulnerable, lonesome. A magnificent bird, Simorgh, comes down to him from his mountain high. God in his majestic mercy had planted the love of this boy in the heart of the mighty bird, and the bird saves the child and raises him as if his own child. The boy grows up and becomes a valiant hero. It was destined that the boy would grow and prosper. He would soon father the hero of all other heroes of the *Shahnameh*, the one and only Rostam. But the pain of being abandoned by his father upon his birth will always remain with him, and with us. What's wrong with having white hair? Why was he left to be raised by animals, however kind and generous like Simurgh, and then how can we explain the love, kindness, and parental generosity with which Simurgh raises this child? *Khodavand mehri beh Simurgh dad*—"God planted love in Simurgh's heart!"

How are we to read the *Shahnameh* at the threshold of the twenty-first century? Since its very composition around the year 1000 in the Christian calendar, the Persian epic has been chief among the accoutrements of power. It has been far more beautifully illustrated and copied and written in exquisite calligraphy than critically read, discussed, and understood. Generation after generation what we have are illustrated manuscripts of the text and scarcely anything resembling critical, analytic, or theoretical encounters with the epic itself. Until very recently it has been far more a talismanic of imperial power than a poetic of resistance to it. It was only during the Pahlavi period that Iranian scholars began to take over from European Orientalists in preparing the critical edition of Ferdowsi's epic and launch a sustained course of critical encounter with the text, and the poetics of its purpose.

It was during this latter phase of critical encounter with the Persian epic that we began to realize how ennobling is the sense of the tragic hero in the *Shahnameh*. The hero here does not dwell on his or her moment of tragic incidence. The hero ennobles the story, and with it the epic, and eventually disappears. What remains is the quintessence and the aftertaste of the heroic incidents. They occur, gather momentum, leave their emotive traces, and disappear, story after story, incidence after incidence, leaving a lasting mark on your soul. The *Shahnameh* is no single postcolonial epic. It belongs to each and every such nation that has emerged from the historical Persianate empires from the Ghaznavids to the Qajars and has dwelled poetically in the inner sanctum of the epic. The Persian epic generates its own "nationhood," or "peoplehood," by virtue of the sustained course of sentiments it sustains and that it has helped its readers imagine for millennia from one end of the earth to the next. It carries its ancient relics forward and around but not into any historical posterior only. It carries them into its own textual interiority in that labyrinth of epic interiority, in that indwelling, of the sense of the tragic epic, the *Shahnameh* heals its own wounds. It is a living organism of truth and narrative.

FROM ALEXANDER TO ANUSHIRVAN

The Persian emperor Darab, according to the *Shahnameh*, was married to Nahid, the daughter of the Byzantine emperor. Soon after their marriage the king discovers his bride has a foul-smelling mouth, which results in sending her back to her father. Meanwhile Nahid is pregnant and soon gives birth to a son, whom she calls Alexander. Darab, however, marries another Persian princess, who soon gives birth to Dara. Dara and Alexander are therefore half brothers, from one royal Persian father and two mothers, one a Greek and the other a Persian princess. When Dara and Alexander ultimately face each other on the battlefield, and Alexander is victorious, this is a clear case of fratricide, a brother overpowering another in his quest for the Persian throne. The dramatic narrative here overcomes the historical Alexander of Macedonia facing Darius III. What remains here is the loving farewell of Dara to his half brother Alexander while dying in his arms. Alexander marries Dara's daughter Roshanak and unites the kingdoms of Rome, Iran, and beyond.

The wise and judicious character of Alexander at the end of the Kianian dynasty in the *heroic* age is then replicated in the figure of Anushirvan the Just at the height of the historical period. Anushirvan's relationship to his wise vizier, Bozorgmehr, is on the model of Alexander's to Aristotle as developed in the Alexander Romance genre, splitting the Platonic idea of the "philosopher-king" into two figurative and intimately interrelated characters. It is imperative to remember here that the historical Alexander is believed to have been fond of Xenophon's *Cyropaedia*, a mirror for princes that would remain for generations exceptionally important in the course of the European imperial imaginary. This transfusion of power and knowledge in the fictional characterization of Cyrus the Great in Xenophon's book is equally (though not identically) present to the text of the *Shahnameh* and its characterizations of Anushirvan and Bozorgmehr, and even to some degree in Alexander and Aristotle. But here, contrary to what Foucault would later argue, power is not the source of knowledge but exactly the other way around: knowledge is the source of power, and the oft-repeated axiomatic phrase of the *Shahnameh*, *tavana bovad har keh dana bovad* (Whoever is wise is powerful), explicitly posits knowledge against brute force.

The cumulative knowledge of wise kings triumphs over their vanishing power when cast upon the transfusion of the three narrative moments of the *Shahnameh*. The three tropes of mythic, heroic, and historical narratives become unified in Ferdowsi's epic and dismantle such European philosophers of history as Vico and Hegel and their respective teleologi-cal philosophies of history. History is not teleological in the *Shahn-ameh*. Its dialectic is integral to its unfolding course. The world of the *Shahnameh* is a decidedly anti-Hegelian world. Its *Geist*, as it were, does not unfold progressively. It flowers in and out and through itself. The dia-lectic of knowledge and power here is dialogical; that dialogical prose and poetry of history fracture the totality of any political or literary claim on the *Shahnameh*, including and in particular that of "World Litera-ture," as it charts its own path predicated on the world and worldliness of its inaugural moment.

Toward the end of the *Shahnameh* Ferdowsi writes of his advancing age and that, upon the completion of his lifetime achievement, he was not properly rewarded or appreciated. But he assures himself that soon his wisdom will be spread around the world and cultured and learned people will always praise him for his *Shahnameh*. All these lines are marked with specific dates—I am sixty-five, he says, and then a few lines later seventy-one, and then he dates his concluding page with the year 400 in the Islamic calendar (1009–1010 in the Christian calendar). He as a poet is here fully conscious of his own mortality, of the time when he finishes his lifework, worries about its survival, wishes for its endurance, praises those who have supported him, criticizes those who did not. His ego has assumed full historical dimensions, his voice yet anxious, his mind restless, his boastful consciousness of the significance of what he has achieved marked by the frailty of the feeling of his own imminent mortality. He is alive when he is writing those lines, full of his fragile humanity, the very glory of a life purposefully lived and meaningfully left for posterity now signing off the very last pages of his masterpiece.

AN EPIC FOR ALL SEASONS

The *Shahnameh*, I have argued and demonstrated, was composed in an imperial age and successively used and abused by multiple other empires that appeared after its composition. It has had a symbolic and almost talismanic significance in consecutive imperial ages, all the way from the Ghaznavids to the Mughals, the Safavids and the Qajars, and even to the Ottomans. The Persian epic, speaking of foregone empires in archetypal tones, finally reached the age of colonial and postcolonial nation-states, when it was made to be useful for occasions of literary national pride and concomitant state-building ideologies and projects. But I have wondered beyond these historic origins and successive uses and abuses to which Ferdowsi's magnum opus has been put how we are to read it today and in what sense we can consider it a piece of *world literature*. Will this designation increase or diminish the historic or contemporary significance of the Persian epic? To answer such questions, I have suggested we must begin with the proposition that the very idea of "World Literature" as we know it today is deeply and irredeemably Euro-universalist and therefore by nature cannibalistic. The instant it approaches any other equally if not even more worldly piece of literature it cannot digest it and perforce distorts it in the totality of its worldliness. We must, therefore, move toward the Persian (or Chinese, Japanese, etc.) text itself—in its original language—where we discover it is neither Hegelian in its historiography nor indeed compatible with the prevalent ideas of epic as either triumphalist or defeatist, linear or episodic, as David Quint has suggested. We need therefore first and foremost to come to terms with the organic totality, the irreplaceable worldliness, of the text itself.

In this historical context, I have therefore proposed the *Shahnameh* to have marked and posited itself, as the established scholarship has for long maintained, through three successive moments of *mythic*, *heroic*, and *historical* narrative textures, which thematic sequence I have then concluded constitutes a whole different mode of layered subjectivity in the *Shahnameh* that is decidedly un-Hegelian, or even counter-Hegelian. Those three periods of the *Shahnameh* are not merely sequential. They are paradigmatic forces of a vastly different conception of history when we take them together. We should also consider the fact that its dramatic unfolding is neither triumphalist nor defeatist, neither exclusively linear nor exclusively episodic—that it is decidedly a defiant epic whose *stories* trump its *histories*, its *poetics* undercuts its *politics*, its *infinity* of disclosing unanticipated horizons overcoming the *totality* of its narratives. The central traumas of the Persian epic, as many scholars have already noted,[26] are those of fathers killing their sons (Rostam and Sohrab, Goshtasp and Esfandiar, Key Kavous and Seyavash are the most prominent cases) and not sons killing their fathers (with the exception of the singular case of Zahhak, who indirectly does kill his father through Iblis). That fact turns the Freudian conception of the civilizing guilt of "delayed obedience" into the defiant disposition of "delayed defiance," as I have argued and demonstrated in the case of Shi'ism, which now appears as a case-specific manifestation of a much larger *Shahnameh* narrative trope. Yes, Shi'ism as a religion of protest is rooted in Islamic history, but its effective dramatization of the trauma of Imam Hossein in Karbala is predicated on a specifically *Shahnameh* narrative trope.

From here I have then moved to point out the paradox of people around the world in which the *Shahnameh* is to be read as "World Literature" are reading it in most cases in English, a fact that must run through the equally paradoxical phenomenon that English is now a globally distributed postcolonial language. More non-British and in fact non-Europeans now communicate in English than the British or even the Europeans do together. Creative writers in Asia, Africa, Australia, and North America (where English is a colonial legacy) have been writing works of poetry and fiction in English at least matching in significance if not surpassing in volume and import those written by the British or in fact by Europeans in general. Here we must be clear: the only reason anybody cares to read what these Western European or North American scholars think of what they call "World literature" is that they write their speculations in English, or in French or German, or some other tongue they believe is a "European language." If they did so in Arabic, Persian, Bengali, or Chinese nobody could care less what they fantasize or insist on calling "World Literature." When they write in English they think themselves "Western" and take English to be a "Western language," and thus they take this whole affair as an entirely "Western" business. But there's the rub. English is not merely a British or exclusively "Western" language but a decidedly colonial and thereafter a postcolonial language. It categorically belongs to the people British imperialism and colonialism once conquered and ruled. We now own this language. It is ours. It is not our colonial rulers' and tormentors' anymore. The T. B. Macaulay treachery in his infamous "Minute on Education" (1835) to train a cadre of Indian intellectuals who looked Indian on the outside but thought like the British inside has indeed turned upside down and we the conquered colonials have now devoured our colonial masters' language, digested it, and made it our own. Fanon wrote *The Wretched of the Earth* in French, Edward Said *Orientalism* in English. But English is not a "Western" language, it is a postcolonial global language. They used it to rule over us as they used the Manchester gun to conquer our lands. But the same way that occasionally Native Americans took those Winchester rifles ("the gun that won the West") and started shooting back at their conquerors, we too, the colonized world too, has now taken English away from them and have long since started talking back at them. We have destroyed this house that they thought was their "House of Being." With this language we have built much more democratically leveled houses, into which we welcome the whole world, to enter and rethink what is *worldly literature*. When an Asian, African, South, or even North American disabused of the myth of "the West" reads the *Shahnameh* in English he or she is reading it not in a "Western" language of conquest but in a postcolonial language of defiance, where the Persian epic now squarely belongs. The innate dynamics of the Persian original, where its *poetics* triumphs over its *politics* and its *epic narrative* trumps its *imperial uses*, allows for its traumas of *delayed defiance* be linked to the paradoxical fact that English as a postcolonial language is where the *Shahnameh* must be retrieved as a piece of *worldly literature*. This reading of the Persian epic will show it for what it is s: an exemplary text to be read against the stale, self-referential, self-defeating, chasing-after-its-own-tail, sad saga of "World Literature."

Zeh niku sokhan beh cheh andar jahan . . ., Ferdowsi writes early in his *Shahnameh*,

> What is better than beautiful words in this world
> To those noble souls who appreciate good words?

If the origin of these words were not God Almighty Himself
How would the Noble Prophet be our Guide?

In his *Shahnameh*, Ferdowsi elevated the very existence, the very texture, the sound and certainty, of words to the status of sublime divinity. Words, good speech, eloquent diction—these were the very quintessence of civilization to Ferdowsi, the very secret of our existence in this world. We came to be through one simple and majestic word of God, who commanded with a single word, "Be," and we "were." The entirety of the *Shahnameh* is an ode to the miracle of words, the poetry of our existence, the key to who and what we are. Ferdowsi never minces words. He knows them inside out, hears their sounds, listens to their echoes, understands the shades of their meanings. For Ferdowsi *sokhan* is coterminous with *kherad*, *sokhan* is "word," *kherad* is "wisdom." He was an archaeologist of words, a gemologist of good diction. "My stories," he once said, "may become old, but they become new every time they are recited in any gathering." Every time I have taught the *Shahnameh* in my classes, and now in this book, the summation of my thoughts and feelings about this precious book, I have thought myself blessed with the accidental privilege of having been born into Ferdowsi's language, whispered into my ears with my mother's lullabies, to be able to occasion one of such countless gatherings around his immortal text.

NOTES

INTRODUCTION

1. In the best and most recent translation of the *Shahnameh* by Dick Davis, Abolqasem Ferdowsi, *Shahnameh: The Persian Book of Kings* (London: Penguin Books, 1997), the distinguished translator has alas opted not to translate these exceptionally important prolegomena of the Persian epic and to go straight to its first stories. Just a few select lines of the opening passage do, however, appear in the translator's introduction (xiv). This is a most unfortunate decision. It is like going to see a Mozart opera and suddenly realizing that the conductor has opted to dispense with the overture!

2. The idea of the *Shahnameh* meaning "The Best Book" is not new. As early as the thirteenth century al-Rawandi, in *Rahat al-Sudur*, speaks of the *Shahnameh* as *Shah-e Nameh-ha*, "the best of books," and *Sar-dafter-e Ketab-ha*, "top among books." See al-Rawandi, *Rahat al-Sudur* (Leiden: Brill, Gibb Memorial Series, 1921), 59, 357.

3. Abolqasem Ferdowsi, *Shahnameh*, Julius Mohl ed. (Tehran: Jibi Publications, 1965), 1:30. My translation. Dick Davis does not translate this crucial passage in his text but alludes to it in his introduction.

4. In this reading I am deliberately limiting myself to the text of Ferdowsi's poem itself, which contains a very gentle and even bashful reference to Zahhak's mother. Otherwise, in a magnificent piece of scholarship, and based on pre-*Shahnameh* Pahlavi sources, Mahmoud Omidsalar has documented that the relationship between Zahhak and his mother, who in these sources is named as Vadak, was actually incestuous. Omidsalar's psychoanalytic reading of this mother-son relationship helps cast the story of Zahhak and his mother to have a much more definitive presence in our reading of the rest of the *Shahnameh*. See Mahmoud Omidsalar, "The Dragon Fight in the National Persian Epic," *International Review of Psycho-analysis* 14 (1987): 343–56.

5. Gilles Deleuze, *Masochism: "Coldness and Cruelty" and "Venus in Furs"* (New York: Zone Books, 1991).

6. With different variations this story appears in many sources. I cite this version from a folkloric account collected by renowned Iranian folklorist Seyyed Abu al-Qasem Enjavi Shirazi in *Mardom va Ferdowsi* (People and Ferdowsi) (Tehran: Soroush Publications, 2535/1976), 37–40.

7. I have examined the impact of these translations and receptions of the *Shahnameh* on European social and cultural history and beyond in *Persophilia: Persian Culture on the Global Scene* (Cambridge, Mass.: Harvard University Press, 2015), 67–79.

8. Despite (or perhaps because of) my deep admiration for Dick Davis's translation of Ferdowsi's *Shahnameh*, it is deeply disappointing to see he has left some of the most precious passages of the Persian epic untranslated. Unfortunately, his explanation of his choices in his learned introduction (xxxiii), that he has followed a *naqqali* tradition of popular performances through prosimetrum, is not only unconvincing but also in fact reveals a deeply flawed understanding of the highly courtly and decidedly imperial disposition of the entirely poetic Persian original.

9. Hamid Dabashi, *The World of Persian Literary Humanism* (Cambridge, Mass.: Harvard University Press, 2012).

10. Dipesh Chakrabarty, *Provincializing Europe: Postcolonial Thought and Historical Difference* (Princeton, N.J.: Princeton University Press, 2000).

1. THE PERSIAN EPICS

1. This homage to the opening sentence of Herman Melville's *Moby-Dick* is my loving tribute to a magnificent modern epic brilliantly discussed by my distinguished colleague Franco Moretti in his seminal book *Modern Epic: The World-System from Goethe to García Márquez*, trans. Quintin Hoare (London: Verso, 1996), to which you will see I have many occasions to refer.

2. For a thorough examination of the relationships between the *Shahnameh* of Ferdowsi and *Khvatay-namak* genre, see Mohammad Roshan, "Khoday-nameh-ha va Shahnameh-ye Ferdowsi" (*Khvatay-namak* and Ferdowsi's *Shahnameh*), *Kelk*, nos. 7, 9 (Mehr and Azar 1369/September and November 1990).

3. Djalal Khaleghi-Motlagh, "Mo'arrefi va Arzyabi Barkhi az Dastneveshteh-ha-ye Shahnameh," *Iran Nameh* 11 (spring 1364/1985): 377–406; 13 (fall 1364/1985): 16–47; 14 (winter 13641986): 225–55.

4. For a detailed account of the pre-Islamic sources of Iranian history, see "Historiography: Pre-Islamic Period," in *Encyclopaedia Iranica*, http://www.iranicaonline.org /articles/historiography-ii.

5. Hamid Dabashi, *Persophilia: Persian Culture on the Global Scene* (Cambridge, Mass.: Harvard University Press, 2015), 148–59.

6. For an exquisite essay on the history of the word *vatan* in Persian poetry, see the eminent Iranian literary scholar Mohammad Reza Shafi'i-Kadkani's "Talaqqi-ye Qodama az Vatan" (The conception of our predecessor from the idea of *Vatan*), *Bukhara* 75, no. 2 (Tir 1389/ June 23, 2010), http://bukharamag.com/1389.04.1241.html.

While fully conscious of the European origin of ethnic nationalism, he compares the Iranian case of the idea of *nation* and *nationalism* to this colonial encounter, but he is also fully aware of the critical factor of collective memory. Yet many of my ideas of the *nation* and *homeland* I propose here, especially as the coded term for a postcolonial public sphere, differ significantly from Shafi'i-Kadkani's articulation in this excellent essay. He completely disregards the transformative power of a bourgeois public sphere in an epistemic shift in the definition of *Vatan*.

7. For more on the origins of Ferdowsi's *Shahnameh* in pre-Islamic sources, see the pioneering essays of Hasan Taghizadeh published in Berlin in the 1920s and subsequently collected and edited by Iraj Afshar, *Maqalat-e Taghizadeh*, vol. 6, *Ferdowsi va Shahnameh-ye Ou* (Ferdowsi and his *Shahnameh*) (Tehran: Heydari Publications, 1390/2011), particularly 71–122. For more recent critical observations on Taghizadeh's pioneering scholarship, see Sajjad Aydenlou, "Yaddasht-ha-'i bar Maqalat-e *Shahnameh*-Shenakhti Ostad Taghizadeh" (Commentaries on Taghizadeh's essays on *Shahnameh* studies), *Ketab-e Mah*, no. 77 (Shahrivar 1392/August 2013): 14–27. For the more recent state of scholarship on these sources, see Mahmoud Omidsalar, *Iran's Epic and America's Empire* (Santa Monica, Calif.: Afshar Publishing, 2012), chapters 6 and 7.

8. For more on the *gosan*, "a Parthian word of unknown derivation for 'poet-musician, minstrel,'" see the entry *gōsān* in *Encyclopaedia Iranica*, http://www.iranicaonline.org /articles/gosan.

9. For details, see Mahmoud Omidsalar, *Poetics and Politics of Iran's National Epic, the Shahnameh* (New York: Palgrave Macmillan, 2011), chapters 2 and 3.

10. See the entry *Ayādgār ī Zarērān* in *Encyclopaedia Iranica*, http://www.iranicaonline .org/articles/ayadgar-i-zareran.

11. See *Kār-Nāmag ī Ardašīr ī Pābagān*, in *Encyclopaedia Iranica*, http://www .iranicaonline.org/articles/karnamag-i-ardasir.

12. "Historiography," *Encyclopaedia Iranica*.

13. "Historiography," *Encyclopaedia Iranica*.

14. "Historiography," *Encyclopaedia Iranica*.

15. "Historiography," *Encyclopaedia Iranica*.

16. Zabihollah Safa, *Hamaseh-sura'i dar Iran* (Tehran: Amir Kabir, 1942), 95–98.

17. Safa, *Hamaseh-sura'i dar Iran*, 98–99.

18. Safa, *Hamaseh-sura'i dar Iran*, 99–107.

19. Safa, *Hamaseh-sura'i dar Iran*, 283–94.

20. Safa, *Hamaseh-sura'i dar Iran*, 294–342. In an erudite essay on one of these texts, *Shahryar-nameh*, Mahmoud Omidsalar argues in detail that most of these epics are nowhere near in their eloquence to the master's original, and most of them are of much later origin. With the exception of *Faramarz-nameh*, *Borzu-nameh*, *Bahman-nameh*, *Kush-nameh*, and of course *Garshasp-nameh*, which are all post-Ferdowsi, all other epics about the family of Rostam, Mahmoud Omidsalar believes are very late, mostly post-Safavid or even of Qajar provenance. See Mahmoud Omidsalar, "Shahryar-nameh," in *Jostar-ha-ye Shahnameh Shenasi va Mabaheth-e Adabi* (Essays in

Shahnameh studies and literary issues), 438–60 (Tehran: Bonyad-e Mawqufat-e Doctor Mahmoud-e Afshar, 1381/2002).

21. For a detailed study of the use of the *Shahnameh* as a mirror for princes, see Nasrin Askari, *The Medieval Reception of the "Shāhnāma" as a Mirror for Princes* (Leiden: Brill, 2016).

22. David Quint, *Epic and Empire: Politics and Generic Form from Virgil to Milton* (Princeton, N.J.: Princeton University Press, 1993).

23. "Our appetite for moral *sententiae*," Dick Davis believes, "is considerably smaller than that of a medieval audience, and I did not feel I could try the patience of the general reader—who I again emphasize is my intended audience—too high" (Abolqasem Ferdowsi, *Shahnameh: The Persian Book of Kings* [London: Penguin Books, 1997], xxxv). All such convenient categories ("medieval audience," "general reader," etc.) are deeply flawed, and so is the dismissal of these crucial, meditative, poetic pauses as "moral *sententiae*."

24. Ferdowsi, *Shahnameh*, 25.

25. Ferdowsi, *Shahnameh*, 24.

26. Ferdowsi, *Shahnameh*, 361.

27. For an excellent examination of the figure of Alexander in the *Shahnameh*, see Haila Manteghi, "Alexander the Great in the *Shāhnāmeh* of Ferdowsī," http://www.academia .edu/3499443/Alexander_the_Great_in_the_Shahnameh_of_Ferdowsi.

28. In some manuscripts and critical editions of the *Shahnameh* this question occurs earlier during Rostam and Sohrab's first encounter. These variations do alter the dramatic impact of such poetic implosions but do not compromise their traumatic endurance wherever they occur. Be that as it may, alternative readings can be offered if one were to use one critical edition of the Persian epic as opposed to another. For an exemplary comparison between two such critical editions, see Sajjad Aydenlou, "Moarefi va Bar-ressi do Tashih Tazeh-ye Shahnameh" (Introduction and comparison of two editions of the *Shahnameh*), *Ayeneh-ye Miras*, n.s., 13, suppl. no. 40 (1394/2015): 1–144.

2. FERDOWSI THE POET

1. For a discussion of this distinction between "Western" and "Iranian" readers, see Dick Davis, *Epic and Sedition: The Case of Ferdowsi's Shahnameh* (Washington, D.C.: Mage Publishers, 2006), chapter 1. For a detailed and insightful review of an earlier edition of this book, see Mahmoud Omidsalar, "Epic and Sedition: The Case of Ferdowsi's *Shahnameh*," *British Journal of Middle Eastern Studies* 20, no. 2 (1993): 237–43.

2. Abolqasem Ferdowsi, *Shahnameh: The Persian Book of Kings*, trans. Dick Davis (London: Penguin Books, 1997), xxxv.

3. Zabihollah Safa, *Tarikh-e Adabiyat dar Iran* (History of literature in Iran) (Tehran: Tehran University Press 1959), 1:371–93.

4. Safa, *Tarikh-e Adabiyat dar Iran*, 531–80.

5. Safa, *Tarikh-e Adabiyat dar Iran*, 580–97.

6.   Safa, *Tarikh-e Adabiyat dar Iran*, 603–6.

7.   For further details on how I offer a systematic periodization of Persian literary culture along these lines, see Hamid Dabashi, *The World of Persian Literary Humanism* (Cambridge, Mass.: Harvard University Press, 2012).

8.   Ferdowsi, *Shahnameh*, ed. E. E. Bertels et al., 9 vols. (Moscow: Oriental Institute, 1966–1971), 9:381–82.

9.   There are two excellent biographies of Ferdowsi prepared by two eminent scholars. One is A. Shapur Shahbazi, *Ferdowsi: A Critical Biography* (Costa Mesa, Calif.: Mazda Publishers, 1991), and the other is Djalal Khaleghi-Motlagh, "Ferdowsi, Abu'l-Qāsem i. Life," in *Encyclopaedia Iranica*, http://www.iranicaonline.org/articles/ferdowsi-i). The latter is more recent and more complete, benefiting from Shahbazi's scholarship and including more references to an extensive knowledge of manuscripts with biographical references to Ferdowsi. Most of my references to Ferdowsi's biography are therefore from Djalal Khaleghi-Motlagh's account.

10.   Khaleghi-Motlagh, "Ferdowsi."

11.   Khaleghi-Motlagh, "Ferdowsi."

12.   Khaleghi-Motlagh, "Ferdowsi."

13.   Ferdowsi, *Shahnameh*, 9:138–39. My almost verbatim translation here sacrifices elegance for accuracy.

14.   Khaleghi-Motlagh, "Ferdowsi."

15.   Khaleghi-Motlagh, "Ferdowsi."

16.   Khaleghi-Motlagh, "Ferdowsi."

17.   As he does in Khaleghi-Motlagh, "Ferdowsi."

18.   For more details, see Khaleghi-Motlagh, "Ferdowsi."

19.   For example, for an entirely spurious discussion of religion in the *Shahnameh*, ignoring its dramatic and literary disposition, falsely comparing it with historical narratives, and then speculating about why Ferdowsi does not start his epic with a Zoroastrian reference, and other such conjectures, see Dick Davis, "Religion in the *Shahnameh*," in "The *Shahnameh* of Ferdowsi as World Literature," ed. Frank Lewis, special issue, *Iranian Studies* 48, no. 3 (2015): 337–48. For another equally dubious attempt at speculating about "Ferdowsi's religion," see Shahbazi, *Ferdowsi*, 49–58.

20.   For more details, see Khaleghi-Motlagh, "Ferdowsi."

21.   As persuasively argued in Khaleghi-Motlagh, "Ferdowsi."

22.   See the discussion under the section "Education" in Khaleghi-Motlagh, "Ferdowsi." See also Shahbazi, *Ferdowsi*, 39–48, for similar speculations about Ferdowsi's education.

23.   For details, see Khaleghi-Motlagh, "Ferdowsi."

24.   As in fact even serious scholars like Khaleghi-Motlagh suggest; see Khaleghi-Motlagh, "Ferdowsi." See likewise Shahbazi, *Ferdowsi*, 123–25.

25.   As Djalal Khaleghi-Motlagh rightly notes in "Ferdowsi."

26.   Khaleghi-Motlagh, "Ferdowsi."

27.   Khaleghi-Motlagh, "Ferdowsi."

28.   Khaleghi-Motlagh, "Ferdowsi."

29. For a general study of such opening and closing gambits in the stories of the *Shahn-ameh* stories, see Richard Gabri, "Framing the Unframable in Ferdowsi's *Shahnameh*," in Lewis, "*Shahnameh* of Ferdowsi," 423–41. I do not agree with the central thesis of this essay, that the narrator is "helpless" in foregrounding a reading of the stories that unfold, but the fact that Gabri actually takes these crucial passages seriously and worthy of critical attention is in and of itself laudatory.

30. Ferdowsi, *Shahnameh*, trans. Davis, 332.

31. Ferdowsi, *Shahnameh*, ed. Bertels et al., 5:6–9.

32. Ferdowsi, *Shahnameh*, trans. Davis, 332.

33. Ferdowsi, *Shahnameh*, trans. Davis, 332.

34. Ferdowsi, *Shahnameh*, trans. Davis, 332.

35. There have even been some entirely baseless and rather ludicrous speculations that this persona that Ferdowsi creates here poetically was not only a woman but also in fact his own wife, on the basis of which speculation an entirely fictitious biography is imagined for her too! See Khaleghi-Motlagh, "Ferdowsi."

36. Ferdowsi, *Shahnameh*, trans. Davis, 332. Though the verb "to tell" in Davis's translation is misused here, for the original clearly says *barkhanam*, "to read."

37. Needless to say, if we were to use a critical edition other than Mohl's, say Khaleghi's, such analysis might vary somewhat, but the multiple voices with which the poet speaks stay the same.

38. Walter Benjamin, "Theses on the Philosophy of History," in *Illuminations*, trans. Harry Zohn, ed. Hannah Arendt (New York: Fontana/Collins, 1968), 256; emphasis added.

39. Abolqasem Ferdowsi, *Shahnameh*, Julius Mohl ed. (Tehran: Jibi Publications, 1965), 3:3–4. My translation.

40. Davis, *Epic and Sedition*, chapter 1.

41. David Quint, *Epic and Empire: Politics and Generic Form from Virgil to Milton* (Princeton, N.J.: Princeton University Press, 1993), 25.

42. For an excellent collection of essays on the presence of the Alexander Romance in its Iranian and wider regional contexts, see Richard Stoneman, Kyle Erickson, and Ian Netton, eds., *The Alexander Romance in Persia and the East* (Groningen, Neth.: Barkhuis Publishing and Groningen University Library, 2012).

3. THE BOOK OF KINGS

1. I have categorically challenged this historiography and offered an alternative in Hamid Dabashi, *The World of Persian Literary Humanism* (Cambridge, Mass.: Harvard University Press, 2012).

2. See, for example, Zabihollah Safa, *Hamaseh-sura'i dar Iran* (Tehran: Amir Kabir, 1942), 151–54.

3. Other texts also suggest themselves for such a comparison, perhaps most immediately the *History* of Abu'l-Fadl Bayhaqi (d. 1077).

4. For further details on this division of the text of the *Shahnameh*, see Safa, *Hamaseh-sura'i dar Iran*, 206–15.

5. The way it is promoted through the idea of "oral poetic performance" by Olga M. Davidson, for example, in *Poet and Hero in the Persian Book of Kings*, Bibliotheca Iranica, Intellectual Traditions 12 (Costa Mesa, Calif.: Mazda Publishers, 2006).

6. *The New Science of Giambattista Vico*, trans. from the 3rd ed. (1744) Thomas Goddard Bergin and Max Harold Fisch (Ithaca, N.Y.: Cornell University Press, 1948), 281–347.

7. There is a recent excellent study of Ferdowsi's "cinematic" techniques in Persian by Seyyed Mohsen Hashemi, *Ferdowsi va Honar-e Sinema* (Ferdowsi and the art of cinema) (Tehran: Elm, 1390/2011).

8. Ferdowsi, *Shahnameh*, ed. E. E. Bertels et al., 9 vols. (Moscow: Oriental Institute, 1966–1971), 3:35–36.

9. For more details, see Mahmoud Omidsalar's introduction to *Ali Nameh: An Ancient Story in Verse* (Tehran: Miras-e Maktub et al., 2009).

10. Safa, *Hamaseh sura'i dar Iran*, 377–90.

11. Hadi Seyf, *Naqqashi Qahveh-khaneh* (Tehran: Sazeman e Miras e Farhangi ye Keshvar, 1369/1990), 80.

12. Leading *Shahnameh* scholar Mahmoud Omidsalar believed this story to be an old but interpolated tale. In all likelihood, he believes, Ferdowsi did not put this part into verse.

13. In some editions of the *Shahnameh* these two young princesses are Jamshid's sisters or wives, not daughters.

14. I have detailed this theory of Shi'ism as a religion of filicide in Hamid Dabashi, *Shi'ism: A Religion of Protest* (Cambridge, Mass.: Harvard University Press, 2012). In that book I worked my way through but beyond the Freudian notion of "deferred obedience" toward "deferred defiance." Here I am proposing to work the same issue, albeit through the far more provocative theory of Deleuze.

15. Gilles Deleuze, *Masochism: "Coldness and Cruelty" and "Venus in Furs"* (New York: Zone Books, 1991), 60–61.

16. Ahmad Shamlou, "Ebrahim dar Atash" (Abraham in fire), in *Ahmad Shamlou: She'r-e Mo'aser; Bonbast-ha va Babr-ha-ye Ashegh* (On *Dead Ends* and *Tigers in Love*), ed. A. Pasha'i (Tehran: Ketab-sara, 1377/1998), 253–58. My translation from the original Persian.

4. EPICS AND EMPIRES

1. Sheila R. Canby, *The Shahnama of Shah Tahmasp: The Persian Book of Kings* (New York: Metropolitan Museum of Art, 2014).

2. For a short account of this atrocity, see Melik Kaylan, "Clandestine Trade," *Wall Street Journal*, December 8, 2011, https://www.wsj.com/articles/SB10001424052970204770404577082842506737230.

3. Franco Moretti, *Modern Epic: The World-System from Goethe to García Márquez*, trans. Quintin Hoare (London: Verso, 1996).

4. Walter Benjamin, "On the Concept of History" (1940), https://www.marxists.org /reference/archive/benjamin/1940/history.htm.

5. I have given a preliminary outline of this typology in Hamid Dabashi, "The American Empire: Triumph of Triumphalism," *Unbound: Harvard Journal of the Legal Left* 4, no. 82 (2008).

6. I have dealt in detail with this decentered subject in Hamid Dabashi, *The World of Persian Literary Humanism* (Cambridge, Mass.: Harvard University Press, 2012).

7. Ferdowsi, *Shahnameh*, ed. E. E. Bertels et al., 9 vols. (Moscow: Oriental Institute, 1966–1971), 2:224.

8. Emmanuel Levinas, *Totality and Infinity: An Essay on Exteriority*, trans. Alphonso Lingis (Pittsburgh: Duquesne University Press, 1969), 22.

5. EMPIRES FALL, NATIONS RISE

1. For an excellent account of the history of the Shah Tahmasp *Shahnameh*, see Francesca Leoni, "The Shahnama of Shah Tahmasp," http://www.metmuseum.org/ toah/hd/shnm/hd_shnm.htm. For a detailed account of the return of the fragmented pages of this *Shahnameh* to Iran, see the authoritative account by Hassan Habibi: http://www.tarikhirani.ir/fa/news/4/bodyView/824/%D9%85%D8%A7%D 8%AC%D8%B1%D8%A7%DB%8C.%D8%A8%D8%A7%D8%B2%DA%AF%D8%B1 D8%AF%D8%A7%D9%86%D9%86.%D8%B4%D8%A7%D9%87%D9% 86%D8%A7%D9%85%D9%87%E2%80%8C.%D8%B7%D9%87%D9%85%D8%A7%D 8%B3%D8%A8%DB%8C.%D8%A8%D9%87.%D8%A7%DB%8C%D8%B1%D8%A7% D9%86.%D8%A8%D9%87.%D8%B1%D9%88%D8%A7%DB%8C%D8%AA.%D8% AD%D8%B3%D9%86.%D8%AD%D8%A8%DB%8C%D8%A8%DB%8C.html (accessed August 14, 2018).

2. Mahmoud Omidsalar, *Poetics and Politics of Iran's National Epic, the Shahnameh* (New York: Palgrave Macmillan, 2011), and Mahmoud Omidsalar, *Iran's Epic and America's Empire* (Santa Monica, Calif.: Afshar Publishing, 2012).

3. I have covered this European reception of the *Shahnameh* extensively in Hamid Dabashi, *Persophilia: Persian Culture on the Global Scene* (Cambridge, Mass.: Harvard University Press, 2015), 148–59.

4. For more details, see "The Shahnameh as Propaganda for World War II," http://blogs .bl.uk/asian-and-african/2013/05/the-shahnameh-as-propaganda-for-world-war-ii .html.

5. I take these citations from an excellent master's thesis on the reception of the Persian epic in the twentieth century by one of my former students at Columbia University, Ali Ahmadi Motlagh, "Ferdowsi in the 20th Century" (master's thesis, Columbia University, 2008).

6. Motlagh, "Ferdowsi in the 20th Century."

7. Motlagh, "Ferdowsi in the 20th Century." For more details, see Isa Sadiq, ed., *Heza-reh-ye Ferdowsi* (Tehran, 1944).

8. Motlagh, "Ferdowsi in the 20th Century."

9. Motlagh, "Ferdowsi in the 20th Century."

10. Motlagh, "Ferdowsi in the 20th Century."

11. Motlagh, "Ferdowsi in the 20th Century."

12. This is not to suggest that Muslims were not aware and conscious of "critical editions" before Europeans. Preparing the six canonical editions of the Prophet's Hadith (*Sihah Sittah*) is a clear indication that Muslims were quite conscious of "critical editions." However, with the advent of mechanized printing, a key apparatus of European Orientalism was preparing a "printed critical edition" of Arabic, Persian, or Sanskrit texts as an insignia of "modern scholarship." It is that "modernity" that is the issue here.

13. See https://www.youtube.com/watch?v=-YrfvhfrDeU.

14. See http://iranshenakht.blogspot.com/2006/05/360_22.html.

15. See http://jadidonline.com/story/09112009/frnk/simorq_operetta.

16. Bahram Beiza'i, *Sohrab-Koshi* (Sohrabicide) (Tehran: Roshangaran Publishers, 1386/2007).

17. For more on Beiza'i, see Hamid Dabashi, "Bahram Beizai," in *Master and Master-pieces of Iranian Cinema*, 253–80 (Washington, D.C.: Mage Publishers, 2007).

18. For more on the Green Movement in Iran, see Hamid Dabashi, *Iran, the Green Movement and the USA* (London: Zed Books, 2010).

19. It would be instructive to compare Moretti's book with a far more poignant study of the relation between epics and empires, unburdened by the hubris of "the West" and "world texts": Celia López-Chávez's exquisite book, *Epics of Empire and Frontier: Alonso de Ercilla and Gaspar de Villagrá as Spanish Colonial Chroniclers* (Norman: University of Oklahoma Press, 2016), in which she examines Alonso de Ercilla's *La Araucana* (1569), about the Spanish conquest of Chile, and Gaspar de Villagrá's *Historia de la Nueva México* (1610), a historical epic about the Spanish subjugation of the indigenous peoples of New Mexico. This book is a far more effective way of thinking about epics and empires. The significance of this study is seeing clearly through the dynamic of conquest and the conquered.

20. For a short account of *Shahnameh* stories adapted for the screen, see Hassan Mahda-vifar, "Ferdowsi va *Shahnameh* dar Sinema" (Ferdowsi and the *Shahnameh* in cinema), July 2011, http://honarbedunemarz.blogfa.com/post-179.aspx.

CONCLUSION

1. Ferdowsi, *Shahnameh*, ed. E. E. Bertels et al., 9 vols. (Moscow: Oriental Institute, 1966–1971), 7:6.

2. Mahmoud Omidsalar makes a strong case that these narratives incorporating Alexander into the dynastic families of Iran and Egypt were invented by his own propaganda. See Mahmoud Omidsalar, *Iran's Epic and America's Empire* (Santa

Monica, Calif.: Afshar Publishing, 2012), 12–40. Be that as it may, Ferdowsi's incorporation of Alexander into his epic fits perfectly in his narrative scheme.

3. David Damrosch, ed., *World Literature in Theory* (Chichester, U.K.: Wiley Blackwell, 2014).

4. Damrosch, *World Literature in Theory*, 518.

5. Damrosch, *World Literature in Theory*, 521.

6. Emily Apter, *Against World Literature: On the Politics of Untranslatability* (New York: Verso, 2013).

7. David Damrosch, review of *Against World Literature: On the Politics of Untranslatability*, by Emily Apter, *Comparative Literature Studies* 51, no. 3 (2014): 504–8.

8. Apter, *Against World Literature*, 8.

9. Damrosch, review of *Against World Literature*, 508.

10. Damrosch, review of *Against World Literature*, 508.

11. David Damrosch, *What Is World Literature?* (Princeton, N.J.: Princeton University Press, 2003).

12. Hamid Dabashi, *The World of Persian Literary Humanism* (Cambridge, Mass.: Harvard University Press, 2012), 251–55.

13. Wai Chee Dimock and Lawrence Buell, eds., *Shades of the Planet: American Literature as World Literature* (Princeton, N.J.: Princeton University Press, 2007), 5. In *What Is a World? On Postcolonial Literature as World Literature* (Durham, N.C.: Duke University Press, 2016), Pheng Cheah correctly zooms in on the question of "World" in "World Literature" and makes the cogent argument that any emerging literature carves out its own world by virtue of its widening readership. Pheng Cheah's excellent point, however, is limited to the world in which a body of literature is received, while in my argument in this book I dwell on two other interrelated worlds of the *Shahnameh*—the world in which it was created and the inner world of the epic itself.

14. Enrique Dussel, *Philosophy of Liberation*, trans. Aquilina Martinez and Christine Morkovsky (Maryknoll, N.Y.: Orbis Books, 1985), 3.

15. Dussel, *Philosophy of Liberation*, 3.

16. Dussel, *Philosophy of Liberation*, 3.

17. Gayatri Chakravorty Spivak, *Death of a Discipline* (New York: Columbia University Press, 2003), 6.

18. Spivak, *Death of a Discipline*, 7.

19. Spivak, *Death of a Discipline*, 9.

20. Frantz Fanon, *The Wretched of the Earth*, trans. Richard Philcox (New York: Grove Press, 1961), 1.

21. Mehdi Akhavan-e Sales, *Behtarin-e Omid* (The best of Omid) (Tehran: Mihan Publishers, 1969), 307–19. This original version of "Khan-e Hashtom" is reprinted a number of other times along with its sequel, "Adamak" (The little man, March 1968), for example, in *Bagh-e bi-Bargi* (The fruitless garden: Mehdi Akhavan-e Sales memorial volume), ed. Morteza Kakhi (Tehran: Agah Publishers, 1991), 544–58. All translations and abbreviations from the Persian original are my own.

22. Gholamreza Takhti (1930–1968) was a deeply loved and admired world champion wrestler known for his nationalist (anticolonial) politics.

23. Rakhsh is the name of Rostam's horse.
24. Sam, Zal, Rostam, Sohrab, Faramarz, and Borzu are all among the *Shahnameh* heroes.
25. As I do in Dabashi, *World of Persian Literary Humanism*.
26. See, for example, Mohammad Ali Islami Nodushan, *Zendegi va Marg Pahlavanan dar Shahnameh* (The life and death of heroes in the *Shahnameh*) (Tehran: Intishar Publications, 1969), and Mostafa Rahimi, *Tragedy-ye Qodrat dar Shahnameh* (The tragedy of power in the *Shahnameh*) (Tehran: Nilufar Publishing House, 1990).

INDEX